A PRACTICAL MANUAL OF
SCREEN PLAYWRITING

for theater and television films

A PRACTICAL MANUAL OF

for theater and television films

SCREEN PLAYWRITING

BY LEWIS HERMAN

A MERIDIAN BOOK

NEW AMERICAN LIBRARY

TIMES MIRROR

NEW YORK AND SCARBOROUGH, ONTARIO
THE NEW ENGLISH LIBRARY LIMITED, LONDON

Library of Congress Catalog Card Number: 52-5175

MERIDIAN TRADEMARK REG. U.S. PAT. OFF. AND FOREIGN COUNTRIES
REGISTERED TRADEMARK—MARCA REGISTRADA
HECHO EN FORGE VILLAGE, MASS., U.S.A.

SIGNET, SIGNET CLASSICS, MENTOR, PLUME AND MERIDIAN BOOKS
are published in the United States by
The New American Library, Inc.,
1301 Avenue of the Americas, New York, New York 10019,
in Canada by The New American Library of Canada Limited,
81 Mack Avenue, Scarborough, Ontario M1L 1M8,
in the United Kingdom by The New English Library Limited,
Barnard's Inn, Holborn, London, E.C. 1, England.

First Printing/World Publishing Company, February, 1963
First Printing/New American Library, December, 1974

    3 4 5 6 7 8 9

PRINTED IN THE UNITED STATES OF AMERICA

To my most ardent though prejudiced admirers:
my wife Marguerite and our children—
Stephanie, Judith, and Helmar.

The sections "Dialects" and "Foreign Language Dialogue"
were originally published in full in
The Screen Writer magazine.

PREFACE

This book is a practical manual of screen-play writing. Its purpose is to supply practical rules and suggestions and to describe practices applicable to the writing of motion-picture screen plays for both theater and television presentation.

It should be obvious that motion-picture techniques are adaptable to television production—especially to filmed television drama.

The television drama, as produced on film, varies from the feature-length film mainly in the matter of the size of the script and, hence, the running length of the film. This difference operates so that ninety-minute films made for theater showings cannot be cut down for television without affecting their quality considerably, no matter how fine they may have been originally.

When this has been done—and it will be done more and more as the major studios release their old films—artistic mayhem results. Violent jump cuts, for example, are the rule rather than the exception. These jump cuts occur not only picture-wise but, what is even worse, in dialogue, in sound, and in music. Characters who have been arbitrarily cut from opening scenes suddenly appear as if from nowhere and disappear again just as mysteriously. Characters introduced in the opening scenes of the theater version are sometimes discussed in the TV version as though they were familiar to the viewer, despite the fact that they have found oblivion on the cutting-room floor of the TV studio.

These as well as other crudities can mean only one thing: that the theater-length film is not ideally suited for television presentation when it is cut down to size. More and more it must become apparent that the only films suitable for television are those that are expressly written for television.

With but few exceptions—which will be duly noted and discussed —all the material written in this book regarding feature-length films for theaters can be applied to feature films for television as well.

There was a time, for example, when the long shot was proscribed to the television film. This was so because the average home TV image screen was considerably smaller than it is at the present time. Thus, the figures in a long shot appeared so small as to make them almost invisible. But with the advent of the large TV screen, this injunction, together with many others, was lifted. So that now it can be safely said that the TV film script is almost the exact counterpart of the feature-film script.

Screen plays must be written for motion pictures other than Hollywood feature films—for documentary films, commercial films, educational films, and training films. Although screen plays for these use certain basic techniques, writing for them requires specialized knowledge that would require another book to detail. Hence, in this book, complete emphasis will be put on the rules for writing screen plays only for feature films for theaters and dramatic films for television.

The techniques given will be those that have evolved through the years into a sort of filmic grammar. As such, they have become almost inflexible rules for the making of acceptable motion pictures. The result is that the noncreative segment of picture makers abide by them with doctrinaire slavishness. A corollary result is bad pictures.

The rules are being presented here, however, in no such light. For the free and creative spirit recognizes no rules. It accepts rules merely as conventions to be shattered if fresh, unfettered creations are to result. Therefore, the rules given in this book should be used only as signposts—or springboards—to creative invention.

Accept most of these rules with reservations. Accept them only as steppingstones. And go on from there to create, if you are able, original and imaginative works.

LEWIS HERMAN

November, 1951

CONTENTS

ix

2   THE FILMIC COMPONENTS

3 WRITING THE SCREEN PLAY

DRAMATURGY

SECTION

The screen play

The motion-picture screen play is a written composition designed to serve as a sort of work diagram for the motion-picture director. He causes it to be photographed as a series of picture sequences. When spliced together these sequences become the finished motion-picture film, after suitable sound effects and background music have been dubbed in.

Unlike the play or novel, the motion-picture screen play—or, as it has been variously called, the shooting script, the script, or the scenario—has seldom become a work of literary art. Like the blueprint in architecture, it has served only as an intermediate stage through which the completed motion picture must go before it achieves its ultimate structure as a movie.

The Hollywood screen-play writer's position in the manufacture of motion pictures is comparable to that of the writer in no other medium in the field of entertainment. The playwright usually sees his drama produced and performed almost as he has written it, unless a play doctor has been called in. The magazine writer's work is published with relatively few corrections by his editor. The book author is rarely forced to make radical editorial changes. Radio writing is affected in not too great a degree by the demands of advertising-agency account executives. But the supposedly creative work of the Hollywood screen-play writer seldom, if ever, reaches the screening stage intact.

There are many reasons for this peculiar difference. The making of motion pictures is a collaborative enterprise. The creative work of dozens of closely knit crafts and arts is necessary—acting, cinematography, architecture, scenic design, costume design, interior deco-

3

rating—these and a multitude of others are all essential to the making of motion pictures.

To give some idea of the varied amount of craft work involved, the following were observed on the sound stage where Maugham's *The Razor's Edge* was being shot.

In addition to the director, his two assistants, the actors and their standees, were: the gaffer (head electrician) and his assistants; the cameraman (director of photography) and two assistant cameramen; a camera operator; a crane operator; a crane steerer; the head grip (stagehand) in charge of five other grips; a script clerk; four electricians; a dialogue director; a unit production manager; a contact man; a fixture man; a greenery man; a special-effects man; a sound engineer and his assistant; a sound-boom man; a sound-cable man; a prop man and his assistant; two make-up men; a hairdresser; two wardrobe people; and a still photographer.

Note particularly that the screen-play writer was not present.

Incidentally, these employees were only those actually working on the set. They did not include the hundreds of others who had been involved in the many other phases of picture making, from the set designers through to the man who swept up the debris after the set had been used and struck. Even in the production of cheaply made television dramas—those produced in accredited studios and with union and guild personnel—the number of workers is surprising.

In addition to this multiplicity of crafts and talents that makes for the differences between screen-play writing and other forms of creative writing, there is still another important variance.

The novel (especially) and the dramatic play (occasionally) are written directly for an audience. The screen-play writer, however, creates only a set of directions for the director, the actors, the cameraman, and the vast horde of other craftsmen. Therefore, a screen play should never be written to be read. That is why so few of them have ever been published. When they are, it is usually with most of the camera directions and actor actions deleted.

The test of a screen play, then, should be not how it reads, but rather how effective it is in describing scenes to be photographed, dialogue to be heard, and actions to be seen.

This accounts for the frequent failure of so many novelists—and even playwrights—who are called to Hollywood to write screen plays.

They write beautiful scripts that read well. Their dialogue—written extensively, as it is done in the discursive novel—has fire, emotion, and realism. And their descriptions of a character's appearance, his actions, and his motivations are indeed immensely apt and readable.

But unless an experienced screen-play writer is called in to do a "polish job" on the script, it will usually photograph very badly. Its dialogue will emerge from the sound track as uninspired and pedestrian. The elaborate directions for the action will, of necessity, have been watered down by the time it is brought to life by the actors. And the inept camera directions will have been ignored by the director, who usually asserts his prerogative of shooting the scenes in his own way.

It can be stated, then, that a successful fiction writer does not necessarily possess the ability to write acceptable and shootable screen plays.

The screen writer. It can also be stated that, because a writer works in a Hollywood studio or at an Eastern television film studio as a screen-play writer, he does not necessarily practice screen-play writing. Of the roster of more than fifteen hundred members of the Screen Writers' Guild in Hollywood less than one-fourth actually write screen plays.

Many are known as "idea men." That is, they are proficient in dreaming up ideas for future motion pictures. Others are "situation" men, who can read a completed script and suggest new scenes and situations with which to enliven the action and dialogue. Still others are "gag" men, whose job it is to insert funny situations or dialogue jokes. And then there are the "polish job" writers whose forte is to take a completed script, juggle scenes and dialogue, add or take out scenes and dialogue, generally clean up rough spots, heighten action, and accelerate tempo.

But a majority of the screen writers, other than the above-mentioned, write master-scene scripts, without camera shots and angles indicated.

Tools of the trade. Primarily, a screen-play writer should be able to write—to express his ideas in words that are amply descriptive and appropriate.

Then, he should have a creative imagination. He should be able to recognize subject material that is intrinsically dramatic.

He should be a good storyteller. He should know those techniques of storytelling that make for a plot that is expertly opened, provocatively developed, and satisfactorily concluded.

He should have developed a catholic power of observation. He should be able to *see* characters, situations, and story developments as they can be related to a screen play.

More important, he should be able to relate outer, physical characteristics and actions to inner, emotional drives, and to integrate them naturally into the screen play so that acceptance of psychological motivation will not be strained and, therefore, lost.

In addition to possessing a photographic eye, the good screen-play writer should have a dictographic ear. He should be able to reproduce living speech in a way that is revelatory and at the same time selective.

He should also be able to use sound effects for the purpose of creating mood, of heightening dramatic action and, as is often necessary, for transitional, scene-capping, and plot devices.

These qualities, though, are not exactly exclusive with the screen-play writer. The radio-script writer and the playwright should possess most of them—the fiction writer some. But the screen-play writer must possess, in addition, a highly developed sense of the visual. He must have the faculty of "seeing" to an extraordinary degree. He must be able to *see* an idea in terms of a picture rather than as a well written, verbally colorful, mentally stimulating—but physically static paragraph of words.

In a recently produced British Technicolor picture, the physiological sensations of a sneeze were reproduced by cutting in a few blank pink frames of film covered with twinkling sparks. Someone— the writer, director, or producer—believed that the sneeze could be made more graphic in this manner. It was a good try even though the desired effect was not completely realized.

Because he is writing a motion picture, the screen-play writer must deal primarily with motion. His story must move swiftly or slowly, the exact pace depending on the nature of the story. His dialogue must move continuously. It must have in it the very essence of dynamic movement—again, either swiftly or slowly according to the pace desired—but *it must move*. His characters must move so that there is sufficient physical action within the framework of each shot to justify its existence in a motion picture.

Then the screen-play writer should be able to develop movement in the order of his individual shots within the scene so that, photographically, a moving progression of shots will result. At the same time, this progressive movement must be injected into the sequence of scenes, into the act sequences, and into the picture as a whole. Much of this movement is contributed by the director and the film editor. But the basis for it should be furnished by the screen-play writer.

The quality of character growth, which has a certain innate movement of its own, is still another means of projecting this progressive movement.

The accomplishment of these factors of movement, however, requires an intimate knowledge of motion-picture techniques. It demands a knowledge of the use of the various kinds of shots; that is, of camera distances and angles. It demands a knowledge of optical effects, like the "dissolve" and the "wipe," which are effective aids for moving from scene to scene and from sequence to sequence. It demands a knowledge of the use of a vast tool chest of technical devices without which a motion picture could not be made.

Historical background

There was a time when such a specialized knowledge of motion-picture making was unnecessary. In the cradle days of picture making, the cameraman was the Koko of the industry—the story plotter, the script writer, the director, and the film editor. He was *it!*

Gradually, as the demand for pictures increased, and as the cameraman's job became more onerous, he was forced to relegate some of his tasks to other specialists. But he retained the story-developing responsibility for some time simply because he never found it necessary to write a formal screen play. In those days, shooting was done "off the cuff," extemporaneously.

The next step was the hiring of a writer—usually a vaudeville or stage comedian—to write down a series of funny situations for the cameraman to shoot. Soon he was required to write "title cards" with which the silent pictures tried to present a minimal amount of only absolutely essential dialogue and descriptive comments, the most typical of which were of the "came the dawn" variety.

Then, as the pictures matured in concept and grew in length from two-reelers to four-reelers and finally to eight-reelers, the outlines became longer and more complex. So specialists were developed to handle the separate elements of a screen play: idea men to furnish the plot kernel; situation men to develop the plot idea into dramatic situations; title-card writers to supply the words to be flashed on the screen as explanatory material, or as essential dialogue; and a general, over-all writer to put together all the separate elements and to write the final shooting script.

The addition of sound and speech automatically eliminated the title-card writer. But it also created a demand for authors who could write dynamic dialogue. At first they were recruited from the ranks of Broadway playwrights. In the first disordered rush of the change-over from silent to talking pictures, the legitimate theater was raided for every type of professional, from actors and directors to dialogue writers. And the first talking pictures demonstrated the error of attempting to transplant what was basically a static medium to "motion" pictures. They were simply stage plays transplanted to the flickering shadow-screen.

Much of the fault lay with the playwrights, who made no attempt to adjust their stage-play writing techniques to the requirements of motion-picture writing. Speeches were windy and wordy. Slow-moving, individual scenes made the movement pedestrian. The close-up fell into disfavor and was supplanted by the medium-shot and the full-shot *mise en scène*.

But gradually, as the picture makers began to assess their errors in the finished product, the level of screen-play writing rose. The long-worded dialogue was trimmed until now, for the most part, it has become succinct and realistic. The full shot, it was realized, had its place, but not to the detriment of one of the motion picture's chief tools, the close-up. And definite techniques for screen-play writing have evolved that produce stories that move along as a motion picture should do.

Present studio procedures

The current Hollywood staff-written screen play is the result of much preparatory work. It begins with the purchase of a bare idea, a published book, a produced or unproduced play, a magazine story, or an original story written expressly for the screen. At one time the last mentioned was bought mainly to star an already contracted actor or to supply a specific market or picture trend. But the original-story screen play is rapidly gaining greater acceptance, especially with television film producers, who cannot afford to pay exorbitant prices for "best seller" material.

The basic story is elaborated—if it is an idea—or boiled down—if it is a novel or play—to a synopsis. This synopsis will run anywhere from five to ten double-spaced typewritten pages. Sometimes, if a producer is too busy to read even these few pages, the synopsis is truncated to a page or even a paragraph. One important producer is known to hire actors to act out the story for him the while he cogitates on more important matters.

Then a story conference is called. This is attended by the supervising producer (who has from two to half a dozen different pictures going under his aegis) ; the individual picture producer; the screenplay writer; and sometimes, but not often, by the director assigned to the picture, although usually the director is assigned only after the screen play has been completed.

The story idea is thrashed out. The writer is given sundry opinions and injunctions. Production values are discussed. There is also much consideration of the stars that might be available for the picture. Innumerable phone calls interrupt the proceedings. Locations and budgets are discussed. Finally the conference ends. The writer returns to his cubbyhole to think, to make notes, to pound out on his typewriter, write longhand, or dictate to a stenographer, his elaboration of the synopsis into what is known as a "treatment."

The writer tries to incorporate into it all the ideas that have been proferred him during the story conference, plus the ideas implicit in the original story and his own ideas about it. This takes the form of a fifty-page short story written in the present tense. It is correspondingly shorter, of course, for the shorter television drama. It should describe the characters, list their individual characteristics, detail their various interrelated actions throughout the story, and, at the same time, try to give the dramatic high spots of the dialogue.

But story conferences continue to be held between the writer and his unit producer. Story values, actions, and dialogue are thrashed out, always to the satisfaction of the producer who, at the same time, bends a quaking ear to the omnipresence—not necessarily physical—of his supervising producer. And the result becomes a finished treatment.

This treatment then goes to the supervising producer. Copies are sent to the heads of the story department, to the studio heads, and to their assistants. That is to say, about twenty-five people then read it, comment on it, make suggestions for it, tear it apart, or build it up. The shreds of the treatment are then returned to the writer for co-ordination. He, of course, is told that he may reject or accept the suggestions as he sees fit. But if he is experienced, he rejects only minor changes and suggestions and accepts most of those made by his salary-superiors, the exact number of acceptances being in direct proportion to the importance of his critics in the studio hierarchy, and to the writer's desire to retain his job and to get further assignments.

A revised treatment is then completed by the writer and sent around. The same group of studio executives read it. Eventually—usually after about six weeks—a completed treatment is written that is acceptable—but always with reservations—to the executives. That done, the writer begins to work on the shooting script proper, which is the master script that will be followed when the actual shooting of the picture begins.

Needless to say, the same procedure is gone through in the writing of the shooting script. Endless conferences are conducted. Multitudinous changes are made. Reams and reams of new scenes, of new dialogue, are written and rewritten. The writer swelters. The stenos sweat. The unit producer gnaws at his fingernails. The supervising producer snarls. But gradually, and miraculously, a completed shooting script evolves, until, from about six weeks to a year later, the final-final-final, last-draft shooting script comes off the mimeograph machine.

But still other things can and do happen. After a year, the script may be discarded. Another writer may then be put on the original idea. And the same weary process is repeated. What will happen almost certainly—even if the finished script is perfectly acceptable— is that still another writer will be called in to rewrite the work of the original writer. This is called a "polish job." That done—if the picture is an important one—still another writer may be hired to rewrite the rewrite. The theory here is that if one writer's work is good, then certainly the work of half a dozen additional writers should be six times better.

Now, with half a dozen or more versions of the story before him, the producer is beset with doubts. Eventually he makes his choice, and the winning script is mimeographed and sent out to the heads of the various departments for their estimates and work on the picture.

Technical workers are assigned. Actors are auditioned and cast. The sets are designed and erected. The shooting schedule is worked out in a script breakdown. Finally the picture is shot. Rarely, if ever, is the writer called on to work on the set with the director, to make on-the-spot changes in the dialogue. When he is, it is usually only for gag material.

While the picture is being shot and edited, the various writers who worked on the script are sent, through their agents, the names of those writers that will appear on the credit cards in the picture. If a number of writers are involved, a squabble usually results. For credits are the screen-play writer's measure of competency in Hollywood. This squabble is usually referred to an arbitration panel composed of three members of the Screen Writers' Guild. The panel reads all the scripts and makes the necessary decisions. The result is usually a compromise. Until recently the compromise was: "Original story by Joe Joakes and Bill Boakes; adapted by Sam Soakes and Moe Moakes; screen play by Frank Foakes and Nellie Noakes; with additional dialogue by Ralph Roakes and Hiram Hoakes, and additional scenes added by Oscar Oakes and Pat Poakes." The names of the writers who were not mentioned were filed away in that Valhalla of anonymous screen credits, "the archives of the Academy of Motion Picture Arts and Sciences."

But the Screen Writers' Guild has tried to limit the number of credits for one picture so that today the names of only a few writers are permitted to be included.

Screen play classifications

The Hollywood screen play can be broken down into a number of classifications. Although they call for the same over-all treatment, insofar as writing is concerned, each is subject to certain variations. Many of these variations will be discussed in forthcoming sections. The same classifications, with few exceptions, can be used for television films. It will suffice now merely to list the classifications for identification purposes.

WESTERN	COMEDY	CRIME
Action	Romantic	Action
Mystery	Musical	Prison
Musical	Juvenile	Social Problem

MELODRAMA	DRAMA
Action	Romantic
Adventure	Biographical
Juvenile	Social Problem
Detective-Mystery	Musical
Murder-Mystery	Comedy
Social Problem	Action
Romantic	Religious
War	War
Musical	Psychological
Psychological-Mystery	Historical
Psychological	

MISCELLANEOUS	
Fantasy	Documentary
Fantasy-Musical	Semi-Documentary
Comedy-Fantasy	Cartoon
Comedy-Fantasy-Musical	Historical
Farce-Comedy	Travelogue
Farce-Murder-Mystery	Musical-Review-Drama
Farce-Horror	Drama
Horror	Serial
Horror-Psychological	Two-Reel Comedy

Before we begin

"In the beginning was the word." This biblical phrase can well be applied to motion-picture making. For in the beginning of every modern motion picture there must be words—the words of the screen-play writer fashioned into a script from which the entire studio personnel takes off and begins to function.

The era of the off-the-cuff cameraman and director has become only a vestigial remnant in Hollywood. With the exception of very few directors—Roberto Rossellini of Italy and Charles Chaplin, in his *Woman of Paris*, are the only two who come to mind—directors can begin to function only after the screen play has been written.

The screen-play writer, then, is the prime mover of every motion picture, whether it be for theater or television presentation. It is incumbent on him to see that his work, which serves as the initial impetus, continues to carry the action forward. His screen play should have overt and covert movement. It should suggest shots that contain action movement and dialogue movement. It should string those shots together so that the movement does not falter, but continues to go forward progressively, in a pattern designed to suit the general mood of the finished picture.

This fact cannot be repeated too often: *The prime consideration of the motion-picture screen play is that it should make for a motion picture that moves.*

Motion is also especially required by the television film play. Feature films for theater projection are displayed in motion-picture houses to what has been termed "captive audiences." That is to say, the audience is more or less forced to remain to watch the unreeling of the picture, primarily because they have paid admission to see it.

The television film, however, viewed in the home, plays to no such captive audience. The members of this audience have not only paid nothing to see the film but, what is more, simply by turning the dial, they can avail themselves of any one of several more attractive entertainments.

And there are other differences. In a dark theater, the audience's attention is almost hypnotically directed toward the flickering screen. Distractions—other than the typical ones of crackling paper bags, popcorn-crunching, cooing lovers, and squirming youngsters—are reduced to a minimum. Hence, the audience's attention can be quite easily held by the picture.

But this is not so with the TV filmed picture. The living room is seldom darkened completely for TV viewing. There is no motion-picture projector drone to act as a soporific. The baby's whimpering in an adjoining bedroom; the bickering of the couple next door heard through flimsy walls; the chatter of traffic coming through an open window; the telephone; the doorbell; the comments from fellow viewers—these and many other distractions serve to sever the tenuous thread of attention which acts as a point of contact between the TV audience and the picture they are seeing. And then there is always the little numbered dial on the set which promises different and, perhaps, better entertainment.

The fact that television is viewed in the home makes for still another difference that calls for special attention by the television screen-play writer. At home, the viewer is surrounded by few fellow viewers. In the theater, though, he is part of a very large group who respond to the picture *en masse*. Laughs that may be missed by some are caught by others, who transmit their reactions to the less acute. In the same way, coughs and throat-clearings—indicating boredom and disinterest—can also be transferred to others. Radio and live television programs, especially the variety and comedy shows, solved this problem by performing for studio audiences whose reactions—rehearsed in a "warm up" before show time and properly coached with applause cards while the show is on the air—are broadcast together with the program. Thus, the herd responses are supplied to the home listener.

The "Amos and Andy" television films use this method too, by dubbing into the traditional sound track an applause track of audience responses. This is indeed a radical departure for, in effect, it becomes a motion-picture drama that supplies its own appreciative applause, thus assuring itself of acceptance. This leaves one to shudder at the possibility of other producers adopting the method for theater motion pictures, where the captive viewers would be subjected to the indignities of an audience-conditioning cheering section.

One other point applies particularly to the writing of comedy drama for television. The usual procedure for motion pictures is to write in a few seconds of "dead dialogue" after a laugh line or situation. This acts as a cushion for the audience laughter and assures their not missing anything pertinent. In television, however, this "dead dialogue" is not required because the viewer is usually at home and the laughter reaction is neither so loud nor so long as it is in the theater.

These are considerations which must be taken into account in the writing of motion into a TV film script that moves. How this movement can be translated from the original idea, through the synopsis, the treatment, and the shooting script, will be discussed in the forthcoming sections.

The story idea

We have already seen that ideas for feature motion-picture screen plays are obtained from a number of sources. When the picture is based on a "best-selling" book, a Broadway-produced play, a short story, or a magazine article, the story idea, synopsis, and plot and character development are already furnished to the screen-play writer. His is merely a job of adaptation.

But an increasingly fecund source of material is to be found in the "original story," written especially for motion pictures, either to a specific order or on speculation. The reasons are many. They are cheaper to buy than the others. The cost of a successful play or book is proportionate to its success. And the more successful it is the greater interest it develops in the studios, who then bid against each other for its purchase and thus run up the cost, sometimes to enormous sums. In addition, costs must be added for adapting the book or play into a screen play.

The original-story screen play, however, is complete in itself. Its original cost is its only cost. What is more, bankers who are approached for backing by independent producers consider a completed original screen play as a property and will often advance money solely on the strength of it.

Ideas for original-story motion pictures can be found anywhere. They can be gleaned from the multifarious activities of people as they are observed by the writer himself.

This is the safest and most advantageous way. For if your story is to concern the actions of people—and it must, of necessity—and if it is to be fresh, realistic, and universally appealing, then it is from real people that the stories of your reel people should come.

Notebook.   This requires, first, an acquisitive and curious mind, and, second, a notebook. Observe details and note them down immediately. To delay this process of notation is to call into play two negative factors: (1) the forgetting of important details, and (2) the embroidering or fictionalizing of them. The contrived story results when these two factors are present. The memory is, at best, a faulty faculty and the only method for making certain that it will function perfectly is to avoid its use completely and resort to written notes.

Idea selectivity.   Selectivity is one of the writer's most important techniques. The amateur writer can be discerned almost always by his lack of it. The work of a finished, professional writer is always evidenced by the orderly compactness of his writing.

Selectivity plays a very important role in all aspects of screen-play writing, and it will be dealt with in succeeding sections of this book. It is particularly important in finding and using ideas for motion pictures. The writer should develop the talent for noting down only those ideas that may lend themselves most easily to screen-play development.

This means that you will not assiduously note down all of grandpa's tales of derring-do, nor all Aunt Prissy's idle gossip of the doings of her Wednesday Night Social Circle. Grandpa has changed his stories so often that, by the time they reach you, they contain all the tag ends of hundreds of other tales with which he has been inoculated over the years.

But the story of cousin Joe, who works at the bank—of how he frustrated a holdup of the bank by a twelve-year-old boy—has in it the basis for a good screen story.

Idea development.   Using this story only as a jumping-off point, you would then start to delve into the family situation that may have forced the boy to attempt the robbery. And eventually, out of this idea may come a dramatic story of juvenile delinquency. You may finish with something that has nothing to do with a bank robbery. But you will have a story—which was what you started out to write in the first place.

Ideas for free.   The printed word is another fruitful source of ideas. Newspapers are ideal for this purpose, particularly the items on the local news pages. Human interest stories are constantly recorded. Avoid the national story covered by the big news services. Motion-picture studios themselves have research units that clip these stories for submission to their story departments and producers.

Once again, try the oblique method. Use the news item only as a springboard for another story by delving into the story's backgrounds, and by developing them.

Sam Goldwyn is said to have gotten the original idea for his picture *The Best Years of Our Lives* from an item in *Time.* The story he read was simply one about a trainload of marines returning home from the wars. What was eventually evolved for him from this starter idea was a trenchant picture detailing the postwar readjustments of returned soldiers.

Jerry Wald, another dynamic producer of Hollywood pictures, subscribes to scores of magazines and newspapers which he scans and clips religiously for topical story ideas from which many excellent pictures have emerged.

Idea twists.   Fiction, plays, and even motion pictures themselves may furnish the germ of an idea for a story. Forget about plagiarism. The important thing to remember is not *where* you got the idea, but *what* you do with it.

Shakespeare cribbed most of his ideas from other authors. His *Henry V* story was derived largely from Holinshed's *Chronicles.* Few know Holinshed. Shakespeare is an immortal.

When reading a book, stop and lay the book down somewhere in the middle. Then try to figure how you think the plot will turn out —or, more important, how you think it *should* turn out. Quite often you'll find, after completing the book, that you have come up with an entirely different ending for the story—and you'll have a new idea, gratis.

Use the same method when seeing a picture or play. Try to figure out the plot development and the denouement in advance, according to your own idea. You'll be amazed at the stock of new ideas you can accumulate by such a method.

Ideas by assignment.   If you are fortunate enough to be working at a studio, you may be confronted with a situation in which your producer throws a title at you, something on the order of "High School Daze" or "Prison Ship." And he'll tell you to write a story for him to fit the title.

Or the studio may have a mock-up (incomplete full-scale model) on the back lot of a New England whaler that has been used in a former picture and has been gathering overhead instead of profits. "Write me a whaling story," you may be told.

The former assignment is the easier of the two. The Hollywood habit of using a title only as bait, without worrying too much about relating it to the story, should enable you to fit almost any idea to the title.

Naturally, you should try to create an attractive title for your story, one that suggests the theme provocatively without revealing it completely. It should contain at least one "color" word, and should be short enough to fit into a movie-house marquee signboard. Even if your original story is bought, the chances are that the original title will be jettisoned for another. A story which started out as "Jane Froman's Story" was switched to "I'll See You in My Dreams," then to "You and the Night and the Music," then to "With a Song in my Heart." It will no doubt be released under still another title—or the original one.

The assignment of writers to a prop calls for a certain amount of ingenuity. Be sure to visit the back lot and examine the mock-up to be used. One screen-play writer was assigned to a prison-ship picture because the studio had the prow of a ship on its back lot. He wrote a complete treatment, using a slave "blackbirding" idea as the theme, only to discover later that the prow was that of a modern oil-cargo ship, with no possibility of being revamped to suit the purposes of the slave-ship story.

Research ideas.   Story ideas may come indirectly, while you are doing research for background material. Suppose you decide a story with a trucking background would be saleable. You do some library research on trucking—its techniques, its peculiar locutions, the character types, etc. Out of this local-color background research may come springboards for a number of story ideas. A magazine article on the trucking business may tell the story of a trucking tycoon and describe his unique experiences. With some judicious adapting, switching, and protective camouflage, these experiences may well serve as the idea for your story.

Remember this: *Ideas proliferate all about you.* They abound in everything you see, everything you do, everyone you meet, everything you read. The British screen-play writer T. E. B. Clarke got the idea for his gimmick in *The Lavender Mob* from a picture postcard.

Ideas are not enough. But the Hollywood studios are crawling with idea men, who do nothing but dream up ideas for pictures. Unless you are well placed in the industry, unless you have the ear of an executive who can say "yea" or "nay" to the purchase of your bare idea, don't try to sell it as an idea alone. Only a Ben Hecht can get away with it. And he has been known to sell an idea verbally, get paid for it, and forget about it the next day. If you can do this, then you are in the wrong business. You should be selling stocks and bonds or real estate.

But if you are just another journeyman writer, like most of us, and can recognize an idea as picture material, adapt it into a fresh conception, and develop it into a cohesive, unified, and dramatic story, then you are well on the road to beginning what may turn out to be an acceptable and profitable sale.

At least you have the basic foundation for going into the next process in the fashioning of a screen play—the synopsis.

Theme outline

The story idea written down in your notebook is only a memory jog. It merely states a situation, a character facet, an ironic twist, a mystery-story clue, a unique method of murder, or any one of the countless other story ideas or devices.

But if you decide to use the idea for a feature-length film, it will be necessary for you to develop it further into a three-act theme outline, and then into a more detailed synopsis.

This process is performed in one of two ways. If the need for the idea is urgent, or if the idea is hot—that is, if it is so compellingly good that you are unable to forget it—then you will think about it continually. It is this "worrying" of an idea in the author's mind that starts a process of plot development which can sometimes result in a complete outline—story synopsis, character development, and all—with which he can go into the next phase of idea development— the laying out of the story treatment. But ordinarily it is better to write out this synopsis, using whatever idea embellishments you may have thought of.

If your idea is to be used as a half-hour television drama, ordinarily you will have to break it up into two acts instead of three. This is to accommodate the insertion of a "middle commercial." As long as advertisers—who make television entertainment possible on a free basis—insist on putting in this middle commercial, it will be necessary for the script writer to write his scripts in two acts, with the first act winding up with some sort of "cliff hanger" situation— either physical or emotional—to serve as an attention carryover from the commercial to the second act. The elimination of this annoying and interest-destroying device will make for more successful television presentations.

Background locale. It will be necessary to introduce a background locale against which the action of your idea can be played.

You may have a background idea to start with. Your idea may be: "What about a picture to expose the advertising-agency racket?" In which case, with a background already set, your next step would be to lay out and develop the idea.

Ordinarily the development would be inherent in or suggested by the basic idea itself. The basic idea may come from another motion picture, as was previously explained. News stories were published about the actor starred in De Sica's *The Bicycle Thief* to the effect that, after his initial success in the picture, he had a difficult time obtaining other screen acting work. Eventually, he was forced to return to his former job of laying bricks.

Now, from this news item it is possible to fashion a screen story that could have the same appeal as *The Bicycle Thief*. It could be the story of a man—a bricklayer or a carpenter or any artisan—who is apparently happy in his work, and with his family. He suddenly finds himself a famous movie star because, and only because, he looks like a bricklayer, thinks like one, can perform the duties of one and, to top it off, can impersonate a bricklayer without appearing to be *acting* like one.

With this springboard the following three-act theme outline, three paragraphs in length, can be evolved.

The first act should consist of a brief resume of the basic situation of the story.

First act resume. A young bricklayer—who is happily married and satisfied with his place in life—is selected to play the leading role in a semi-documentary motion-picture being directed by a famous Hollywood personality who believes in using real people in real situations. As a result of his experiences, subtle changes take place in the bricklayer's character. He becomes dissatisfied with his own work of bricklaying. His relationship with his wife and son undergoes a change. He actually believes he possesses great acting ability despite the fact that it is the director's talent for handling amateur actors that is responsible for the bricklayer's fine performance. He is no longer carefree and philosophical but nervous and anxious as he awaits the great day of the picture's release when, he is sure, the world will recognize him as a great motion-picture star. The attentions of his wife and child are nothing compared with the acclaim of the world.

The second act should leap from this springboard into a gradual development of the story, and should wind up with the climax.

Second act development. After the usual delays, the picture is eventually released, and with great critical and popular acclaim. The young bricklayer is feted and honored. He is asked to make personal appearances—the usual star buildup. And his relations with his wife and son become very strained. He becomes infatuated with the director's wife, who encourages him only because he is in the limelight and because she is in the mood for light flirtation. He is approached by a studio to make another picture. But the original director refuses to work on it because he has other commitments and also because he knows the bricklayer cannot interpret the part.

The bricklayer accepts the offer confidently and, of course, continues his affair with the director's wife. However, despite his immense enthusiasm for acting, his limitations are realized and his contract is dropped. He tries to get work at other studios but to no avail. His discouragement is capped when the director's wife jettisons him with a revelatory payoff. Now, he is right back where he had started except that as a successful has-been he doesn't know which way to turn. He's licked.

The third paragraph should present the denouement, the final revelation that will clarify the outcome of the story and supply a solution to the situation.

Third act denouement. After an argument with his wife, he stalks out of the house followed by his son. Eventually, they find themselves at the entrance to the zoo. The bricklayer is furious because his son prefers to watch a caterpillar rather than a magnificent lion or the exotic birds. The child's simple answer—that he likes to watch the caterpillar and it makes him happy—strikes a soothing chord in the father. On the way home he begins to take notice of the brickwork along the way and comments on it. He stops self-consciously by a building some of his fellow-workers are erecting and, having been taunted, proves he is still a better bricklayer than most. When he arrives home, his wife is startled by his more cheerful attitude and extremely confused when he explains it by telling her he found a caterpillar. We leave him, happily tackling life once more, on a construction job receiving a golden Academy Award Oscar for the part he had played in the picture. Unceremoniously, he throws the Oscar into a refuse dump and returns to his job of laying bricks, a completely satisfied man again.

Write for story analysts. There is a definite reason for writing the theme outline in this way. For that is just what the story analysts will do if your treatment or completed screen play is submitted to the studio on a free-lance basis. It is their job to read everything submitted, and to break down each story into a one-paragraph plot theme, condensing the story so that it can be easily and quickly read by the studio's story chief and the producers.

After boiling down the story to one paragraph, the story analyst reverses the process and enlarges the theme to a three-paragraph summary, on the order of the one given above. If the story is well constructed, it should be able to withstand the sloughing off of the verbiage with which the average writer festoons his stories.

The story analyst's next step is to enlarge the theme summary to a synopsis. He does this only if he likes the story well enough to submit it for possible consideration by the studio. In this synopsis he will write from ten to twenty-five pages, giving a more detailed elaboration of the story outline, the dramatic conflicts, and the characterizations. He sees to it that all excess wordage is eliminated. He stresses the integration of the characters into the story, and makes certain their dominant characteristics are presented, because most of the studios scan story submissions as possible vehicles for stars already under contract to them. Primarily, the theme outline should stress those aspects of the story that would best make for a moving motion picture, and not for a fine piece of writing.

Because the story analyst is your first hurdle at the studios, it is advisable to write your story so that it will stand up under his expert probings. He looks, primarily, for a good basic idea. Then he'll appreciate a rational and moving development of the idea. He'll spot story weaknesses immediately, so make certain that all story holes are plugged up. Finally, he seeks constantly for honest, rational, and orderly character development, perfectly integrated into lively action.

With these facts in mind, your next step should be to develop your story line from the three-paragraph theme outline, to a more detailed synopsis.

Names are important. Now it will be necessary to identify your characters by name. This should not be done haphazardly. Their names should fit them and should be as identifying as their clothing or their speech. Names carry with them certain associations that have come to possess an almost inflexible acceptance by audiences. A "bitch" character, as the industry labels a villainess, would be misnamed "Mary." Conversely, a warm, sympathetic character would hardly be suggested by the names "Daisy" or "Mamie." To the average audience these are names of chorus girls or the girl friend of a Brooklyn character.

The same care should be used in choosing names for national types. But avoid typing within the type. Do not call your Frenchman "Duval" or your Swede "Petersen." These may be common names for those national types, but all Americans or Englishmen are not named Smith or Brown. Try, when possible, to suit the name to the character, by obtaining a translation of the name. The German name "Schoenberg," for example, would be "Belmont."

In the matter of surnames, especially when the name of the protagonist is also to be the title of the picture, strive for euphony. "William Faversham," for instance, ripples. "Martin O'Grady," with the "O" as a grace glide, has a pleasing rhythm. "Simon Bocanegra" has a compelling sonority. "Dan Cott," on the other hand, has a staccato beat. It could be used for a character who is abrupt in his speech and actions. Study Dickens for his superb handling of surnames.

Avoid name clichés. The name "Jason," somehow, has come to represent a skinflint banker. It is almost always used to identify the eccentric millionaire in murder mysteries whose strange will brings together a variegated set of misbegotten relatives. Not all ancient New England codgers are named Caleb. Not all Brooklynite girl friends are named "Mamie." Not all GI's are named Joe. Not all Frenchmen are named Jacques. Not all Russians are named Ivan.

But there are certain names that in themselves suggest the character to be portrayed. Names on the order of Anastasia, Agatha, Abigail, Arabella, Bessie, Elvira, Flora, Hepzibah, Henrietta, Lavinia, Mathilda, Melissa, Nettie, Martha, Tabitha, Sophronisba and Zenobia suggest, somehow, an old-maid aunt, especially when she is a comedy character. Perhaps it is because they are old-fashioned names. But the suggestion is present and must be taken into account when choosing names.

Avoid Tom, Dick, Harry, Joe, and Bill for men unless you intend to use them for comedy purposes, or to symbolize American types. The same applies to Mary, Jane, Sue, and other too familiar names for women.

Use a telephone book to obtain your characters' names. Try to give them names that are not only characteristic but, in addition, have the quality of realism. "Pat Collins," "Robert Montagu," "Phil Rabin," "Rudie Spivak," "Edna Ward," "Kate Woodson"—these are the real names of real people. They are familiar without being cloyingly clichéd.

Do not use a name that might be misinterpreted or misunderstood at normal speech speed, unless for comedy effect. Try to vary the syllabic content of your cast names so as to avoid monotony. Be careful about giving two characters names with the same initial letter. Try not to use the names of actual people in the news. If you do, and if you hold that character up to ridicule, you are inviting certain libel suit. Do not make acrostics out of real names, or reverse real names. They always have a phony, manufactured ring. Unless you have a specific purpose for doing so, give Smith, Jones, and Brown the go-by. Instead, use names that are distinctive, graphic, and easily understood. Above all, do not get snared into the currently popular name trend. Some time ago an epidemic of "Peters" popped into all casts. For women, it was "Lisa." England contributed "Gogo" and "Jiji."

And do not use names for puns. Puns are all right in their place, especially if they are bright and fresh. But puns on names are in bad taste and are resorted to only by rank amateurs.

A last word about names: All character names must be in capitals (GEORGE) when first introduced—in the synopsis, the treatment, and the screen play—for identification purposes. Some prefer to continue capitalization throughout the screen play. Others use only the initial capitalization.

The synopsis

With the names of your characters set, your next job is to enlarge on the three-paragraph theme outline and develop a more detailed synopsis. The result will not contain the complete action of the story as it will go into the finished screen play. For, in the process of continued development of the story, other factors always enter to change the story line, sometimes radically. But, with the synopsis, the writer will have a detailed blueprint to aid him in building the finished edifice of the screen play.

Your first task in this process is to establish your characters. Using the given outline as a basis, you will establish: (a) a young, happy bricklayer (b) his understanding wife (c) his adoring young son (d) an eccentric motion-picture director (e) his beautiful and bored wife (f) an earthy, older bricklayer as a foil and for comedy-relief (g) a cynical know-it-all assistant director to be used as a foil and for comedy relief; together with various minor characters necessary to the development of the story.

Personality shading.   With the characters established, the next step is to develop characterization. In establishing the traits of your characters, care must be taken not to sacrifice realism. No evil person is ever all black. No good guy is always all white. There are nuances of gray that shade off from the white and from the black. More important, there must be reasoning and emotion and often submerged memories behind your characters' actions.

The gangster-villain of your piece should not be shown as a completely broad-stroked blackguard. He should have some redeeming qualities, but they must not be so startlingly at variance with his evil nature as to throw the character completely out of kilter. The oft done movie killer who loves and breeds canaries, goldfish, or angleworms is an example of this fault. An extreme leap from black to white, without the humanizing effect of a gradual gray carry-over, makes for character incredibility.

In *The Prowler* Van Heflin played a gambler who was willing to risk his neck to achieve his ends. In his final breakdown, he is made to say, "I did it for the $62,000—but I love you. You've got to give me credit for that." He was a self-admitted villain, yes, but a human one.

This, too: your good folk should not be so utterly good that they will float away on angel's wings. Then they would become unbelievable and even their virtue would be suspect. "No one was ever that good!" would be the mental reservation of most of the audience, who would like to think themselves all good but realize that they have all sorts of devilish, negative traits as well.

All cats are gray.   Here again, when endowing a good character with negative traits, the method is not to show them in violent opposition to the good qualities, but rather to fashion them so that there will be a gradual graying-off from the white into the black, if there is to be any black at all. Gray qualities usually suffice to round out the character of an ostensibly good person.

These detailed, motivating traits of character, however, need not be brought into the synopsis itself. But a basis for their use must be introduced into it. Later, when the treatment is written, there will be no awkward and unfounded action that must be forced to remain in the script because later plot developments will be based on them.

Conflict from complexities. There is another important reason for not limning a character with one-track traits. The more complex his character, the more conflicts he will engender and be confronted with, and the more variety will there be in those conflicts. Complexity of character breeds conflicts which, in themselves, make for emotion which, by itself, makes for motion, a prime necessity for motion pictures and television dramas.

Puppets are not people. Remember this: Your characters must not be puppets patently manufactured by another. They must be credible human beings with all the physical and emotional wrinkles, wens, warts, and freckles that disfigure most people—so that what they do is the result not of the author's expert plot manipulation, but of an inherent drive within the "real-person" character. Contrived characters make only for contrived situations. When it becomes obvious that it is the writer who is putting his characters into a fix—and is also trying to extricate them from it—then the resultant story becomes contrived, unnatural, unrealistic, and unbelievable.

Is it contrived? The favorite dodge of many story readers, agents, producers, and critics is to label a story they don't like as "contrived." When asked to elucidate the generality with specific examples, most of them back water with a weak, "Well, that's how it strikes me. I just feel it, that's all."

Actually, all stories are contrived, in that they are the creations of writers. Writers brought them into being. But there are certain faults written into many stories that result in mechanized, robot-like action. One of these faults comes with coincidence. An accidental meeting obviously arranged for by the writer makes for a situation that is too pat. Such a situation is the one in *The Third Man,* in which Joseph Cotten is picked up by a tough cabby, in a cab with barred windows, and driven at breakneck speed to—of all things—a lecture on James Joyce. The rigmarole of trying to establish the cabby as a menace and the wild ride as a kidnaping, in order to justify the innocuous pay-off, was a creaking contriving and, what was worse, audience cheating. The menacing cab driver was never established as such and, as a result, his sudden injection into the plot was completely unmotivated. To have introduced him previously, however, would have killed the effect of the pay-off; hence his precipitous arrival.

What makes for a least contrived story, then, are real characters who involve themselves—through the alembic of the writer's imagination—in a crucial situation which they themselves must resolve, either for good or for bad.

Conflict by opposition. Given a set of real characters, your next job is to have the characters become enmeshed in a set of seemingly unsolvable problems and situations. They must be opposed by someone or something. There must be conflict. If there is no appreciable conflict there is no story for motion pictures or television, for only conflict can beget action and only action can endow a drama with motion.

It should not be difficult to do this. We live in a world that teems with opposites capable of generating conflict. For every aspect of life that is good there is a corresponding aspect that is bad. In opposition to health, for example, there is sickness.

The story conflict: a healthy man suddenly finds himself faced with a siege of sickness. How he solves his problems attendant on the sick spell will make your story.

Let's take another set of examples. In opposition to youth there is old age. The story conflict, then, could be: A woman who has been beautiful in her youth finds herself confronted with the problems of old age—loss of love, health, friends, etc. How she goes about solving those problems will be the burden of your tale.

Even colors can make for dramatic conflict. Let's take black and white. The story conflict: a light-skinned Negro who is passing as white is suddenly exposed as a Negro.

The most exploited set of opposites is to be found in the poor-rich pair. In fact, most success stories use it in obvious and clichéd ways.

There is no end to this involvement of characters with "positive" traits in conflict with characters with "negative" traits. You need only a good book of synonyms and antonyms to have an inexhaustible fund, enough to last you for your entire lifetime of writing. Take each set and see what you can do about working out a story conflict.

Once you have mastered the technique of establishing conflicts by contrasting opposites, you should find it comparatively simple to endow your characters with values that represent either positive or negative aspects of their opposite, and to set their conflicts in motion by juxtaposing the opposite aspects.

It is in the synopsis that these basic conflicts must be definitely established. For without conflicts, there will be no story—no motion-picture or television story, at least, which demand that emotional and physical conflict be present if motion is to result.

Problems breed conflicts.   To make certain that your story contains conflict, it is essential that your basic idea possess the seeds of conflict. It must involve the characters in a problem or in a series of problems which must be solved. If they are solved, your screen play will end happily. If these personal problems remain unsolved at the end of the picture, as far as your characters are concerned, your screen play is a tragedy and will have an unhappy ending. But there will be a solution to *your* problem, even though it may be an unhappy one for your characters.

Credible problems.   These problems must stem naturally from the character of the people you are portraying, from their backgrounds and present milieu.

Universality.   At the same time, these problems must have universality. That is to say, they must affect the audience so that they can identify themselves with the character and his problems, and so be made to feel that "there, but for the grace of God, go I."

Empathetic problems.   Also, these problems must have significance, not only to the character, but to the audience, which expects to be entertained. This capacity to entertain can be measured by the natural, human reaction of "empathy," in which each member of the audience is caused to project his separate and individual consciousness into the consciousness of the character. The audience must be made to want to *care* about the character, to become involved in his struggles and in the manner in which he solves his problems and overcomes his conflicts.

To do this it is absolutely necessary that your character possess traits that are personally important to the audience. They must be made to feel that they know each character intimately, that they love or hate him according to his nature and the part he plays in the story—that he could be living down the block, or next door, or even in their own households.

Character dossiers. Before you begin to develop your characters and their story for your synopsis, you must do one thing—prepare a dossier of each of the important ones, containing an extensive background for each, even if you don't intend to use it all for your script. List everything you can think of: milieu of birth; predilections; age, shape, coloring, and general appearance; taste in clothing, art, music, etc.; occupation and hobbies. The dossier should contain everything, in fact, that will aid in obtaining a well-rounded character who can become involved in motivated conflicts that both you and the audience can understand and believe in.

In Mankiewicz's otherwise excellent picture, *All About Eve,* the character of Eve was never fully realized, because her actions were never *fully* motivated. This gave a cast of improbability to her behavior which resulted in making her eventual success somewhat unbelievable. You never understood what it was in her background that made her act as she did.

Plot vs. character

One of the greatest differences between Hollywood films and those made in Europe is to be found in the plot vs. character dilemma with which the screen-play writer is constantly being confronted.

Where the Hollywood product emphasizes the *actions* of the people involved, the European picture—and especially those from the British studios—hew to the *character* line, to the inner motivations of the characters.

The Hollywood method, therefore, in stressing action to the detriment of character, produces a picture that may move but, like an

ineptly handled marionette, often moves erratically and unpurpose-
fully. The European film, on the other hand, in stressing character
to the detriment of action, sometimes slows up to a pedestrian pace
so that the characters lose identity and actuality for want of revelatory action.

Plot and character.   Actually, both extremes err in that neither
takes cognizance of the obvious facts that plot and character should
be interrelated, and that the ideal form would be to combine plot
with character so that each stems from and flows into the other.

What is plot?   The plot of a story is the outlined pattern of action
taken by a certain set of characters. This pattern must involve a
central character—or characters—in a situation that appears to be
hopeless. Then, after being brought into *conflict* with powerful
forces—within himself, in others, or in Nature—the central character
becomes enmeshed in certain *complications* which make the solving
of his hopeless situation even more hopeless. He is forced to do—or
not to do—certain things by the conflict-creating force. These things
he is forced to do create a series of *crises* in his life—turning points
in the story—which build up to a dramatic *climax,* which is the
most important of the *crises.* This climax—resulting from the solving
or from the not solving of the problems—resolves the story in that
it brings the central character to the end of that particular episode
in his life.

No beginning nor ending.   This fact must be noted: There is no
beginning nor ending in most stories. It would be impossible to
picture a person's lifetime from the moment of his birth to the
moment of his last breath. Therefore, a motion picture actually
depicts only a highlighted episode, or episodes, in a person's life.

   This being so, the audience should be given to understand that
the character was living his life before they get their first glimpse
of him on the screen. Also, when they see him in the last fade-out,
they should be made to realize that he will continue to live—if it is
a happy ending—despite the picture's ending.

   If a story can accomplish this—if it can present a character, or a
set of characters, in the complete round, by implication and by
indirection—then it can be said to possess true stature.

It is for this reason, then, that character should not be subverted to the purposes of plot. If a subject can be naturally and realistically characterized in that segment of his life which has been picturized and viewed by the audience, then it would not be difficult for that same audience to visualize not only his pre-picture life, but his post-picture life as well.

The pre-picture elements can be subtly indicated by means of dialogue "hark backs," or by certain present actions that will hark back to similar actions of the past.

The post-picture elements can be suggested, at the picture's end, by means of dialogue and action. The fairy tale's "they lived happily ever after" is an example of writing that suggests the nature of the hero's post-story life.

But aside from these elements, there should be implicit in the character of the hero certain intimations of his pre-picture experience, together with certain implications that will suggest the nature of his actions after the end of the picture is reached.

With pre-picture, picture, and post-picture elements written in unobtrusively, and suggested as intrinsic character components, it is possible to present the picture of a person who, as a certain popular magazine has it, is "unforgettable."

Be chary with crises. In the composing of the plot, care must be taken not to interpret every sequence as a crisis and concluding as one. Instead, the sequence should end in some sort of pay-off. And the various sequences should build to a crisis which, in turn, should be part of the build-up to the climax. To top a crisis with another crisis which in turn is topped with still another crisis, and so on to the actual climax, will result in a picture that loses interest and gains only monotony.

Plot patterns

The plot patterns mentioned above can run the entire gamut of human emotions and actions. Generally speaking, though, they fall into a number of broad classifications. Georges Polti attempted to classify them in his collection of "Thirty-six Dramatic Situations." But these thirty-six can be simplified by even broader grouping.

1. *Love pattern.*   Here, boy meets girl, boy loses girl, boy gets girl is the order of events. It is the tried and true formula of many pictures.

2. *Success Pattern.*   This deals with the attempts of a person to achieve success, which he either does or fails to do, according to the nature of the story. Any of the pseudoscientific, pseudohistorical pictures on the order of *The Magic Bullet* falls into this pattern.

3. *Cinderella pattern.*   Here, the ancient story of the ugly duckling being metamorphosed into a beautiful girl is retold in countless forms. One of the most outstanding examples of this pattern is to be found in the picturization of Shaw's *Pygmalion*.

4. *Triangle pattern.*   The interrelated loves of three protagonists have formed the set pattern for innumerable film stories. That these stories are cut to a pattern should not militate against their quality. The British picture *Brief Encounter* is a fine example of this pattern and is, at the same time, a superb picture. Too often, though, this pattern has degenerated into banalities.

5. *Return pattern.*   The dramatic return of the prodigal son, the wandering father, the missing husband—of Enoch Arden, to use a classic example—is a pattern that has been used in many diverse forms.

6. *Vengeance pattern.*   This is the basic pattern for most murder-mystery stories. A crime is committed and vengeance must be wreaked on the criminal, either by the forces of law and order, or by the person most affected by the crime.

7. *Conversion pattern.*   The story of the reformation of an evil person to virtue has been the subject of countless pictures, good and bad. The bad ones err in that the conversion is usually affected too quickly, and with insufficient motivation. The writers of the good

pictures see to it that the conversions are planned so that they grow out of the character into action, slowly and naturally.

8. Sacrifice pattern. The converse of the vengeance pattern, this pattern revolves around the actions of a person who, by sacrificing himself or his own personal aims, helps another to achieve some desired end. The difficulty here, as far as most pictures are concerned, is that such sacrifice calls for a greatness of character which picture producers, somehow, are either unable or unwilling to permit for fear of sacrificing dynamic character mobility to static character development.

9. Family pattern. That there is drama in the interrelationships of a family group has been proved by the plethora of stories using the family pattern. Such families need not be related by blood. The story can concern the doings of a group of boarding house lodgers, insane asylum inmates, shipboard fellow-travelers; in fact, any group of people thrown together by circumstances whose lives are brought to a dramatic point by those same circumstances. *The Royal Family, Dinner At Eight, Orient Express, You Can't Take it With You,* and many others, successful and unsuccessful, are fitting examples of this extremely popular pattern.

These, then, are the most important and oft-used plot patterns available to the screen-play writer. When they are embroidered with an emphasis on action alone, the results are negligible and add nothing to the stature of the writer. But when attention is paid to character and action, the pattern can become a richly colored work of art.

Minor-character development

Because no human being lives in a vacuum, but is affected by his relations with other human beings, it is necessary, when creating a story, that your central character or characters move in a milieu in which other characters live. Even Defoe had to introduce his man, Friday, in order to vary the conflicts with Nature with human conflicts. These minor characters must be involved somehow in the lives of your major characters or else their presence would be gratuitous.

Minors are human too. But at the same time, these minor characters have lives of their own which cause them to become complicated with those of the major characters. To round out these minor characters so that they can become clothed with essential depth and third-dimensional realism it is necessary that they too be motivated by well defined, natural character traits. For unless they are well developed, their connections with the major characters will become clouded with unreality. As a result, the actions of the major characters, no matter how realistically they may have been presented, will suffer because they will reflect the unreality of the minor characters.

But because they are minor characters, and because they are presented only for brief periods, they must be developed quickly. This can be done in dialogue and action. Often this is accomplished with foreign or regional accents—by making the characters Brooklyn cabbies, Irish cops, or cockney maids.

But this is not enough. It is necessary to present them, not only as sounding like Brooklyn cab drivers, but *acting* like them as well. In addition, they must not be presented as clichéd types, to be seen in hundreds of other pictures, but as individuals. The cab driver, for example, can be given to complaining constantly of traffic cops— a persecution complex. Or, instead of dialogue, he can be characterized by a bit of identifying pantomime—a peculiar grin, an ugly leer, or even a tic. Una O'Connor's mincing walk, in the minor role of the cockney maid in *The Barretts of Wimpole Street,* was a fine example of this type of characterizing. The same actress' nervous cough in *Cluny Brown* was another excellent bit of characterization that gave major proportions to a minor character's part.

Each minor character should be given something—either in dialogue or action—that will endow him with a quality of reality, so that in his relations with the major characters, his genuineness will be reflected in their scenes together.

The writer has a difficult problem, though, in presenting minor characters for a half-hour television film. Because of the comparative lack of time, there is insufficient footage available for developing them. But they should be present to be used as foils for the major characters and also for comedy relief. And the lack of time available makes it imperative that the writer know his minor characters thoroughly, so that though presented briefly, they are believable.

Subplots

Contrast is necessary in every art form. In painting, warm colors are contrasted with cool ones. In motion-picture writing, the good is contrasted with the bad, the slow with the speedy, and the rich with the poor. There must always be some means of comparison, some frame of reference, if any quality, good or bad, is to be presented truthfully and effectively.

That is why in all dramatic forms subplots are resorted to as foils for the main plot. Shakespeare was addicted to far too many of them, which accounts, at times, for the confusion in his plays, especially his comedies. When he hews to the story line, as in *Hamlet* and *Antony and Cleopatra*, Shakespeare's art is seen at its best.

Basically, a subplot is a divagation from the main story line, concerning minor characters whose doings are tied in with the main story line and with the actions of the major characters.

Integrate subplots. To be most effective, a subplot must be integrated into the main story line. It must contribute to its development, influence its crises, or affect its climax. In many screen plays this is accomplished by having the minor characters in the subplot involved as friends of the major characters. Thus, the girl in the story usually has a wisecracking girl friend who, while the heroine is involved with her own young man, is also having romantic complications, in a subplot. That is a basic formula.

Variations are unlimited, their freshness being in direct ratio to the creative ability of the screen-play writer. But the girl friend's subplot must be integrated with the heroine's main story line so that its developments are contributory, in some way, to the developments of the main story line. The wider the divergence between the two the less correlation there will be, and an element of confusion will be introduced that will destroy unity and coherence and make for utter confusion in the audience.

Other subplot uses. Subplots and minor characters have this added virtue—they make excellent vehicles for comedy relief, crisis relief, and time-lapse cutaways. When the major story line becomes too tense, the action can always be cut away to the antics of the characters in the subplot.

Play majors against minors. In addition, minor characters in subplots can be used as character foils for the major characters and their story line. Every comedian must have a straight man off whom he can bounce his gags. In the same way, the characters of those taking part in the major story line can be heightened tremendously simply by playing them against the characters of those in the minor roles. The quick-thinking executive can always be made to appear quicker thinking if he is permitted to play against a slower thinking person as a foil.

Major treatment of minors. A word of warning: Don't slough off the writing of minor characters in subplots. They must be well motivated persons with definite, individual characters—with traits and actions that are reactions of inner compulsions. The same attention must be given to them as to those in the major story line.

And the same attention must be paid to the subplot story line as well. Not only should it be a story in itself, but it must be carefully worked out and integrated into the main story line. It should build within itself and, simultaneously, within the framework of the main story line. But its importance must never be permitted to get out of hand so that it will intrude into and take precedence over the main story line.

Obviously, the more subplots in a story the greater the possibility of losing the main story line. In the British film *Laughter in Paradise* three or four separate subplots served to make the main story quite confusing.

Love in the minors. Minor characters have a peculiar habit of charming the writer. Because they are usually parts written for character actors, because they are sometimes more real than the major characters, the writer unconsciously finds himself falling in love with them. Before he is aware of it, he discovers he is writing his best lines and situations for them. The result is disproportion in regard to the emergence of the main characters. Such dispro-portion tends to throw emphasis from the main story line to the subplot and its minor characters. In most films in which a minor character obviously steals the picture from the star this failing is usually to be found in evidence in the original scripts.

In half-hour television scripts, the subplots must be limited both in number and in length. Once again the time factor intrudes, so that it is impossible to do justice to the major story line if too much attention is paid to the subplot. Subplots are admissible, but only if they can be used to point up the main story without digressing too far from it.

Dramatic values

Your synopsis should now contain certain inherent emotional values inculcated into its story line. But emotion is not enough. Emotion in itself is static unless it is related to action.

Motivate actions. Conversely, any action need not be dramatic in itself. It too must be motivated by specific emotions, emotions that could only result in the concluding action.

Shock dramatics. Dramatic values, in other words, must contain certain factors that make for an empathetic reaction from the audi-ence. They must have shock value. They must deviate from the expected norm so that, when presented, they will create a definite reaction in the viewer.

A car driving along a road is a normal phenomenon. It has in-herent movement. But it is not necessarily dramatic movement. It can be dramatized, however, and thus thrill the audience, simply by having it swerve off dangerously as it hits a soft shoulder on the road.

A slum child staring into a bakery window is an ordinary sight. But dramatic value can be injected by having the child's nose flat-tened against the windowpane—thus high-lighting the child's yearn-ing and also stimulating the viewer's sympathy.

An act of courage, in a war picture, can be given heightened dramatic impact, and can achieve truly heroic proportions, *if it is shown* that the heroism was performed in the face of dangerous obstacles—exploding shells, rat-tat-tatting machine guns, barbed wire, etc.

The horns of a dilemma. Dramatic values are especially present in a situation in which a character finds himself, as it were, on the horns of a dilemma. He must be confronted with a situation in which he is forced to make a decisive choice. Then, as Hollywood puts it, "he's in a manhole" out of which he must extricate himself or perish.

Structural unity. But these points of impact, of dramatic values, must have continuity, unity, and coherence and, in addition, they must build to a climax. Once the story theme has been made clear, the developments should flow from the theme, through the theme, and around the theme. Everything in the story should contribute to its structural unity. The characters, their actions and reactions, their speech, the milieus in which they operate—everything should be made a part of a life that flows from the FADE IN of the picture to the FADE OUT.

Straight-line story line. The story line, however, must not progress in a straight line. It can appear to wander off at times, but only for planned, definite purposes.

The straight-line story line is the commonplace story, the development of which forces the characters to follow hackneyed patterns of behavior which result in hackneyed situations and, therefore, in definitely undramatic values. This subject will be treated more fully in the section entitled GIMMICKS. But here it will suffice to mention that the story line must never be one of straight, to-be-expected developments.

For the straight-line story reveals its plot prematurely. It excludes the important element of suspense—of which more later. This factor of suspense is not confined strictly to "who-dunnits" and psychological thrillers. It is an element that should be present in every story if audience interest is to be maintained.

Telegraphing.   A major fault that robs many stories of suspense is to be found in "telegraphing"—revealing a story point prematurely so that an imminent incident is robbed of its full dramatic value. A prize fighter is said to "telegraph" his Sunday punch when, as a preparatory maneuver, he cocks his fist, wrist, and elbow in such a manner as to inform his opponent that an intended haymaker is on the way. This same fault is to be found in many badly written stories.

Telegraphing can be visual and verbal. It would be verbal telegraphing, for instance, to have one of your characters announce, "I'm afraid we're going to have trouble with that guy!" The audience will then expect that trouble and be on the *qui vive* for it, so that when it does eventually come it will have lost its dramatic impact.

Other common errors of this type are such statements as, "You'll be sorry for this," and, "He doesn't know what's in store for him," and, "You'll find out soon enough"—in short, any predictions of dire consequences that tend to vitiate suspense.

Suspense

The quality of suspense involves degrees of mental uncertainty, curiosity, anxiety, and, in an oblique manner, sympathy. When these qualities are evident in a picture they can be transferred to the audience so that they, too, by empathy, can suffer the same anxieties and uncertainties as the characters.

Suspense can contribute to the flow of continuity. By forcing the audience to *want* to know how things are going to turn out, suspense thus makes for a constancy of attention that moves along with the unreeling of the picture.

In the British film *The Spider and the Fly,* for example, the audience's curiosity, anxiety, and sympathy are centered on Phillipe in that extremely suspenseful scene in which he tries to make a desperate getaway after the bank robbery by walking across the overhead girder. The device is simple and old. The old-time serials used it at the end of every episode.

But when your hero is thrown into a seemingly inescapable situation, he must be able to extricate himself not by accident, nor by a coincidental happenstance, but by his own devices. It must be his own strength and ingenuity that result in the solving of his problem. The long bow of coincidence twangs inharmoniously when the marines just happen to be around, or when the hero accidentally discovers a ladder in the manhole.

Someone to root for. It is necessary, first of all, to present the characters so that they will gain the sympathy and interest of the audience. Without an understandable and sympathetic character, there can be no audience interest. If there is no interest, then there can be no anxiety for that character's present and future. Few people can attend a horse race, for example, without placing a bet on a horse, even if it's one chosen at random. This gives the bettor a horse to root for in the race, a horse in whose immediate future the bettor becomes vitally interested.

The motion-picture onlookers must be vitally concerned with the character if they are to be expected to root for him and with him in his struggle to achieve his ends, or to overcome his difficulties, or to solve his problems. Once this interest is created—once this link of sympathy is welded—then it is a simple step for the audience to suffer the tenseness that accompanies temporary setbacks or moments of indecision and uncertainty.

These moments of indecision, however, can be created only when your hero is opposed by a force that is either more puissant than he, or is his mental or physical equal. Doubt as to the outcome of any conflict—which creates suspense—can result only when the opposing forces are equally aligned, or when the evil force appears certain to have the upper hand.

Story-line suspense can be achieved in many ways. With the combined factors of the visual and the verbal available to the screenplay writer, the possibilities are increased tremendously.

Write—don't telegraph. At no time, though, should the audience be given an inkling of *exactly* what is going to happen. They can be teased with vague presentiments, with indefinite suggestions, and at times even with misleading clues—a favorite dodge of the master, Hitchcock—but never with telegraphing, suspense-killing giveaways of the climactic action that is to come.

Anything the audience sees but which it is unable to understand readily, will add to the suspense. But suspense must not be injected for the sole purpose of creating suspense. It must be completely justified. It must flow out of the characters and out of their actions. And it must flow smoothly into the eventual revelation which suddenly makes the audience aware of the full significance of what has previously been unknown.

Don't withhold. Suspense cannot be sustained if important—but necessary—items of plot information are deliberately ignored by the writer and conveniently withheld from the audience. This fault is apparent in many mystery stories where important clues are not given, or are glossed over, so that the real killer's identity can be continued to be hidden. Such suspense may work for a while. But the time will come when the revelation is essential. And the audience will sense a definite feeling of having been cheated. The result will be a denouement that will fizzle out completely.

The otherwise fine work of William Irish—also writing under the nom de plume of Cornell Woolrich—contains numerous examples of another type of suspense which, if used ineptly, tends to confuse, mislead, and disappoint. His people always become involved in situations which seemingly have little to do with the main story line. Occasionally, at the end of the story, the author justifies the use of these irrelevant scenes by tying them in with the denouement. But more often than not, most of these extraneous episodes remain unexplained, even to the very end of the story.

Such suspense defeats its purpose. Too much of it, for instance, becomes boring. At the same time, any and all unexplained suspense episodes that are not *paid off* at the end remain like stickle burs in the audience's subconscious, and tend to detract from the effects of legitimate suspense episodes the author has created.

The pay-off. Every dramatic element in the story must pay off. That is to say, they must all come to some satisfactory conclusion after the denouement. The running gag—which will be dealt with shortly—must be capped with a "topper" (a humorous denouement). The hidden papers must eventually be found. The missing heir must turn up. The character traits of an individual actor must result in something positive. Information that has been withheld must be revealed to achieve its full measure of suspense value. If minor characters or subplots are introduced for suspense effects, a return must be made to the major story line at the end of the story and they too must be paid off.

The telegram fashioned into the shape of an airplane in Reed's *The Fallen Idol* flies lazily through space, lands at the detective's feet, and is then kicked about by him. But eventually he picks it up. After he creates a terrific amount of suspense by fingering it idly, unfolding it casually, and then glancing only at its contents, he pays off the gimmick by revealing to Baynes, the accused butler, that he has read the contents of the telegram, thus upsetting the butler's chief alibi.

This element of suspense must be introduced into the synopsis first. Later on, in the screen play, it can be developed further by the judicious use of angles and shots. Film editing can add tremendously to suspense. These methods will be dealt with in their respective sections. But here the fact must be stressed that the element of suspense is vital to the synopsis story—love story as well as mystery, comedy as well as tragedy.

Suspense tricks. There are innumerable little tricks that can be introduced later on, in the treatment and in the screen play, that can add a fillip of suspense.

1. The entrance through a door of someone other than the one expected.

2. The tire blowout, machine breakdown, or any minor accident.

3. The messenger or emissary delayed by a casual stop engendered by curiosity, arranged for or otherwise.

4. The ignoring of an important letter, package, or any other vital item, by a number of people who could profit were they to stop, recognize, and identify it.

These and many other similar devices—anything, in fact, that interrupts what appears to be the inevitable—are all legitimate tricks that can be adopted and adapted for suspense purposes.

Fight against time. One of the most effective and most often used of such devices for sustaining suspense in motion pictures is the so-called "fight against time." This is so because it contains all the virtues of movement, of violent action and reaction so essential to the forward flow of a good motion picture.

A crude but effective application of this device has the baddie say, "If you don't hand over the papers by the time I count five, well . . ." Then he starts to count as the shot changes to an extreme close-up of his trigger finger squeezing relentlessly on his gun. And as the dread "five" approaches, suspense mounts almost to the breaking point.

When the fight-against-time device is used in a static situation, the result is suspense. When, however, it is used in a situation that requires sustained movement, the result is a chase (which see) containing the elements of suspense. This device has been used so often, however, that its effectiveness has been considerably blunted by repetition. It has been particularly handy in crime pictures, where the governor must be reached for a pardon before the innocent man is electrocuted; in Westerns, where the posse must be informed of the imminent arrival of the cattle rustlers; and in comedies where the husband must get home in time to warn the little wife, who cooks from tin cans, of the unscheduled arrival of his boss, who dotes on home cooking.

Regardless of its overuse, though, it can be adapted in some form or other as a device for carrying the movement forward and of thus sustaining interest through suspense. The creative writer should be capable of taking over this hoary mechanism and creating a freshly slanted twist, the originality of which can more than compensate for its ancient lineage.

A classic use of the device came up in Hitchcock's *The Woman Alone,* which featured the journey of a little boy carrying a time bomb that had been set to go off at one o'clock. The camera followed the boy in his meandering through the London streets, as he stopped to have his hair shampooed by an itinerant soap grifter, as he paused to get a puppy, etc., until finally he boarded a bus. All the while, the audience had been shown various shots of different clocks indicating that the time was dangerously approaching one o'clock. Finally, after an almost excruciating, ever mounting peak of suspense—and as the last clock indicated the creeping but insistent stream of minutes, then seconds—the time bomb exploded and the crowded bus blew up.

Actually, every story—if it is to show a struggle to achieve a definite end—must have some form of this fight-against-time element in its make-up. Someone must do something before something or someone else intervenes to frustrate his intentions. By adding a definite limit to the time in which the intention is to be executed, the suspense can be heightened and the interest strengthened and sustained. Even without setting a time limit, suspense can result.

The chase

The fight-against-time device is usually part of another dramatic device, one that has been popularized by, and is best suited to, the motion picture. It is the chase.

Movement in the extreme.   The chase was used in the first feature motion picture ever produced—*The Great Train Robbery*. It has been an effective stock in trade ever since.

Griffith used it effectively in the ice floe scene of *Way Down East,* in the ride of the hooded men in *Birth of a Nation,* and in the chase to save a man doomed to the gallows in *Intolerance,* which he also used in Danton's ride to the guillotine in *Tale of Two Cities.*

The chase, of all filmic devices, is basic motion-picture material. By its very nature, because it presents movement in the extreme, it furnishes motion to every picture in which it plays a part. There was a time, in the early days of picture making, when the chase was imperative, because the producers were fully cognizant of its sure-fire propensities.

Universal application.   Even today the chase is still being used in almost every picture. Westerns, especially, dote on it. Even documentaries, which supposedly eschew the hackneyed feature-film tricks to create cinematic devices of their own, often rely on the chase. O'Flaherty's *Louisiana Story* used it in a number of variations in the scenes between the boy, the alligator, and the tame coon. And De Sica's magnificent *Bicycle Thief* was a chase from beginning to end, with Maggiorani and his son chasing the bicycle thief through the murky streets of Rome.

Western chases.   The broad-vista setting of a mountain range as a backdrop lends itself admirably to a chase of any sort, especially when the sound effects of clopping hoofs, horses' snorts, and jingling spurs and harness add to the sense of excitement. Years ago it was the cowboys who chased the Indians who, in turn, had chased the unwary settlers in their Conestoga wagons. Nowadays cowboys chase cattle rustlers, posses chase stagecoach robbers, and the villain chases Li'l Nell as she approaches the dynamited mine.

Sam Wood's last picture had two chase sequences—one in which the soldiers wiped out most of the Indians, and the other where the escaped Indians set a trap for the whites, killed most of them, and were in turn wiped out by the Reserves.

Comedy chases. The chase is especially effective in comedies. The old-time two-reelers featured a chase in almost every sequence. The Keystone Cops came into being because they were needed to chase baggy-pants comedians. When the camera was slowed down to twelve frames a second (which increased the number of photographed frames and thus sped up the action) the chase was made to appear even faster and the action more hilarious. In photographing Westerns, the normal twenty-four frames per second are gradually cut down to eighteen frames in chase scenes. Cross-screen action need not be slowed down to increase the speed but head-on shots are usually photographed at twenty frames per second to increase speed. A wide-angle lens is also used to accomplish the same effect. More about these matters later, however.

Murder chases. In murder-mystery stories the chase usually begins with the discovery of the crime and with the uncovering of the first clue. Here the chase is more subdued, slower paced. It becomes not so much a chase from one place to another—where the movement is obvious—but a more subtle procedure, one that is slowed down to a stalk.

Very often, though, especially in suspense or crime-without-murder stories, the chase can become as frenzied as in a two-reel Western comedy. In the British film *A Run for Your Money* an effective, sustained chase was used in which one character was pursued by another while the girl was being tracked down by her victim and a harassed copy boy, vainly trying to capture his charges, wound up being captured by the police himself. This double chase has been successfully exploited in Hitchcock's films. In his *The Lodger* the

Ripper is chasing the young girl, or his next victim, while, at the same time, the Ripper is being chased by the Scotland Yard man who is in love with the young girl.

The Carol Reed picture, *Odd Man Out*, was a sustained chase from beginning to end, suspenseful to the very moment when the chase ended with Mason and his girl framed in the pitiless glare of the police-car headlights.

Build your chase.   To be effective, the chase requires top-notch film editing, to which the screen-play writer can contribute by writing in suitable shots and shot descriptions.

The chase calls for, in the first place, careful attention to "building." It must be introduced after the characters in the chase are fully identified, and after their place in the scheme of the story is well established. There can be variations of this dictum, of course. The hunter, for example, need never be identified until the very end of the picture. Then, again, the identity of the hunted need never be established until the picture's closing shots, as was done in *The Mask of Dimitrios*.

But by and large, if the chase is to be integrated, its characters and their relationships must be fairly well established. That done, the exposition of the plot can then be developed slowly at first, but gradually mounting in speed by shortening the length of the scenes until the actual chase begins.

Dialogue impedes chases.   The chase itself then, should serve as the high spot of the build-up. It should be written briskly. The dependence here should be not so much on dialogue as on action. The audience should be permitted to see the story rather than to hear it being told in dialogue form. In Western chases, minutes often elapse before a word of dialogue is heard, and then the dialogue is usually staccato, on the order of a laconic, "He went thataway!" the cliché which has come to typify most Western chases.

For dialogue tends to slow up the action necessary to the chase. But where the action has been breathlessly fast and where a halt is called for, dialogue—and only that of the terse, staccato type—can be introduced, in much the same manner as a jockey checks the speed of his horse in order to reserve enough strength for a burst of speed in the home stretch.

Suspense chase. The chase should never be permitted to go along unimpeded so that the outcome will always be known to the audience. Suspense must be added. This can be done by having the hunted just miss falling into the hunter's hands, eluding him by some accident or, preferably, by a resourceful stratagem. These episodes of near capture and near escape should be shortened—in scene length—as the action of the chase progresses, so that by the time the capture, or escape, is imminent the pacing is such that the escape or capture occurs at a high spot.

This pacing on the part of the writer can be accomplished by writing the scenes so that they will time progressively shorter and shorter; by cutting away from shots of the hunter to those of the hunted; by using the techniques of suspense outlined in the section devoted to shots.

Chase sound effects. The use of sound effects is very important to the chase—is almost an essential adjunct to it. In comedies, the rattles and bangs of the trick auto add a sort of comic verisimilitude. In the Western "hoss oprys" chase, the clop of horses' hoofs, the squeak of saddle leather, the click of hardware, the grind and groan of the swaying stagecoach, the snuffling of the horses, the punctuating pistol shots are all accouterments to the chase. In murder mysteries the use of such sound atmospherics as echoing footsteps, creaking doors, disembodied shrieks in the night, and dogs baying at the moon, can all be used to give an effect of third-dimensional chase tension. Sometimes, in suspense pictures, a desired mood can be achieved by the complete absence of sound, or by the sudden injection of a slight sound into tense silence.

The British picture *It Always Rains on Sunday* concluded with an astounding chase when the hero tried to escape capture by the police. It was climaxed by a terrifying melange of railroad sounds when he was cornered in a switchyard—the puff of locomotives, the click of steel rails, the screaming of sirens, the clank of boxcars—these sounds, played as a sort of aural backdrop to the chase, served to give it a sense of tense expectancy that made it the redeeming sequence of what was a pretentious and otherwise unsatisfactory picture. The section devoted to sound will suggest additional uses of this important element in chase sequences.

Chase direction. A very important factor in a chase sequence is the direction which the chase takes. This is actually within the province of the director and the film editor. But the screen-play writer should have some knowledge of the techniques involved so that the script material he supplies will be as usable as possible, and so that rewrites may be avoided. This subject will be dealt with more fully in other sections, so it will suffice to say here that the direction the action takes on the screen—from left to right or from right to left—must be consistent throughout so that the audience is able to accompany the hunter and the hunted as they approach each other.

Anything can happen. The chase has a peculiar virtue in that, in it, anything can happen. Where the other elements of a picture must hew to the line of normality, the elements of the chase can be atypical. They can be comic, humanly realistic, outlandishly burlesqued, even maudlinly sentimental. Chaplin's comedies—even the later ones—drool with bathos of the worst sort. Yet, because much of the bathos is introduced in a fast-action chase, the frenetic, supercharged effects engendered by the chase tend to offset the false sentiment, so that it loses some of its objectionableness.

So, in the chase, the writer has an opportunity to go hog-wild, as it were, with his creative imagination. Because anything can happen in a seemingly uncontrolled chase, even the most fantastic situations and developments can be resorted to. Hitchcock and René Clair have both fully realized this virtue of the chase in many of their pictures.

In the old days almost every comedy company hired what it termed a "wild man," someone who knew nothing about picture making but who was capable of suggesting the most outlandish, the most impossible things to be done. The results were chases that bordered on the maniacal—but they were funny.

Picturesque chases. To be most effective, chases should take place in picturesque locales, places that are not necessarily pretty but, rather, out of the ordinary. They can occur on murky docks, through towering theater fly galleries, across impassable canyons, through underground water mains (*He Walks by Night* and *The Third*

Man), over mist-hung moors (*The Hound of the Baskervilles*), in ghost towns (*The Prowler*), in cavernous warehouses, up and down grand staircases, through the length of a transcontinental train, up and down the muck of slum streets, in the tortuous corridors of a mine, through the halls of Madame Tussaud's Wax Museum, among the ruined headstones of a cemetery, across the arctic tundras, through impenetrable jungles, up and down the escalators of a department store, from basement to attic of a deserted old house, up and down the various floors of a skyscraper, on circus grounds, up and down the elevators of the Eiffel Tower (*The Man on the Eiffel Tower*)—anywhere, at any time, with anyone, anything can happen in a chase.

Of late, there has been a tendency to conduct chases through streets glistening in the night from a previous rain. Carol Reed's *The Third Man* used it, as did his *The Fallen Idol*. The French *Such a Pretty Little Beach*, directed by Yves Allégret, leaned heavily on the photogenic quality of wet pavements adopted, no doubt, from the originator of the effect, Marcel Carné, whose latest picture, *Marie du Port*, features this excellent chase background.

In ordinary circumstances, it would be considerably out of place in a dramatic picture to have action call for dumping a policeman in a stream. But in *The 39 Steps*—which certainly could not be classified as a comedy—this was done and the director got away with it because it was performed in a chase sequence.

The importance of the chase to any screen play cannot be overestimated. To master its intricacies is to be well on the road to success.

The serial

Although the writing of weekly juvenile serials is done by a few specialists, it would not be amiss here to discuss some of the aspects of serial screen-play writing. It is apropos at this time because all serials consist of a chase that extends over fifteen two-reel episodes of film. It is also appropriate because eventually such serials will undoubtedly become television fare—if they are not so already. The principles which apply to the theater presentation variety will also apply to those that will be made especially for television.

The first serial to be made was *Fantomas,* a French production, in 1913. The first American imitation came with *The Adventures of Kathleen.* Since then, thousands have been ground out to regale juveniles and, more often than they care to admit, adults as well.

In the old days, such serials as *The Man with the Iron Claw, The Voice on the Wire,* and *The Perils of Pauline* were replete with death-dealing buzz saws, dynamited dams, lava cauldrons, alligator pools, flaming buildings, locomotives, and the like. Nowadays, the trend is to death rays, atomic bombs, poison steam, bacteria, nerve gas, and other such modern forms of civilized persuasion.

The serial screen-play writer's job is to dream up new and ingenious perils—fabulous "manholes" in which the hero or the heroine become entrapped. In addition, he must also supply the method by which the good guy is able to free himself.

The escape must come shortly after the introductory recap of each episode. This recap recounts the details of the previous episode's climactic point, in which the hero is left dangling over the cliff's edge the while a cougar nibbles at his straining fingers. Then comes what is known as the "take-out"—the rescue, in other words.

To accomplish this, it is necessary to cheat the audience with what is known as a "cheater cut." This is done by cutting in a few feet of a scene that introduces the means of escape which had been carefully ignored in the closing feet of the previous episode: that is, the hero's leaping from the wagon immediately before it goes crashing over the cliff, or succeeding in de-activating the death-ray machine seconds before it is to be detonated.

All this preliminary material must be brought out in the first two or three minutes of each episode. From then on, the action becomes once again a wild, headlong chase which, in the closing feet of the film, ends with the hero hopelessly entrapped by the baddie.

The first few minutes of this twelve-minute section should be devoted to exposing the course the new action is to take. The bad guy, for example, orders his henchmen (they're always henchmen in serials) to waylay the hero's girl as she wends her way to her father's scientific laboratory. Suspense is then introduced for about two minutes, as we see the girl being stalked by the mobsters, and as we yearn for the marines to arrive, in the form of the bemuscled but shapely hero. Of course, he does arrive, in the nick of time—to coin a cliché—and, after a desperate brawl with the baddie's mobsters, succeeds in succoring the fair maiden.

This leads us into what is called the "middle action." This fight with the tough guys must always be a sadistic, knock-'em-down, drag-'em-out ruckus. Balsa-wood chairs are smashed over heads, breakaway tables are broken to bits, plaster-thin pottery is scrambled into shards and sugar-glass windows are broken. Then various and sundry gymnastics are indulged in by the hero and the toughest tough guy—always performed by doubles, in long shots (intercut with close-ups of the real actors), so as to make them unidentifiable. These invariably end with the tough guy landing a lucky, one-punch knockout blow on the hero's chin.

The girl is then spirited away by the henchmen and the place is set on fire with our hero still unconscious in it. But he recovers in time to avoid cremation and undauntedly lopes out to chase the heroine-snatching villains.

This is where the high spot of the chase comes in. It should run for about seven minutes of film and should call into play the use of any vehicles that move, and the faster the better. By this time, nine minutes of the serial should have elapsed, so that when the hero reaches the baddie's hangout, he should have about two or three minutes of time to become embroiled in still another fight with the henchmen, in an attempt to save the girl from a fate worse than death. Once again the hero should receive a lucky clout on the jaw. Once again he finds himself chin-deep in a manhole situation. Once again the girl is whisked away as the water slowly fills the manhole, to kill off the hero for certain this time.

It should be obvious from the foregoing that the accent in serials is on action. One inflexible rule in the making of serials is: *Keep it moving!* Only a minimum of dialogue should be written—about seven hundred words per episode—and only enough to carry the plot forward. There must be no idle repartee, no wisecracks.

Characterization, of course, must be sedulously avoided. The hero must always be a clean-living, typical American lad. The leading heavy, or menace, must always be sinister and suave. And his henchmen must always be "dirty dog" heavies, with leering countenances, innumerable facial scars, and heavy eyebrows. The heroine must be blonde, frail, comely, capable of displaying a perpetual "badge of sufferance" and, at the same time, sturdy enough to withstand the rigors of being mauled and of mauling back. Never must there be even the slightest leer of sex to besmirch her relations with the hero. This is so because all serials are made for only one kind of audience—the Saturday-afternoon kid trade, particularly in rural areas. City kids get their blood and thunder from the radio and television serials. British kids, somehow, aren't taken in by them unless, of course, they are Western serials, with cowboys and Indians. On the other hand, South American audiences have been known to see fifteen complete episodes at one sitting!

The making of serials is definitely a budget proposition. Only the most economy-minded producers are put on them. Cheap screenplay writing is used. Shots calling for big sets fall back on the use of sets that have been used in other pictures and have not been struck. Stock film is a must: wild animals, train crashes, conflagrations, and the like. If horses are called for, only a few are rented and they are mounted by a few riders who are photographed separately, to give the impression of a mob of horses and riders. Shooting schedules are hectic sessions, with action comparable to the action in the scenes shot. A good serial unit should be able to get an average of 125 shots in the can—about 18 minutes of running film—in one day's work. The average cost of a serial runs to anywhere from $300,000 to $500,000—that is for 30 reels of finished film or about four feature-length pictures.

A word about the serial's opening episode: it must introduce and establish the characters first. Then it must introduce the "weenie." This is the thing, the object, the papers, the will, the secret formula, the treasure map, the pearl of great value which sets the suave bad guy off on his trail of mayhem and arson against the good guy and his gal. It is the seesawing struggle to obtain this weenie which motivates the action of the serial. If you can think up a new weenie, and devise new methods of torture, new manhole situations, and new take-out devices, you can be kept busy at the Columbia, Universal-International, and Republic Studios, where most serials are made.

But your creative faculties should stop there. For from then on you must conform to the strict rules of serial-making. They are inflexible. Like the rigid, formalistic movements of a ceremonial dance, they must be adhered to with complete conformance.

Westerns

Because most Westerns are made for the same juvenile trade as serials, they must also conform to certain traditions. The hero must always be brave, forthright, honest, trustworthy, kind, obedient, cheerful, thrifty, clean, and reverent—like his Cub Scout fans. The villain must always be a "yeller-bellied polecat." The girl must always be long-haired, of sweet disposition and with sufficient histrionic ability to portray a sunny disposition. Love is only sissy stuff, and woe be it if the hero ever dares kiss his girl friend. He may nuzzle his horse, but love with a girl is not countenanced.

The pattern remains unchanged since the days of Bronco Billy's "hoss oprys" or "oaters," as they are termed in the trade. That it pays off is proved by the fact that about thirty-five per cent of all American films are of the Western variety. A cheap-budgeted straight Western picture, costing between thirty-five and fifty thousand dollars to produce, is sure of netting a fifty per cent profit.

The pattern, of course, is the old familiar conflict between the hero, as represented by the cowboy, and the villain, as represented by the cattle rustler, the crooked sheriff, the rapacious banker or, in fact, any low character. The same pattern can be found in the three types of Westerns: the low-budgeted straight Western; the musical Western which usually features a recognized name star and which is produced on a medium budget; and the deluxe, top-budget, million-dollar production put out by the big studios. Basically, as far as plot pattern is concerned, there is little difference between a Monogram Studios *Riders of Gower Gulch* or Republic Studio's *Gun Totin' Sheriff* and the major studios' *The Plainsman, Stagecoach,* and *Duel in the Sun.*

Within the narrow framework of that pattern, and encumbered with a variety of taboos and musts, the screen-play writer must fashion a story that will result in a picture that is fresh, provocative, and cheap. Usually he compromises with all those qualities but the last. The hoss-opry audience wants nothing better. It cannot recognize quality or value. When a superior Western, *The Oxbow Incident,* dared to stray from the accepted formula, it received wide critical acclaim—but died in the box office. Its people were depicted in shades of gray. It was real. But the audience stayed away in droves because it did not give them what they seek in all Westerns—escape.

The moral is this: Forget about any ideas you may have about doing something new and different if you are ever assigned to do a Western picture. Not that this is a common occurrence, for most Western screen plays are written by specialists willing to accept seasonal employment. Westerns are shot only in the outdoors when the weather is clement enough to warrant continuous days of shooting.

But if you can turn out reasonably different variations on the same theme pattern; if you are hep to cowboy lingo (and it must be authentic, and not of the Coney Island variety) ; if you are conversant with the mores of the old West; if you have seen sufficient hoss oprys and read enough Western novels to be able to limn Western characters with reasonable likenesses of same; if you are quick on the typewriter trigger finger and can turn out a Western opus in, at most, two weeks; if you know some of the many methods for cutting production costs; if you have a faculty for visualizing and for depicting exciting horse chases; if you can remember not to permit cowboys to fire their six-shooters more than six times without reloading; if you are able to write scene after scene without resorting to action-impeding dialogue; if you are aware of the limitations of a horse's mentality so that you do not give it too many script lines to read; if you can remember that cowboys are sexless, silent, strong men of impeccable scruples; if you are willing and able to forget that you are a creative writer, and to compose drivel of the corniest kind—then you should be able to make a pretty good living.

The gimmick

The search for the weenie is not confined to serials and Westerns alone. Known variously as the "gimmick," "old switcheroo," "weenie," "boff," "yak," "topper," "twist," "routine," "formula," "heart," and "bleeder," this device is used in other types of pictures. It is simply an arbitrary reversal of the usual elements in a situation designed to achieve a shock effect. It is not a new literary device. It has been used as a writer's tool for centuries. It was brought to the apex of perfection in O. Henry's short stories.

In Hollywood the gimmick is the most overused stock in trade. It is because of the gimmick that Hollywood pictures stress plot to the detriment of genuine characterization. Few story conferences have been held in which the discussion did not revolve around some sort of "switcheroo" for the story under discussion.

A supervisor will suggest, "But suppose we make it so the girl ain't his daughter."

"Can't," the writer will reply laconically, "the father's character hasn't been written that way."

"It'll make a better story if it is."

So our writer returns to his cubbyhole and rewrites his story until it is completely out of joint, in order to squeeze in the gimmick. And the result will be a surprise ending that will have shock effect —but nothing more.

One independent producer purchased a radio drama solely because of the unique gimmick which he thought would make for a good picture. His writers evolved a completely new story to fit the gimmick. Then the picture was shot. After viewing the answer print (the last temporary print made before the final release print is OK'd), the producer decided he didn't like the gimmick after all, reshot the end, and made it, of all things, a dream topper.

The gimmick has its place in the screen-play story. There is no denying it. The impact of the surprise—if it is used in the right place, at the right time, and with the proper character build-up—can be entertaining. But the gimmick must not be used for itself alone.

Integrate the gimmick. It, too, must be completely integrated into the flow of the story. As surprising as its revelation may be, it must be realistic in that it should be within the realm of probability as far as the characters and their actions are concerned. It should be presented so that the audience will accept it as something that could very well have happened.

If the gimmick is not integrated into the story, does not flow from a legitimate character development, and is used solely for surprise effect, it will overshadow the main story line. The audience will then come away from the picture with the impression of the gimmick alone. And although they may have been entertained by the gimmick's novelty, they will be puzzled at the same time because they will be unable to connect the gimmick's denouement with any definite plot or character development. Usually such an unmotivated gimmick is brought off only by leaving an unexplained story hole in the plot. This, in itself, breeds audience dissatisfaction.

Scene-tag gimmicks.   Another type of gimmick is used as a tag to top off a scene or a sequence with a laugh, a shudder, or any other kind of violent or semiviolent audience reaction. Thus, in the picture *The Return of Rusty,* in a scene which showed a bully browbeating a group of smaller boys, the scene ended with one of the tykes shaking his fist at the bully, after his cohorts had been frightened off, as though he were threatening him. But when the bully made a feint at the moppet, as if to leap at him, the little boy turned on his heel in fright and ran off squealing, "Mama!"

These tag gimmicks need not be visual. In comedies especially, a verbal gag can work the trick. A combination of both the verbal and the visual, however, is the ideal.

Sequence gimmick tags in mystery stories may wind up with a gag too, for comedy relief. These can be mixed in with visual *shock* gimmicks—the sudden revelation of an important clue which has been previously planted, or with the revealing of a new corpse.

Such gimmicks should be written into the synopsis and treatment so that eventually they will become integrated into the screen play. The creative director can ad lib or plan such gimmicks from the script. But if he is furnished one that is tailor-made to the story, the chances are that, where he would ordinarily ignore the screen play as far as camera angles are concerned, he will be more than glad to accept the effective tag gimmick.

No gimmick, though, should be pulled out of a hat to be used solely because of its shock value. They must all be carefully integrated into the story so as to flow from the previous action and into the succeeding action.

A case in point where a gimmick was thrown in indiscriminately is the excellent picture *Sunset Boulevard.* Its opening sequence ended with gruesome shots of a screen-play writer's body floating in a Hollywood swimming pool. Then, inexplicably, the dead man began to tell the story of how he got that way. The story of how he got that way made for an adult motion picture. But it was spoiled because of the gimmick which necessitated the return, at the picture's end, to the dead man floating in the pool—the gimmick being that now the audience realized that the unidentified corpse at the opening was actually the hero and narrator of the picture. What bothered everyone, though, and detracted from the picture's worth, was the question: How was the dead man able to narrate the story if he was as dead as he appeared to be in the opening and closing shots?

Plants

Still another type of gimmick used in screen plays is the plot plant. This is an item of information—either in the form of dialogue or picturized action, or with a combination of both—that is introduced at the story's opening, developed in the second act, and then exploded by a sudden revelation, as a denouement.

In Hitchcock's *The 39 Steps,* for example, the fact that the master spy had an amputated little finger was introduced in the first act in the two-shot between the dying female spy and Donat. In the second act the fact was brought out again so that it remained in the audience's subconscious. Then, at the end of the second act, as Donat was discussing with a presumed pillar of British society his search for the man with the amputated little finger, the pillar calmly asked, "You mean this one?" as he raised his hand and showed Donat a hand with a portion of the little finger missing. The impact was such that the denouement always resulted in audible gasps from the audience.

In *The Third Man,* the fact that the cat licked Welles's shoes was planted early in the picture so that, in the identity-uncovering scene, when the cat repeated its shoe-licking of the unseen man lurking in the shadows, the audience realized suddenly, without seeing him, that the skulker was Welles.

Plant with care. The seed for a plant must be sown with care, subtly and unostentatiously. The audience must never be permitted to realize that later on the plant will be developed and paid off. Otherwise they will wait expectantly for it to appear, pounce on it when it does, and thus destroy the effect of explosive suddenness

which the denouement or pay-off of each plant must possess to justify
its use. The planting of the cat licking Welles's shoe, for example,
seemed to be a perfectly natural thing when it was first introduced.
The camera did not linger on it nor was there any reference made
to it in the dialogue. It was introduced naturally and then dropped.

Plants must flow.   The plant must be written so that it flows natu-
ally out of the preceding scene, action, or dialogue, and then flows
just as naturally into the succeeding scene, action, or dialogue.

Plant without telegraphing.   Be sure that all plants are integrated
without telegraphing their presence. The introduction of any foreign element—foreign, that is, insofar as what has gone on before is
concerned—is always dangerous because it makes that element stand
out too noticeably. In the little-finger plant of *The 39 Steps,* a
masterful motivation brought results. It came in the description of
the master spy given by the dying lady spy. One of the details—given
with sufficient importance to remain in the audience's subconscious
but with not so much as to make it outstanding—was the detail of
the missing little finger.

Build your plants.   At the same time, however, care must be taken
not to throw off the plant with such careful carelessness that it will
be buried. If the plant loses its significance, so that when it is finally
paid off its denouement is lost to the audience, the resulting fizzle
will be as disappointing as a dud giant firecracker. That is why a
second-act development—or repetition—of the plant is almost imperative. For if the initial plant is lost, the repetition can serve to
return it to the audience's awareness and thus justify its use in the
pay-off.

Pay off your plants.   And your plant must pay off. If you condition
the audience to expect something to happen, the expectation must
not be frustrated. To pay off with an ill-conceived, shoddy revelation is to admit to creative insufficiency. It is bad enough to write
inconsequential gimmicks into a screen play without preparing for
them with introductory and developing plants, but to use them as
pay-offs after they have been pointed up with preliminary preparation is to court certain disapproval.

The running gag

One of the most effective plants is to be found in the running gag. This is usually a humorous bit of business—verbal or visual—that is repeated a number of times throughout the picture.

In the British film, *A Run for Your Money*, a decrepit and down-at-the-heel musician who suffers from a constant dearth of alcohol, tries to manipulate his prize possession, a harp, into pubs, buses, and trains, with, of course, hilarious high jinks.

Character and humor. Ordinarily, the running gag is used as a character developer or as comedy relief, rather than as a device to advance or develop the plot. Thus, in the picture *The Gorilla* the detective chief was given the cry, "Where the devil is Mulligan?" as a running-gag line, which he repeated whenever his dumb aid decamped on a scatterbrained clue quest of his own.

In Hitchcock's *The Lady Vanishes*, the running gag presented was a seemingly disconnected discourse between the two cricket enthusiasts who, because of an important cricket match they were on their way to see, bewailed the fact that their train was being delayed. Whenever the action became tense, and when the suspense was almost unbearable, Hitchcock masterfully introduced the innocuous pair and their more innocuous cricket chirpings, as comedy relief. At the end, he paid off the running gag by establishing the fact that after all the concern of the two cricket fans, the game had been called off on account of rain.

Running-gag pay-off. The running gag must always pay off. Constant repetition of this device induces an expectation in the audience for something to happen to cap the gag—something to make it complete.

In the French picture *The Procession of the Hours* Fernandel plays a cadging deadbeat who tries to live by borrowing money and drinks from his bistro friends. Instead of paying him off at the end of the picture—by having him come into money, perhaps, and then having him turn down his old friends—the picture concludes with his singing a few naughty French ballads.

The pay-off is especially necessary to the oft-used running gag which has a strange character barge into a party (he's usually drunk) and wander in and out aimlessly, completely unknown to any of the confused guests and to the host. This mysterious myrmidon was excellently paid off in the picture *Hi Diddle Diddle,* in which a strange girl wandered on and off the set. When someone asked Adolphe Menjou who she was, he replied, "Oh! she's the producer's girl friend."

In *The Set-Up* intermittent shots showed a fat man in the boxing audience eating progressively larger snacks of hot dogs, popcorn, etc. As the excitement in the ring mounted, the interest in him increased, but these shots were not paid off at the end and thus lost much of their effectiveness. Simply by topping off the gag by showing the fat man daintily swallowing an antacid pill would have paid off the running gag sufficiently.

One warning: the running gag should not be repeated too often or it will tend to take precedence over the main story line and thus shift the interest to a divergent theme.

Build with running gag. The running gag need not be humorous. It can be used in a serious picture for the purpose of building a series of scenes or situations. It is almost a must—as a visual element—in mystery and horror pictures when successive shots of shadows, footsteps, creaking noises, and the like, are introduced at well chosen spots to build suspense. In the original play, and in the picturization of Wexley's *The Last Mile,* the intermittent dimming of the electric bulbs to indicate that another doomed inmate of Death Row was being electrocuted had a horrifyingly cumulative effect on the audience.

Transition running gags. The running gag can also serve as a connecting device to tie together scenes, or as a transition technique. In Ford's *The Informer,* the figure of the blind man and the sound of his tapping cane (adapted freely from Joyce's novel *Ulysses,* as were a number of other elements in the same picture) were used as a connecting device to tie together varied Dublin street scenes. This sort of device was peculiarly necessary to the picture because it was a sprawling, many-scened film adapted from a very discursive novel.

When both sight and sound are used for transitional purposes the running gag pays off handsomely. The remarkably effective build-up

to McLaglen's death—from the beginning to the end of the picture—
was achieved in part with the running-gag device.

Running-gag props.   Props—and live ones especially—furnish excellent material for the running gag, as was evidenced in the splendid
byplay created with the dog in *My Favorite Wife,* and in *The Awful
Truth.*

Running-gag props can also be used to establish surface characterization. George Raft's persistent coin-flipping is one example that
comes to mind. There is a danger, though, in overdoing this device
for characterization. It may take on so much importance that the
audience may misconstrue it as a plant, which calls for a pay-off,
instead of as a character-developing running gag. This was true in
the British *Storm in a Teacup,* where the judge was characterized
as a knuckle-cracker. He was seen—in big close-ups, too—cracking
his knuckles so often that in time the audience must have won-
dered whether the action had any significance, and undoubtedly
believed that shortly it would pay off into something funny or dramatic. But nothing of the sort happened. And there was a definite
feeling of being let down.

The knuckle-cracking may have been intended to furnish comedy
relief perhaps, but because it was highlighted to such an extent and
repeated so often, even its value as comedy was lost.

A running gag that is worked too long can fall flat despite the
pay-off. In another British film, *Laughter in Paradise,* in the scene in
which the old solicitor is reading the will, Guy Middleton continued
to supply the aged lawyer with the words for which he constantly
groped. This went on and on until it became very unfunny. And
even with the pay-off, when the barrister stopped in the middle of
the post-will singing of "For he's a jolly good . . . " and waited for
Middleton to supply the last word, audience exasperation was sufficient to kill the laugh.

Comedy relief

Why comedy relief?   It is almost obligatory that comedy relief be
used in some form or other to help sustain interest. It would be

asking the impossible of any audience to expect its collective attention to remain riveted to a sustained scene that does not vary its
mood in any way. For there is only a limited amount of sticking
power in the interest of any audience. The mind is obliged to
wander when it has been forced to concentrate on any one thing or
subject for a length of time, especially in the darkened sleep-pro-
ducing confines of a motion-picture theater. Therefore, immediately
following a particularly dramatic scene, there should be introduced a
short scene that will relieve the audience tension.

In the picture *The Hasty Heart* comedy relief was furnished by a
gag sequence in which the ward patients tried to learn what the
Scotsman wore under his kilts. The attempts were interspersed so
that stark tragedy was relieved with humor.

It must flow.   This relief need not always be humorous. But it must
flow naturally from the previous dramatic scene into the succeeding
scene. And it should be kept in only long enough to relieve the
dramatic tension without breaking it entirely.

Although much of this depends on the film editor, it helps for
the screen-play writer to insert his relief scenes into their niches, to
prevent tampering by the director and the film editor.

Played by minor characters.   Ordinarily, comedy relief should not
be written in to be played by the characters who have just under-
gone a grueling emotional experience. The switch-over to comedy
should be made by minor, though essential, characters. The former
would be incredible to an audience and would result in the complete dislocation of character, mood, and story-line development.

As natural reactions.   The best way to make certain that comedy
relief is integrated with tense dramatic action is to arrange so that
it comes as a natural reaction to it. The reactions of an onlooker—
a hotel clerk or a cop—can be used for comedy relief after showing
an argument between a man and his wife. Even the reactions of a
pet dog could be shown in a cutaway shot, for comedy relief. But
if it is necessary to the plot development to cut away from the scene
of the dramatic action to other characters in another scene of action,
something in what they say or do must be *tied in* with the dramatic
scene the audience has already witnessed. The cutaway must in

some way advance the story line so that no break will occur to bring confusion as to the direction in which the plot is developing.

Relief without comedy.   It has already been stated that it is not necessary to relieve a tense dramatic situation with comedy alone. Comedy may be completely out of place under certain conditions, where the dramatic intensity must be sustained, but only in a limited degree. This can be done by cutting away to another scene, with other characters, who are not necessarily involved in a humorous incident. But here again the flow of unity must not be disrupted. The new scene, its characters, and their actions and speech should all contribute to the story line and should be written so that the situation can be accepted by the audience as the next logical development.

Relief in some form, however, is essential. When you find an audience laughing during a tense moment in a dramatic picture, the reason, in most cases, will be that they were not furnished with sufficient relief and were forced to give vent to their supercharged, pent-up emotions even at an inappropriate time.

Humor

In the days of the old silent pictures, it was necessary to flash title cards onto the screen to effect transitions and also to furnish high spots in the dialogue, which could not be heard, of course, but which was essential to the understanding of the action. It was found that these titles had to be written brightly to hold attention. Their composition, therefore, was relegated to vaudeville writers, who gagged them up.

Later, when the talkies arrived, the heavy dramas were so overladen with dialogue that only the comedies purchased from Broadway were able to survive as acceptable box-office material.

The wisecrack is king.   The vaults of most studios are filled with treatments that were purchased only because they were witty and read well, but which could not be developed into acceptable screen plays.

Even now the wisecrack persists. It is not considered necessary that a person talk like an ordinary human being; he is allowed to mouth quips and gags that are as spontaneous as a burlesque chorine's dance routines. Make it funny, is the criterion.

In the smart, breezy comedy film, such verbal gags have their legitimate place. Such stories make no attempt to present real people in real situations. Their sole purpose is to entertain by titivating the audience's risibilities.

But Hollywood pictures frequently do not stop there. It has become almost axiomatic that screen-play writers must be prepared to pepper their dialogue with smart cracks, sophisticated retorts, humorous gibes, double-entendre jokes, puns, malapropisms, and the like, in the belief that because they are funny they are, *ipso facto,* entertaining.

But the average person does not converse with sparkling, ad lib humor. Even Oscar Wilde, who was supposed to have been a supreme master of the witty retort, actually composed his witticisms carefully, long before he found—or made—an appropriate opening for their use.

Pictorial humor better.   If humor is to be used, it should be preferably of the pictorial kind, for motion pictures are, by nature, almost completely visual. It should be situation humor rather than verbal.

Don't contrive humor.   These situations, however, must not be patently manufactured contrivances. They too, like all the elements of a film, must be perfectly integrated with all the other elements. They must not be inserted only for laughs. Instead, in addition to creating humor, they must advance the story, develop character, or create a mood.

Real people mean real humor.   And they must be real if they are to be concerned with real people. Good, acceptable comedy—not of the comic remark variety—must be, to quote Lincoln, "of the people, by the people, and for the people." It must concern itself with the antics of people caught in the tentacles of modern society, who react with natural evasions and subterfuges.

Consider the Italian masterpiece *To Live in Peace,* which concerned itself with the grim subject of war but which was presented as a comedy. The exceedingly funny humor was introduced in a situation in which the citizens of an entire Italian village quaked in their boots because a drunken German soldier might awaken from his stupor and remember that the night before he had sullied his Nazi racial beliefs by dancing with an un-Nordic, American Negro soldier.

Remember the situation in *Foreign Correspondent* when Joel McCrea was chased over the roof tops by the Nazis? As he scurried past a hotel sign, he accidently broke off the tubing that formed the last two letters of the word "hotel," thus making the sign read "hot," an ironic comment on his precarious situation.

The dearth of real humor in our motion pictures may be accounted for by the fact that we are afraid that people will resent being made to laugh at themselves. They know that they do not drip flip cracks with every tenth word, so they disassociate themselves completely from the reel characters who do. They may laugh, yes, but it is the sort of laughter that is forgotten, like last night's off-color story.

But people can laugh at themselves. That has been proved by the success of Shaw's plays, by Ring Lardner's bitter but comic gibes at the genus *homo americanus,* by Gilbert and Sullivan's comic operettas, by such pictures as *It Happened One Night, The Awful Truth, The Great McGinty, The Baker's Daughter,* by all the Chaplin comedies, and even by many of the Marx Brothers pictures and the early W. C. Field mordaunt comedy satires.

Yes, there is a time for comedy and it is right now. But it must be the *comédie humaine,* of the real people, and not the stultifying wisecracks of the flicker folk of the reels.

The flash back

Filmic realism is often killed with still another popular device—the flash back. Why it should be necessary to go back in time to pick up incidents that occurred previous to the beginning of the picture, is a mystery. When used legitimately, the flash back can be an effective device, but when it is resorted to in pictures that could do much better without it, the flash back has serious drawbacks.

Flash backs impede movement. For one thing, the flash back definitely impedes the forward flow of a picture's action. Because it is retrogressive, it halts progression. That in itself defeats the primary rule of motion-picture making—the picture must *move*.

Flash backs fritter suspense. Flash backs also tend to destroy attention-getting and attention-holding suspense. To be most effective, suspense should build to a climax. Anything that interferes with that important gradual build-up saps suspense and fritters away audience interest.

The audience always wants to know "What happens next?" That is what makes for a suspenseful, attention-compelling flow of continuity. But in a flash back the audience is given, not what happens next, but what happened some time ago.

Newspaper editors recognize the fact that "nothing is so dead as yesterday's news." The same applies to yesterday's events in a motion picture. For it is the motion picture's task to create a *sense of immediacy* that will create the illusion in the audience that the shadows they see cavorting on the screen are real people undergoing real experiences, *in the immediate present,* at the time the audience is viewing the picture. A picture which can accomplish that has most of the ingredients of success.

Flash backs lose immediacy. More often than not, the flash back destroys that sense of immediacy. Because, unless it is actually *told* by a narrator and in the form of a story, the flash back does not happen in real life. Life is a continual flow of events that begin and end without going back in time. Unless the flash back is sufficiently motivated in a picture, the continual flow of events which the picture must try to represent in its delineation of life will be interrupted unnaturally.

When an entire picture is written as a flash back it is necessary that the story be told, either by one of the principal characters, by a minor character, or even by someone who has no part in the story line itself.

Thus, in *Wuthering Heights,* the picture we saw was actually a series of flash backs constituting the story told by the old housekeeper. Now in order to keep this fact in focus, it was necessary to return occasionally to the *old* housekeeper, as she retailed the story of Wuthering Heights to the traveler who had wandered into the forbidding house. Then it was necessary to return to the succeeding episodes of the story she was telling, until it became necessary to return to her again, to re-establish her identity, and go on from there again to the story proper.

What happened, as far as the audience's view of the housekeeper-narrator was concerned—and she was more than a minor character in the story—was to see her first as an old woman, then as a young woman, then again as an older woman, and again as an old woman (as the narrator), and then again as an aging woman. This may have been a remarkable tour de force by the make-up department, but it added nothing but confusion to the audience's attempt to understand the housekeeper's role in the story. She was presented in fits and starts, first young, then old, instead of by means of a slow character build-up. As a result, she never emerged as a distinct character although Heathcliff and the others did, despite the shattering flash-back technique. They came through, but what could have been a perfect picture without the flash back was just a rather good picture. Consider the picture *Sunset Boulevard,* made some time after *Wuthering Heights.* Now *Sunset Boulevard* is a great picture—a modern classic. But how much better it could have been had its writers not succumbed to the insidious attraction of the flash back. The picture opened with shots of a squad car speeding to the scene of a crime. Then came shots of a man's body floating in a Hollywood swimming pool. Then, as if from nowhere, came a man's voice—William Holden's—telling the story of what had happened to the man who was now lying dead in the pool. Following that came the real story of the picture, the one that presented one facet of prismatic Hollywood and its fantastic denizens in its true light. It was picture making of the most supreme kind. But, at the end of that story, and at the picture's end, the audience was suddenly given to realize that the corpse they had seen floating in the pool, in the opening shots, was the hero of the picture and, to their consternation, was also the voice of the narrator! Just what mumbo-jumbo was resorted to to conjure up this trick of reincarnation was never explained by the script writers. They had concocted a trick ending that had sock, and they were satisfied.

Flash backs make money.   There are concrete reasons why producers use the flash-back device so often. It has audience-acceptance value. Pictures in which it is featured make money despite the shortcomings of the technique. But the producers realize that they would make money even if they were to return to title cards. For picture makers have created a hunger for motion pictures that cannot be put off by inferior quality. The "B" picture has thrived because audiences demand pictures—any pictures—as long as they can relieve the tedium of humdrum life and furnish a colorful vehicle of vicarious escape. Popular success, therefore, should be no criterion for quality.

What is more, the flash-back picture is easier to write than one using normal techniques. For cutbacks to the narrator serve as transition devices to connect the component flash-back sequences that go to make up the picture as a whole. And fresh, effective transitions are not easy to come by.

Flash-back transitions.   But there is the root of the flash-back error. The reorienting cutback to the storyteller more often serves as a transition device *for the flash back,* instead of for the original and main story line. In other words, smooth transitions between the important story-line sequences—the heart of the matter—are sacrificed in order to carry the flash backs, which are an artificial form, to make them work satisfactorily. Transitions are made not because the story itself calls for them, but only because the form makes it necessary to cut back to the storyteller in order to reorient the audience to the device.

It can be stated categorically that no picture told wholly in flash-back style could not have been told just as well, and even better, were a simple beginning, middle, and ending technique to have been used. But the flash back is flashy. So it attracts screen-play writers and producers who see in it only a tricky, novel manner of presenting mediocrity. Perhaps their reason for resorting to the flash back is that it gives them an opportunity of dressing up in novel attire what is actually threadbare.

Flash back uses limited.   Under certain conditions, though, the flash back may have its legitimate uses, and then only in a limited way. It may be necessary in some stories, for example, to withhold certain background information from the audience in order to build suspense, or to create a delayed dramatic impact. In the main, this is a device that is confined to mystery stories, where the audience has been conditioned to being cheated in this manner. In such cases, and where it is imperative to reveal the withheld information to make its use pay off, the flash-back technique can be resorted to despite the obvious fact that, in being used, it destroys the continuity build-up, unhinges the pacing, and shocks the audience's attention receptivity by forcing them to reorient themselves from the present to the past, and then back to the present again.

When used for this purpose, the flash back properly belongs near the picture's end, almost immediately before the climax is reached. In no case, though, should the flash back itself be used as the climax, for then it will lose the quality of immediacy which is so essential to dramatic impact. The denouement must be shown to be happening, not in the past—as far as the time of the picture is concerned, of course—but in the present.

When the flash back is thrown into the opening sequences—as has been the case quite often—the audience becomes confused by the indirect line of action. Even before they have been completely oriented to the characters as they see them involved in events that are happening in the immediate present, orientation is snapped and they are wrenched away to a time in the past, peopled by characters who, because they are younger and differently attired, are of necessity considerably different from those whom they have met at the picture's opening.

Start at the beginning. The flash back's only excuse for being is that it can depict characters in actions that took place some time before the picture's story began. If the flash back concerns these people in incidents that took place only a short time before the opening of the picture, there is no reason for its use. The picture could just as well have started with the previous incident presented in the normal manner, with a time lapse to connect it with the ensuing action.

Flash backs within flash backs. Confusion can be confounded with flash backs. In some pictures (*The Passionate Friends*) screen-play writers have thought it necessary to write a flash back within a flash back! *Lady in the Lake* contained a flash-back sequence in which one of the characters told a story which was dramatized as a flash back. This made it necessary to reorient the audience first from the interior flash back to the major flash back, and then from the major flash back to the regular story line.

Tricky but unnecessary. Avoid the flash back. It may look pretty, but it can do more harm than good. It's tricky. On the stage, in *Death of a Salesman,* the flash back was used so often that, although it appeared to have a positive effect on the audience, its use began to pall. The play could have been written in a straightforward style —with the first act in the distant past, the second act in the early past, and the third act in the immediate present. The flash backs were gaudy tricks that were impressive only because they were tricks. They added nothing to the basic quality of the play itself. Here again, too much emphasis was put on construction and form. And the only reason why the play was a popular success was that innate honesty, sincerity, and superior writing came through despite the flash backs.

In television, the flash back creates an additional problem. Because television plays are usually broken into two parts (for half-hour shows) and three parts (for hour shows) to accommodate the advertising commercials, the character narrating the flash back must be brought back at the end of each act and at the beginning of the following act. The breaks in time and sequence necessitated by the commercials make reorientation to the narrator an absolute essential.

Repetition

You may have noted in the foregoing section that the words "orient" and "reorient" were repeated time and again. This was done designedly. For a lack of orientation on the part of the audience makes only for confusion. That is why, at all times, they must be made fully aware of *what* is going on, *why* it is going on, *who* is involved in the goings-on, *where* the goings-on are taking place, *how* the goings-on affect each of the characters, and *when* the goings-on are taking place in time.

One method of accomplishing this is by repetition. Because the motion-picture image is so fleeting, it is necessary for the screen-play writer to resort to constant repetition throughout the story in order to retain audience orientation and to make certain that the important story elements will remain integrated with the picture's theme throughout the picture.

Character traits.   Character traits must be repeated, not necessarily in kind, exactly, but definitely in pattern, if the character is to be sustained. Thus it would not be necessary to have a character kick a dog three times throughout the film to establish his cruelty. Nor would it be necessary to have him fondle a canary to establish that, although he is a low-down cad, he is also possessed of a sentimental streak. It should be part of the screen-play writer's creative ability to work out repeatedly different aspects of the same character trait, which could recognizably fall into the same pattern of behavior.

Repeat figures.   What must be especially repeated are facts and statistics that figure prominently in the story line. If the plot hinges on the fact that 10,500 shares of stock must be sold to prevent the hero from being thrown into bankruptcy, then that figure must be repeated often enough so that when it is actually brought into the denouement the audience will recognize it immediately and associate it with the next plot development without too much retrospection.

Avoid undue recapitulation.   There is a certain type of repetition that must be avoided. At no time should an entire scene or conversation be *entirely* recapitulated for the benefit of a character who has not been in on the scene previously, and who must be brought up to date on what has already happened.

If the audience has already seen something happen, or has heard it in dialogue, they should never be subjected to a repetition of it. Thus, if the audience has already heard a character tell of how he has gotten into a certain predicament, and if it is necessary to have him repeat the details of the situation to still another character, then some device must be used to spare the audience and to telescope the retelling so that their reaction will not be an annoyed, "Oh! we've heard all that already—let's get on with the story!"

Use dissolves.   The most common device for surmounting this difficulty is the "dissolve," (see p. 135) a filmic device which can indicate the passage of time which the retelling may consume. Indicate
that the picture should fade out at the beginning of the retelling
and then fade in at its end, thus eliminating much unnecessary
detail without losing attention.

Another device is simply to dissolve or wipe out at the beginning
of the retelling and leave it up to the audience to fill in the balance
with their previously obtained knowledge.

Condense repetitions.   Still another device makes use of condensa-
tion, a retelling of the already told facts in summarized form. Thus,
if the action already witnessed by the audience involves the beating
up of the character retelling the incident, instead of having the unfortunate character meander through all the details, it would be
sufficient for him to say something on the order of, "And then the
guy beat me up."

When recapitulation is unavoidable.   There may be times, however, when recapitulation becomes unavoidable. When that situation exists, it is good practice to repeat the known information over
a cutaway shot (see p. 127) to some significant detail in the same
scene, or over an extreme close-up of the character who is hearing the
recapitulation, to take advantage of reactions expressed on his face.

Quick conversions

Repetition is a handy device for offsetting what is a common be-
setting sin in a great many pictures—the quick conversion. This
ineptness can be attributed only to faulty writing. For in using it,
the writer neglects to furnish a solid, realistic basis for the conversion of a character from evil to good, when the plot calls for such
a conversion. Usually this switch occurs at the climax and leaves
the audience with a vague feeling of dissatisfaction. In *Sirocco,*
after practicing assorted skulduggery through almost the entire
picture, Humphrey Bogart undergoes a last-reel conversion and per-
forms the customary noble gesture.

Time is the essence.   There are reasons for this failing. The motion picture—and especially the half-hour television film—is afforded only a short period of time in which to present its story as compared, say, with the novel. A novelist can devote a considerable number of pages to the development of the motivation and character revelations necessary to accomplishing a satisfactory conversion.

Action vs. character.   Then again, the current Hollywood insistence on action progression to the detriment of character development provides the writer with insufficient footage with which to prepare the audience for the character's conversion by means of a slow, cumulative process. For people do not respond on the spur of the moment even when they may appear to be doing so. Their actions are usually the result of an accretion of thoughts and afterthoughts, actions and reactions, questions and answers, accusations and self-accusations, conversations, arguments, proofs by example, injunctions, threats, promises—in fact, by a vast arsenal of moving elements that are part and parcel of the process of conversion.

Arguments are not enough.   Usually only one, or a few at best, are brought into play to bring about a quick conversion. When little time is available for it, a very quick conversion is accomplished by the use of "argument." The evildoer is made to see the evil of his ways by having a good character—usually someone on the order of a priest, a teacher, or any other older person of accepted moral stability (and sometimes a child)—convince him by argumentative persuasion that what he is doing is bad and that if he is to enter the Kingdom of Heaven he will have to mend his ways and confess to having been the real perpetrator of the act of which some innocent character has been accused. It stands to reason that a hardened character whose evil has been developed over a long period of time would hardly be so receptive to moral suasion.

Plant conversions.   It is necessary, therefore, to make such a conversion seem genuine. To do this, the breakdown of evil should begin some time before the actual conversion takes place. Also, there must be planted in the character of the evildoer those elements that could make for a conversion. He could, for instance, be shown to be vacillating in intention, simply by dramatizing one of his vacillations. He could be *shown* reacting to the results of his evil-doing so that it will not be necessary to tell the audience about it. His final answer to the request for a conversion could be delayed for some time, while he deliberates, with self-probings, on the possible results of his conversion, both to himself and to those who are affected by his actions. Before his final conversion he could be visited by a number of people—people who are in some way connected with his evil-doing—and remonstrated with, argued with, pleaded with, and implored.

Dramatized motivated conversions. Better still, before the evildoer makes his final decision he could be *shown* (and this is very important) acting and reacting to certain results of his fell life. If these preliminary preparations are made before he is actually brought around to goodness, our evildoer's conversion will be documented so that what he does will flow out of his character and will be sufficient motivation for the story's climax.

In Wilder's *Ace in the Hole,* Kirk Douglas played the part of a newspaperman who was a double-dyed, unregenerate heel, liar, cynic, and conniver—selfish, cruel, arrogant, vicious, ambitious, and pathologically insecure. He was that from the beginning of the picture until almost the very end when, after undergoing a flash of unmotivated remorse, he was stabbed and fell to his death. This unwarranted last-minute conversion spoiled what was otherwise a splendid picture.

On the other hand, in *St. Benny the Dip,* the conversion of three confidence men who donned ecclesiastical costume early in the picture to escape the police was a gradual reformation—the first becoming a chaplain, the second returning to his old job as a taxi-driver and the third becoming a happily married man.

Realism

No matter how hard the screen-play writer may strive to inject realism into his script, he labors under a constant disadvantage. For how real, how true to actual life can a motion-picture story be? To be absolutely realistic a motion picture must be concerned with the happenings of a set of people within the limits of the running time of the picture.

In other words, the picture would have to concern itself with happenings that take place in an uninterrupted period of about twenty-seven minutes for a half-hour television drama, fifty-four minutes for an hour-length television drama (about an average of ten per cent of the time should be allotted for advertising commercials) and about seventy-five to ninety minutes for a theater feature film. Hitchcock's *The Rope* attempted this with its long-playing single scenes in which the camera roved at will around the big set. But even Hitchcock was forced to break up his scenes with cuts because of the limited amount of film his camera could hold, thus destroying the utter realism he strove for. For real life does not operate like a series of film cuts cemented together by a film editor.

The omnipresent camera. To be *pure realism* a picture must, of necessity, follow its characters around from set to set, from the beginning of the picture to the end, without resorting to such filmic tricks as cuts, wipes, fades, montages, and dissolves. This, however, is a physical impossibility. Hence the need to temper pure realism with filmic conventions—with expressionism, for all cinematic devices are nothing but expressionistic representations of the real.

Candid realism. The purely realistic film would also have to be shot in newsreel style—candid camera, as it were, with little consideration being given to lighting, camera movement, and make-up. The semi-documentaries *Boomerang* and *The House on 92nd Street* followed the techniques of the *March of Time,* and attempted a form of candid-camera shooting—quite successfully, it may be added. But they did not go whole hog with the method, for many of the scenes were studio-mounted and shot. The result was that in blending the unreality of the studio scenes with the reality of the candidly shot scenes the former suffered by comparison, and a sustained sense of realism was frustrated.

Infinite details. The purely realistic film must also be all-inclusive. Although the screen-play writer's sense of selectivity should continue to be operative, at the same time he should not slough off essential details that develop character and plot, details that may slow up the picture's pace, but which are essential to the reproduction of reality.

British pictures offer many good examples of this almost fanatical attention to realistic details. In *Brief Encounter,* what could have been a tawdry, ordinary story of middle-class marital infidelity, had it been produced with the customary pseudorealistic techniques, turned out to be a remarkable cinematic experience because of the systematic attention given to character-developing and story-progessing details.

The Italian films *Open City, Bicycle Thief, Paisan,* and *Shoe Shine,* and the Swiss film *The Search* are good examples of this painstaking devotion to significant details. For in them, life was so realistically portrayed that what the audience saw was a living, breathing reproduction of life as it was actually being lived by characters who were, in many cases, indigenous to the countries in which the films were made.

Dialogue selectivity. Again, the purely realistic film must have dialogue that does not scintillate with witticisms. Most real people just don't talk that way. Instead, their speech would be hesitant, groping, repetitive, and quite undistinguished.

Their dialogue would be similar to Joyce's stream of consciousness' inner monologues. Again, though, the writer's sense of selectivity should operate so that, although the effect would be that of a realistic groping for words, the dialogue would not actually be slowed up. Long speeches would be out. Suspended lines would be a must. Interruptions would be written into almost every other speech.

Reel realism is not realistic. If the realistic film is desirable, then it should be as completely realistic as it is possible to make it. *Lost Weekend* was fairly realistic in that it delved into the inner compulsions of a chronic inebriate. But when it edged into the fantastic —as when it portrayed the drunkard's delirium tremens by picturing his hallucinations of a bat flying about his room and killing another creature on the wall—it destroyed the unity of the realism engendered in the rest of the picture. It is difficult enough to sustain a tenuous mood under ordinary conditions. Deliberately to

snap the sustaining thread of unity—of realistic unity, in this case
—is to court a drop in attention. Which accounted, in part, for the
decided letdown in the picture's closing sequences.

Don't gild the lily. But in the ordinary motion picture, such extremes of realism would be out of order. As an art form, motion
pictures are necessarily subject to certain limitations. To gain realism, for example, by painting sculpture—as was done by the Greeks
—is to court a definite esthetic loss in that the pure medium of
sculpture has been encroached on by the similarly pure medium of
painting, even though added realism may result. The sculptor must
recognize the limitations of his medium and work within their
scope. In the same way, the screen-play writer should recognize the
limitations of his own art form.

In Von Stroheim's *Greed,* for example, a definite and deleterious
shock of audience disapproval came with the shot of the hoarded
gold under Zazu Pitts' mattress. Suddenly, in a black and white picture, the real color of gold was injected. Someone had suggested
that the shots of the gold pieces be hand-tinted, frame by frame, to
make them more realistic! To have done this was, indeed, tantamount to penciling a mustache on the Venus de Milo.

Answer? Compromise, of course. The screen-play writer must temper his creative urge with self-preserving selectivity. Some verbal
fumblings, some interrupting interjections, a few introductions of
realistic character byplay—enough, in other words, to add the third
dimension of character roundness, without resorting to the more
effective fourth-dimensional utter realism would be appropriate.

Such a compromise was seen in the television film presentation
of Budd Schulberg's adaptation of the newspaper article concerning a dramatic operation conducted in a submarine. The utter realism of the newspaper description was not completely carried over
into the television film production which, in spite of the compromise, remained an engrossing and satisfying film drama.

Semi-documentaries

There has been a world-wide trend toward the making of what have been called semi-documentary pictures. Before discussing these it would, perhaps, be advisable to determine, first, what a documentary picture is. According to what Robert Flaherty, the dean of documentary pictures, has said about his own work—*Nanook of the North, Moana* and, most recently, his *Louisiana Story*— a documentary picture is a fact film in which the story stems out of a real and, therefore, realistic locale, photographed on location at the actual scene of the story and using the actual people concerned with that story. The documentary, as it has been developed through the years, has become much more than this. But, for our purposes —to examine the semi-documentary picture—this definition is sufficient.

The semi-documentary picture compromises with a strict adherence to the documentary tenets. It photographs exterior scenes only on location, but shoots interior scenes on stage. It uses professional actors in the main and, only occasionally, and for bit parts, resorts to the use of local, non-professional actors. It is not averse to injecting stock shots to simulate verisimilitude. Its cameramen let up a little in their constant drive to lighting perfection to permit for a sort of newsreel immediacy in their lighting of both exterior and interior sets. But, mainly, in the semi-documentary, the story takes precedence over the background material, the reverse of conditions in the documentary film.

The British film, *Brief Encounter,* for example, is an ideal example of an excellent semi-documentary which recorded what appeared to be the true, unromanticized events in the lives of two real people, with all the real details of the milieu in which they moved as a realistic background for their tortured peregrinations. The Italian *Open City, Shoe Shine, Bicycle Thief* and *Bitter Rice,* and the Swiss *The Search* similarly presented unvarnished life. To all intents, facts were not juggled in these films to suit the purposes of the story.

In most American semi-documentaries, however, far too often the facts are tortured in order to present a more palatable story. In de Rochemont's *Boomerang,* for example, the hero of the story was purported to be the actual and real Homer S. Cummings, a former Attorney-General, although the facts as limned by the picture did not follow the actual life of Mr. Cummings. In Sturges' *Sullivan's Travels,* a screen writer of fatuous comedies (Mr. Sturges, himself) decides to desert Hollywood to make a hegira through the distressed areas of the country in order to gather material for a stirring picture on the plight of the masses. Eventually the author (née Sturges) comes to grips with life by realizing that, in making Hollywood comedies, he is adding to the gayety of the nation. So he returns to Hollywood to grind out his comedies once again. These are not facts but gross misrepresentations. For it would take far more than a screening of a Mickey Mouse cartoon (as shown in the picture) in a southern jail to make its inmates forget their woes of racial discrimination, social injustice, and anti-social manifestations brought on by a multitude of modern society's muddling attitudes to its children and its adults.

In the semi-documentary *The Beginning or the End,* which concerned itself with the atom bomb, the introduction of a supposed newsreel clip (presented as a historical fact), of a group of scientists burying a secret file of atomic records in a sort of time-capsule, fiction was fobbed off as fact.

And in *The Sleeping City,* another Hollywood semi-documentary, a common, mine-run, cops-and-robbers story was glossed over with the sugar-coated surface facts of location shooting and presented as a true story.

If the semi-documentary picture is to be assured of its full stature —as it has and can be if we are to judge by the standards set in Italy and in England—then it is incumbent on the screen-play writer that he adhere, as closely as is possible, to the methods and procedures of writing real documentaries, and without compromising too much to the demands of the mass audience for fictional fripperies.

The writer must, first of all, be fully steeped in the background he is to portray. He must visit the locale, observe the people, talk with them, research in their newspaper files and libraries, and try to get under the skin of both the community and its inhabitants so as to discover not only *what* they do, and *how* they do it, but *why* they do it.

He must then make notes of certain people who possess the

ability to act in the projected film—people who are fully representative of the characters to be portrayed and who are typical of the locale.

Then he must scout out locations for the shots he intends to describe in his screen play, locations that are best suited—from a production standpoint as well as a story standpoint—to the delineation of the events that are to be photographed.

He must be particularly observant of revelatory details—those little things which people do and say which can be developed into little gems of epiphany. For it is the intelligent and effective use of such details that make for the difference between a solid documentary film and a so-so fictional motion picture. Graphically presented, even a series of manufacturing details can be made inordinately absorbing to any audience. What could be quite banal and commonplace in the completely fiction film could, in the semi-documentary, be presented interestingly and even suspensefully.

Dialogue in the semi-documentary must be extremely realistic, must sound as though the microphone had recorded candid conversations, as it were, but with the felicitous use of authorial selectivity, of course.

Candid photography is a must. In de Rochemont's *13 Rue Madeleine* the most impressive scenes—in an otherwise unprepossessing cloak-and-dagger melodrama—were those, shot with a hidden camera, of the spies in operation and conversation. For shooting scenes in the documentary *The City,* New York's millions were dramatically caught by a camera hidden in a suitcase. Camouflaged trucks (as used in the picture *Berlin*) can be used. One resourceful director set up a dummy camera and crew at one street corner to attract crowds, so as to leave the street free for him to shoot scenes, with a real camera and crew, at an adjacent scene, using the crowds meandering past to get to the dummy camera as the crowds for his real shots.

Obviously, many of these candid shots cannot carry live sound dialogue. Hence they should be written so as to be shot silent, with narration to carry over. But remember this: let the picture tell the story. Only when additional narration is an absolute must should narration be resorted to.

Much of the information given in the section on DRAMATURGY is adaptable to the writing of the semi-documentary screen play.

Only the obviously tricky effects should be elided or considerably watered down, to permit for as much realism as is possible. The section on character and character development is especially useful. Plot, on the other hand, should not be given precedence over character. The less plot, and the more character, the more suitable the script will be for semi-documentary development. Sub-plots are admissible but they should not be too involved and should not introduce too many minor characters.

All the elements discussed under "dramatic values" apply to the writing of semi-documentary pictures. The same applies to those under "suspense." Because of its semi-documentary nature, a picture need not eschew suspense, which is in evidence constantly in real life. Even the chase can be adapted. The pure documentary, Flaherty's *Louisiana Story,* used it very effectively in the scenes between the boy and the alligators.

Go easy with gimmicks, however. At best, a gimmick is contrived. And real life is devoid of such patent, literary contrivances. Plants, the running gag (to a limited degree), comedy relief (especially), humor (of the real-life variety and not the wisecrack), and repetitions—these are all appropriate to the semi-documentary film.

Avoid the flash back, however. It is *not* true to life. Instead, use an *established* narrator, one, preferably, who is a character in the action rather than an ephemeral, disassociated voice. Definitely avoid quick conversions which just do not happen in life as it really exists. Also avoid fantasy. Try to be as real as possible, in other words. Try to present what amounts to a creative interpretation of actuality.

The screen-play writer of semi-documentaries can refer to his full arsenal of camera shots. But he should pay particular attention to the full shot because the documentary quality can only be fully realized by presenting real individuals in their real milieus. The moving, panning camera is especially called for, as witness its excellent use in Rossellini's *Germany—Year Zero.* Trucking shots, however, and obviously in exterior scenes, should be limited to a minimum. As for angles: try for the startling ones when the action borders on the pedestrian, and especially in montages of manufacturing methods, technical techniques, repetitive actions, and the like.

Try to avoid too many optical wipes and dissolves. Such filmic conventions—although they are completely acceptable to most audiences—tend to dull the edge of realism because, in themselves, they are fundamentally unrealistic. Cut away for short time-lapse but use time-lapses for unconscionably long hiati of time. But above all, do not resort to the time-lapse clichés. Try to integrate the time-lapse with character.

Transitions especially should be carefully attended to. Because of its nature, the semi-documentary can use a limited Cook's-Tour transition to establish or re-establish the all-important locale details. Avoid, though, where possible, match-dissolve transitions, stock-shot transitions, and title-card transitions. The simple, deviceless transition is a must.

Most of the material in the section under "Writing the Screen Play" applies to the writing of semi-documentary films. Especial note should be made of the discussions under "Building." The use of props for amateur actors is definitely called for. Subjective-camera techniques can be applied quite successfully to semi-documentaries.

Sound and its use are subjects that cannot be stressed too much in the writing of semi-documentaries. For real people, living in real places, create certain realistic sounds. Realistically portrayed, these sound-effects can add tremendously to the effect of realism to be desired. Exteriors especially call for a realistic sound-treatment. And where the scenes are shot silent so that appropriate sound-effects must be dubbed in later, make sure that these sounds are carefully included in your scene descriptions, and even integrated with the action and dialogue, so that they cannot be sloughed off.

It can be stated that, with the semi-documentary film, the scriptwriter possesses a means of overcoming many of the prejudices held against current motion-picture making. For with it he can bow to the dictates of the money-minded producer, who insists that only entertainment can sell. At the same time, however, the screen-play writer can serve as an honest medium of public information and education.

Fantasy

Strangely enough, what passes for realism in most Hollywood pictures is actually fantasy. Take *Here Comes Mr. Jordan*, for example. This picture was supposed to be a combination of realism and fantasy. But was it? Fantasy it had, yes. But realism?

What realism can there be, for instance, in the average film portrayal of a poor working-girl's cold-water, walk-up flat in the East Fifties as a plushy, modernly furnished suite of rooms which, under realistic conditions, would have been too rich, even, for her employer's blood? The average heroine's hair is never permitted to be mussed, not even after she has engaged in a drag-'em-out tussle with the villain's henchmen; her fingernails are always long and impeccably manicured, although she may have been scrabbling in rocks for hours; her make-up is always ultracorrect, even in the steaming African jungles. Only with a few rare exceptions—as in *The Snakepit,* where Olivia De Havilland was permitted to look like a deranged mental case—are American heroines permitted to appear like anything but American heroines.

The emphasis is ever on the false trappings of the rich—the elusive bluebird of happiness. It is all part of a grandiose fantasy deliberately foisted on Everyman to appeal to his escapist wishes. It is no wonder, then, that pictures which blend fantasy with supposed realism succeed in entertaining audiences when what they are actually getting are varying degrees of pure fantasy.

This does not mean that there is no room for motion pictures other than those that are realistic. Basically, the motion picture, with its artificial shadows-for-people, is make-believe. The audience, therefore, does not demand that what it sees be always true to life. They can be entertained in many other ways—by farce, by out-of-reality adventures, by musical comedy, by murder mysteries, by any of the varied classifications of motion-picture fare.

They can even be entertained by pictures that are pure fantasy. Cocteau's *Beauty and the Beast* is laid in a country in which no sign is ever given as to its actual identity. Nor is the time identified except for a vague suggestion established by the medieval costumes. The characters are prototypes of the fairy-tale people of Grimm. And their actions are all the dreamy, insubstantial, ephemeral kind of which only fairy tales tell. Disembodied arms act as candelabra; slow-motion, fluttering, wraith-like curtains endow the heroine's walk through grim castle corridors with a floating, dreamy quality; and the Beast, with a human body but with a brutish cat's head—whiskers and all—is the stuff of which fairy tales and fantasy are fashioned. It all made for a good adult motion picture, one that was enjoyed by millions. But it was frankly designed as fantasy and made no pretense of being anything else.

When Hollywood tries its hands at fantasy, however, it does not always fare so successfully. In the picturization of Sutton Vane's *Outward Bound,* it introduced quite the wrong note by tacking on a realistic scene after the dead hero's modernized version of the Styx journey. The original play sustained the mood of fantasy by keeping the action confined strictly to the heaven-bound boat. The Hollywood version shattered the tenuous illusion of fantasy—in which the audience had become steeped and had accepted fully— by wrenching them out of it at the end and bringing its hero, and the audience, back to what was at best a matter-of-fact, squalid existence.

On the other hand, Hollywood's version of *Beggar on Horseback* was pure fantasy, and was accepted by audiences as such and enjoyed by them because it pretended to be nothing else.

To succeed as entertainment, a picture must possess unity of content and form. There is no place in the accepted Western picture, for example, for realism. Audiences demand the old West, not the new one. And when they are given the new West—as in *The Oxbow Incident,* where the entire film was saturated with realism that was not emasculated by overdoses of violent gunfights and fast-paced horseplay—they will not accept it because they have become set in their beliefs as to what the West is supposed to be.

When realism is injected into a sophisticated farce-comedy, for example, the result is a hodgepodge that is neither sophisticated, farcical, nor comical. The action and dialogue in farce-comedy should be believed by no one, particularly by the actors who perform in it. Its plot and development are deliberately artificial, brittle, and unrealistic. And it is just that artificiality and transparency that make for audience enjoyment. For if farce is presented in a dry, crackling, stylistic manner, the audience will accept it only for what it is and will join in the fun. To inject realism in the form of believable comedy is to destroy the fragile artificiality necessary to sustaining what is, at best, a very difficult job of tightrope walking. Imbalance created by combining realism and farce negates both and makes for neither.

Expressionism in pictures is another matter. Because the film shadows of motion pictures are expressionistic—as distinct from the realism of the stage where actual flesh and blood appears—expressionism, in certain limited amounts, can be very effective, even in a so-called realistic film. The conventions of film editing, and of such filmic devices as fades, dissolves, montages, and superimposures, have already been accepted by audiences as means of effecting time lapses and transitions. Dream sequences—such as were presented in *Lady in the Lake* and other films—add to the general effect of expressionism. They are, in fact, legitimate filmic material and should be used whenever needed; and the more inventive and expressionistic they are the more entertaining can they be.

The motion-picture camera is peculiarly adaptable for expressionism, and its inherent capacity for it should not be strangulated. The tricks of having the whisky bottles in *Lost Weekend* become magnified in Milland's alcoholic eyes served to bring the audience into his drunken psyche.

The stream-of-consciousness flash backs in *Best Years of Our Lives,* in which one of the returned GI's re-experiences his war years in a fighter plane, were an ideal method of putting the audience into his mind to show what made it tick.

The *avant-garde* picture makers of the '20's and '30's, in Germany and France, brought expressionism to its peak, especially with such films as *The Cabinet of Dr. Caligari.* Used for certain prescribed purposes—such as a sequence to portray a dream, or a phantasmagoric confusion during unconsciousness, or a febrile hallucination, or a flash back in time—the expressionistic treatment can work very well into a realistic picture. Such creative resourcefulness is particularly germane to the art of the screen-play writer. But, at the same time, the writer should not forget that selectivity is one of his prime literary tools. His choice of scenes to be produced expressionistically should be appropriate in time, in place, and in subject matter.

More important, for expressionism to operate at peak efficiency, it should be used sparingly. It should never be dragged in by the heels, for effect only. Its length must be timed so that it will not interfere with the over-all pacing of the story. Its content matter should flow naturally from what has gone on before into what happens afterward. And it should be motivated so as to make it completely credible and acceptable to the audience. For, because of expressionism's unrealistic nature, if it loses content credibility it will become only so much dead footage that will slow down action, destroy unity, disturb mood, disrupt pacing, and alienate the audience from a complete enjoyment of the picture.

Story holes

There is still another fault common in motion-picture stories that may have deleterious effects—story holes. These are the result of laziness on the part of the writer. They are those unexplained errors in action or dialogue that are illogical and untrue. Especially in murder mysteries the audience is often left at the end of the picture wondering "What on earth ever happened to that funny little man who sold Joe the rabbit" or "But I thought the copper was outside all the time, so how could Mamie have gotten out without being seen?"

These story holes are to be found in stories other than those of the murder-mystery genre. They are errors in plotting that somehow escaped the writer and all who were involved in making the picture. Some of them are not mere holes—some are big enough, as the saying goes, "to drive a truck through."

In the otherwise splendid picture *The Winslow Boy*, for example, the audience is never quite clear about how such a tremendous amount of apparently incontestable evidence could have been amassed against the boy.

Such errors are attributable only to bad plotting—which is bad writing. The expert author who outlines everything his characters will be and say and do rarely falls into these holes. This shoddy writing results from a writer's saying to himself, "no one's going to remember Johnny's losing his gun in the last reel—so why worry about the fact that he uses it again at the end of the picture?"

Such story holes engender vague dissatisfaction in the audience with the story as a whole. A well planned, well plotted, holeless story leaves the audience with the feeling that they have witnessed a completely unified, satisfying tale of events that could have happened to anyone, even to themselves.

Everything in any story must be completely understandable to the audience, at least after the denouement. There is only one way to avoid falling into these holes: check and double check the actions and dialogue of every character in the story. They must all jibe with one another. Care must be taken that every hole is plugged; that every loose string is tied together; that every absence is fully explained; that every entrance and exit is fully motivated, and that they are not made for some obviously contrived reason; that every coincidence is sufficiently motivated to make it credible; that there is no conflict between what has gone on before, what is going on currently, and what will happen in the future; that there is complete consistency between present dialogue and past action—that no baffling question marks are left over at the end of the picture to detract from the audience's appreciation of it.

Happy ending vs. unhappy ending

A serious fault intrinsic in the happy ending is that it must, of necessity, be telegraphed because the audience knows beforehand that the hero will overcome the obstacles that beset him, with the girl, and obtain the papers. This fault is intensified by the obnoxious "star system," where the hero must always win through to success. Rarely, if ever, is he permitted to lose out. When he does it is only in a situation where, by losing his seemingly main objective, he attains another more worthy objective, of heaven on earth or in the far beyond. Although the hero may lose the rich girl, for example, he wins the love of the poor girl who, we know, will make him a better wife and thus make for an eventually happier life.

As Fred Zinnemann stated, "It spoils the illusion for them (the audience) if your actor is Gregory Peck. They know all the time that he isn't Pfc. Quass (the name of the hero in Zinnemann's excellent picture *Teresa*)."

Television films can partially overcome this fault. Because they must be economically made, they cannot afford to pay for high-salaried stars who must be kept alive, in the film shadows, so that they can "live to fight another day."

The happy ending will always be with us, though, because audiences want it. This is no mere conjecture. Box-office statistics prove that no matter how inartistic a happy-ending picture may be, it will always get a better box office than a more artistic unhappy-ending picture. That is because the average person wants desperately to have the good guy win over the bad guy. He always associates himself broadly with the good guy, naturally—with virtue rather than vice. He wants to see the bad guy get his just deserts because he believes that crime does not pay, that evil must be overcome, that the means does not justify the end, that virtue is its own reward, and so on.

It is this triumph of good over evil, then, that makes for the happy ending. If the triumph, however, is left entirely up to Fate, if it is the result of inept and convenient contriving, then the happy ending will be telegraphed and suspense and dramatic impact will go down the drain. But the defeat of evil and the triumph of good must be brought out in a well developed struggle between the hero and the protagonist of evil; their characters must be naturally developed; their actions and reactions must flow smoothly out of their separate characters; and the forces of evil must be stronger than those of the good or, at least, its equal. If these conditions exist, then the expected happy ending will be welcomed by the audience as being in the natural order of things, as being something they would have wanted to happen to themselves were they to have been put in similar adverse circumstances. The unhappy ending, tacked on as a concluding sequence in *The Third Man,* was a mistake since the audience felt that in the end Cotten should inevitably have got the girl.

In the picture *The Best Years of Our Lives,* a happy ending was achieved by all three GI heroes solely because of forces that operated outside their own spheres of influence. Fate was given the job of deciding that their picture lives should all have happy endings. Thus the dramatic impact was considerably weakened. Had at least one of them been permitted not to succeed, then the negative effect would not have been so noticeable. Or, better still, had the three heroes been permitted to work out their own lives, struggled themselves to achieve their own happy endings, the effect would have been far more realistic, far more credible and, therefore, immeasurably more entertaining to the audience.

But it is an onerous task, indeed, to overcome this tendency to telegraph the happy ending. One way is to cover up the denouement as much as possible—by holding it off to the very end of the picture, if necessary; by introducing the poor-girl theme not too soon in the story; by permitting the hero to fail almost up to the climax and then by a sudden but well motivated switch, throwing him back into the happy-ending pattern again. If the certainty of a happy ending is withheld almost to the very end, if the hero becomes engulfed in enough situations that are seemingly impossible to overcome, and if the happy ending is so fashioned that it flows naturally out of the series of catastrophes that have befallen the hero, then it is quite possible to defer the telegraphing and retain audience absorption. Then the expected happy ending will have been forgotten, temporarily at least, so that while the hero is in the throes of his soul-searing troubles the audience will suffer with him without being bothered with the knowledge that somehow, somewhere, at some time, he is certainly going to extricate himself from his woes and win the girl.

Treatment

These, then, are the elements that must be considered when elaborating your idea into a synopsis and eventually into a treatment. If they are not considered for the synopsis they will be forgotten and will never get into the treatment, which is the next step after the synopsis has been completed.

Actually, the treatment is nothing more than a long short story, told in the present tense. Its length may vary from ten pages to as many as one hundred pages. It must contain only certain elements of dialogue—not all the dialogue extensively treated, but just the dramatic highspots, enough to carry the story forward and to suggest the style in which all the dialogue will be handled.

Quite often screen-play writers include directions for some of the master shots, or for dissolves and fades. But these are not essential. Trick shots and effects are also suggested but they, too, can be left out.

THE FILMIC COMPONENTS

SECTION

The shots  Up to this point we have dealt only with literary aspects of the motion-picture story as they relate to the writing of screen plays.

The writer who is interested only in producing master-scene scripts denuded of all camera directions can cease reading from here on in and can settle down to writing only what is expected of him, and no more.

But if he aspires to being more than merely a screen-writing journalist, if he believes that the screen-play writer should be exactly what the title signifies—a screen-play writer—then he will read further.

For in the following material he will find the vital substance of the screen play. He will find detailed discussions of almost every element necessary to the fashioning of a shooting script—a scenario a film editor may use as a basic outline with which to put together the bits of film shot by the director, who may well have followed the script word for word in its entirety.

The writers of television films will find themselves confronted with a number of problems that do not ordinarily concern the writers of films for theater presentation. These problems will all be discussed in their proper places. But a general discussion of the television film in relation to live television production and theater feature-film production might be appropriate at this time.

There is no doubt that televised film plays can be far superior to live television dramas. This is so for the following reasons:

1. Whereas the live show is transitory, the film is a concrete record that can be shown again and again. Although live show definition is superior to that of filmed shows, at the present time, the

kinescoped version of live shows—that is, photography off the television screen—is far inferior to both. With a film, a sponsor can present his entertainment in whatever locale he chooses and at whatever time he desires, since he is not forced to present a live show on the coaxial cable, at arbitrary times which vary across the country.

2. Because television films can be edited, they are free of the accidents to which the live drama is prone, as when actors blow their lines; cameras go out; directors signal for the wrong camera; sound booms fall into the camera's view; a grip is caught on the set; drawers stick, actors trip.

3. The scope of live television, as compared with the filmed variety, is almost negligible. It cannot include the all-important chase, for example. While a filmed drama can roam at will—across moors, through a maze of tunnels, across roof tops—the live television drama is confined to the four or five sets the average television stage can accommodate. And when filmed inserts of a chase are included, they merely highlight the obvious disadvantage under which live television suffers.

4. To offset these patent disadvantages, live television does possess one major advantage—immediacy. Like plays produced on the stage, live television dramas project a sense of actuality few films have ever achieved. Despite this film lack, audiences have accepted motion pictures without reservation, including those not worthy of esthetic consideration, primarily because of their technical excellence. Hence there is every reason to believe that audiences will eventually prefer the more perfect filmed versions of dramatic entertainment to the more imperfect and more restricted live versions.

To conform to the comparatively limited budget of the advertising sponsor, television films must be made considerably cheaper per reel than their movie-house prototypes. These economies can be effected only by making drastic changes in customs and techniques. Since the average "B" picture produced by Hollywood costs from about $150,000 to $400,000, and runs for about 90 minutes, it is obvious that, to produce a half-hour film for television, using the same production techniques, would cost about one third of the B feature film, or from about $50,000 to $130,000. Sponsors cannot and will not pay more than $20,000 for a television film of this length. It is quite apparent that feature-film producers must revamp their production setups completely if they expect to compete with the television film companies that are currently turning out films at costs within the advertising budgets available.

To make television films cheaply enough, these producers have resorted to every cost-cutting dodge and device available. They have limited the number of sets; reduced the size of the casts; refrained from using high-salaried stars; resorted to P.P.P.P. (pre-production planned preparation) so that the casts are perfectly rehearsed before they come onto the set, thus reducing the time and money spent on the set for actual production.

They have also devised such shooting methods as the "multicam" system, which shoots each scene with three cameras instead of one, so that a medium-long shot, a medium shot, and a close shot can be photographed simultaneously, thus making for obvious shooting economies. When such a system is used, the detailed shooting script must give way to the master-scene script. But, like all stopgaps, the multicam system has its faults. No one will contend that it is possible for a cameraman to light a set that will be photogenic for a variety of shots. Extreme close-ups, and inserts, for instance, will have to be shot in the conventional manner. Pans and other camera movements will, of necessity, be restricted by the presence of other cameras which can obtrude in the "take" and thus "n.g." it.

So far, the films produced by this method have been found wanting in many respects. The all-important chase has been studiously avoided; in the main, action has been confined to interior sets; pacing and tempo have suffered because film editors have not been furnished with sufficient shot material, with varying angles and image sizes to make for effective montage and building effects; and what would have ordinarily been n.g. takes from one camera have been cut into the film because no more satisfactory shot was available. Also, it is difficult enough to dress a set for a single camera with the actors and props in their right places so as to obtain the most felicitous composition possible; to expect to obtain esthetically satisfying composition from three cameras, while the actors are in motion, is to expect the impossible. The only way to accomplish it is to limit the action of the actors, which is tantamount to obstructing the flow of action necessary to a motion picture.

Therefore, it can be seen that for television films to be produced both economically and esthetically, the traditional methods of production are indicated. Savings must be effected in ways that are already available to the screen writer of television films. These ways will be discussed in the following sections.

The average feature film for theaters is composed of a length of 35 millimeter film that runs from between 7000 to 8000 feet. For a half-hour television drama, it would run for about 2500 feet if presented on 35 millimeter film and correspondingly less on 16 millimeter film. It is about 30 per cent cheaper to shoot pictures on 16 millimeter film than on 35 millimeter, although the results—both aurally and visually—are considerably less in quality than pictures shot on 35 millimeter film. Television films will be shot on 16 millimeter film, but, for the purpose of clarity, from now on all references to film footage will be based on 35 millimeter.

This footage is composed of a number of "clips" of film cut down from the original footage of "take" shots, which usually average about six feet for every foot of film used in the picture.

Each film clip consists of a number of "frames," which run sixteen to every foot of film. These individual frames are exposed in the camera twenty-four frames to the second, and they are projected on the screen at the same rate of speed.

It is the job of the screen-play writer, then, to indicate exactly what image is to be exposed on every frame of the picture.

After listing certain details in the opening lines of the screen play—to be found in the section under FORMAT—the writer describes the first shot of the script as follows:

EXT. MERIWETHER HOSPITAL—DAY

This is a generalization which indicates—to the assistant director, whose job it is to break down the script for shooting purposes—but more particularly to the director—that the scene is set in exterior surroundings, as distinct from an INT. (interior), which is set inside a house, a vehicle, or any other edifice or covered place.

Following this comes the *specific* place, in this case the MERIWETHER HOSPITAL. It could be the ROBERTS' DINING ROOM, LOBBY OF WEST HOTEL, or PRISON CELL, but it must specify the exact place in which the action is to be played.

Then comes the time of day in which the action of the shot occurs. In most cases—and especially in television films—DAY or NIGHT will suffice. But for the more important pictures, and es-

pecially for those made at the larger studios, a more definite desig-
nation of time can be made—on the order of TWILIGHT or
EARLY MORNING—because there is more money available in the
budget to cover the time the cameraman must devote to achieving
more subtle lighting gradations.

That done, the screen-play writer indicates, on the next line,
something on the order of:

> MED. SHOT on JANE, as she lifts her baby from the crib, hugs it
> to her breast, and looks around frightenedly.

Now, how does the writer know that a medium shot would be best
suited for this action? What can he accomplish, visually, with it?
Would a close shot suit the purpose better? Should the camera pan
Jane from the crib to the door, when she exits, or should she simply
walk out of the frame, to be picked up a second later as she enters
the frame with the camera focused on the door? Or should a cutaway shot be indicated, to someone else either in the same room or
in a different locale?

These and many other plaguy questions will come up to bother
the screen-play writer. The answers to them will be attempted in
the following pages.

Let us look into the business of shots, then, discussing first the
proper distances between the camera and the subject being photographed. Unfortunately, despite the hundreds of thousands of motion pictures that have been produced, no accepted standards of
exact measurements have been evolved. A medium shot, to one
director, may be a shot resulting in an image that will include the
subject's knees. To another director it may mean an image in
which everything from the hips up is to be seen.

The cinematographic societies have tried to formulate exact
measurements, but to date there has been no strict conformance to
any of them by the entire industry.

The following material, then, should not be interpreted as the
final word in such matters. It merely represents one writer-director's
interpretation of the many conflicting dicta gathered from research
and experience. The principles have worked for him. There is no
reason why they cannot work for anyone else. At least it is an honest
attempt to establish standards, a task which has heretofore been
sadly neglected and almost studiously avoided.

The full shot

When it is necessary to show all the action in an entire scene, the full shot is resorted to. Thus, if an entire room is to be shown, or the complete action on a wide street, the full shot would be indicated.

The full shot is also referred to as an "establishing shot," which term should indicate its use: to establish in the audience, as a sort of frame of reference, the locale and the action in which closer, more detailed shots take place.

Every new set must be represented, either at the opening of the sequence of shots or very early in it, with an establishing, full shot. This is so because unless the audience is fully oriented to the *place* in which the action occurs, the full significance of the closer shots may not be realized.

In traditional film editing it is almost axiomatic to return to a full shot after a series of medium shots, close shots, and close-ups have been used, in order to re-establish the entire scene for the audience so that once again they may obtain a fuller understanding of what they have been seeing in *detail* when compared with the *general* action in the frame-of-reference, re-establishing shot.

The scenic full shot is peculiarly adaptable to Westerns, where it is often necessary to show violent action—as, for example, a chase on horseback—against a background of scenic beauty, such as a distant range of mountains, or a closer formation of foothills, towering rocks, gullies, and gulches.

The same effect can be gotten when a violent fight is in progress: by establishing first with a full shot of the room—if it is an interior fight—or the street; then by going in for closer shots of the fight for revelatory details such as chins being hit by fists, knockdowns, etc.; and then by re-establishing toward the end of the scene with a medium shot or another full shot.

Ordinarily—and especially in the cheaper-budgeted pictures—the full shots are taken at one angle, from only one camera setup, so that closer shots can be cut in by the film editor. But varying angles should be used, if time and money are not of the essence, because the entire action must be repeated for each new camera setup.

It is suggested that the single-setup method be indicated for television screen plays. At the same time, the full shot must not be cluttered up with too many people or things. Television's small screen militates against the practice.

In pictures with urban backgrounds, the full shot can be used to achieve an effect of mass and multitudinous activity. In the British film *It Always Rains on Sunday* an excellent impression of the market in London's Petticoat Lane was obtained with a full shot. With the camera on a boom, so that it was able to move in from the general effect of the full shot to the specific details revealed gradually in a fluid succession of uncut long shots, medium shots, and close shots, the effect of dynamic violence was heightened because it was contrasted with the static quality of the background scenics.

The full shot has tremendous dramatic possibilities in urban scenes, especially when it is made from an extremely high angle, as from the top of a building. In Rossellini's *Germany—Year Zero,* and in Carol Reed's *The Fallen Idol,* full shots—taken from high balconies—of a small boy crossing the street served to emphasize the helplessness of each lad when contrasted with the engulfing vastness of the city's streets.

When suggesting such high-angle shots for a television script, the screen writer should keep in mind the fact that the figure of the person seen on the street must be large enough to be identified. This identification can be assured by giving the person some easily discernible prop—a white scarf, a large picture hat, or the like.

Because the quality of scenic backgrounds is usually static, it is often more desirable to obtain a sense of movement by moving the camera in a slow, panning sweep, to follow the action taking place in the foreground or middleground. This is often resorted to in Westerns. The same sense of movement was obtained in the aforementioned Petticoat Lane shot, not by panning, but by dollying in to more detailed, closer shots.

The long shot

The long shot is not necessarily a full shot, although, with it, the camera lens is also set at infinity and the angle is widened. It has effects similar to those of the full shot. It is used to show the subject or subjects in *full length,* but not necessarily in relation to the surrounding background locale.

When the subject is held in a long shot, the angle of the lens remains constant. But when the subject comes closer to the camera, it is necessary for the camera operator to "follow focus" so that the subject will continue in sharp focus on the screen.

Thus, when a subject is in a long shot, but when there is action in the foreground, much depends upon what is to be highlighted. If the foreground action is more important, then it will be in focus, while the background, long-shot action will go out of focus. It may be necessary to open a scene with the long-shot subject in focus at first, and then to change focus to bring out the reaction of a subject in the foreground.

This can be done by the operator's adjusting his focal length in the lens. Orson Welles has used this effect advantageously, especially by having the foreground subject come into the shot in an extreme close-up, while the background long-shot subject remains in focus, so that the action in both planes is also in focus. This is done by using a wide-angle lens—and with judicious lighting, at which Gregg Toland was a master—so that both the action up close and in the extreme background remain in sharp focus simultaneously. With this kind of "forced focus" or "shooting in depth" it is quite possible to see objects that are both 18 inches and 200 feet from the camera.

Here again the television screen-play writer should be extremely cautious. In the early days of television, when the ten-inch screen was the rule, the long shot was completely restricted. Nowadays, with home TV screens running to twenty inches or more, and with larger screens promised, the long shot has lost many of its pariah qualities. A few long shots—preferably of a medium-long quality— can be injected into a half-hour script provided the action it covers is not too important to the story line. Also, screen definition in them is considerably better than in the closer shots. This superior definition carries over from the long shots to the closer shots, a psychological effect known as "apparent definition."

The medium shot

The most commonly used shot in motion-picture shooting is the medium shot, usually condensed to MED. Instead of showing a full figure, as in the long shot, the medium shot presents the figure only from the knees up. In this shot, the vertical planes are such that the action in both the foreground and background can be carried in focus without focal adjustments.

The medium shot is ideal for carrying movement. Unlike the full shot, the action of its central characters is not lost in the vastness of the background panorama. Nor does it lose a certain amount of its centering action to its surrounding locale, as in the long shot. Instead, it concentrates the action and contains it. In addition, the medium shot presents the action within the reference framework of action or scene in the immediate vicinity of the central action.

Thus, with the medium shot, it is possible to evoke from a scene its full content of dramatic conflict. For the medium shot manages to retain facial expressions and physical gestures—partially lost in the long shot—and relates these, dramatically, to the action involved, which can also be included in the scope of the medium shot. The medium shot is virtually the work horse of all the shots available.

The medium shot can also be used as a re-establishing shot, to reorient the audience to the scene as a whole after they have been subjected to the detailed scrutiny of a series of close shots. At the same time, if a return is made to a re-establishing full shot, it is almost obligatory to use a medium shot as an intermediary phase, to avoid the sudden change in camera distance and image size.

Use of the medium shot for orienting and reorienting purposes is particularly necessary for television scripts, where a preponderance of the shots used are close shots or close-ups, all of which must be fully established for the audience to avoid confusion.

The medium-close shot

At times it may be necessary to show what is known as a "tight two-shot"—the heads and shoulders of two people. This would be done in a medium-close shot, which places the camera in a position between that of a medium shot and that of a close shot, enough to accommodate the two heads. This is another "must" shot for television scripts which, together with the closer shots, comprise a majority of the total shots in a TV script.

The close shot

The close shot is often confused with the close-up. In the former, the camera distance is such that the figure shown includes only everything from the shoulders up. However, it is still possible to include in the picture a few details, such as props or set dressing, which can be used either for pictorial, for compositional, or for thematic or story purposes.

Thus, although the close shot has a tendency to slow up the forward movement and impede dramatic action, it carries with it other advantages that compensate for the loss.

For the close shot *can particularize.* It can say to the audience, in effect, "Look here! See what's happening now. It's really important!"

The close shot should be to the television script what the medium shot is to the theater feature-film screen play. It should be used again and again, but do not forget to re-establish, after a series of close shots, with a reorienting medium shot.

Up to this point, the various shots discussed have been, to a certain degree, only slightly different from those obtained in a stage play. In fact, when motion pictures were first made, these shots were used exclusively, especially the medium shot. But when Griffith adopted and perfected the close shot and close-up, motion pictures took their first step out of their swaddling clothes.

For it was with these cinematic devices that the screen writer and director became cinematic creators.

The close-up

This was so especially with the close-up, which goes even closer to the subject and shows only full-screen heads, faces, hands, feet—in fact, any *significant detail* that can *point out* and *point up*, for the audience, and thus heighten the dramatic impact.

With the close-up at his disposal, the writer has a tool that is unique, in so far as contrast with the stage play is concerned. For in the theater, the size of the actor or his props remains constant, and allows only for a size variant limited by the depth of the stage and by artful spot lighting which was the stage forerunner of the cinematic close-up.

In the motion picture, however, the audience's attention can be drawn to, and centered on, any revelatory or significant detail. Thus, the screen-play writer's opportunity for selectivity is increased tremendously.

It is the close-up that has made the motion picture the singular art form that it is today, and that can make it the supreme expression of art in the future. For dramatic impact to top off a scene, there is nothing so effective in the entire lexicon of cinematic devices. In David Lean's British picture *Great Expectations*, the boy, Pip, is shown running wildly through marshes, past gibbets and into a churchyard cemetery, the camera traveling with him. It holds on him when he gets to one of the tombstones. Then suddenly it pans around from Pip to an abrupt close-up on the leering, menacing, distorted features of the escaped convict. The result is an electric shock to the audience and a high spot in a film replete with high spots.

Although the close-up results in a larger screen image, for television it is suggested that it be used only when added particularization—more than could be obtained from a close shot—is called for. Here, also, remember to re-establish with a medium or medium close shot for an orienting frame of reference.

Inserts

But that is only one use of the close-up. Others will be discussed in other sections. Here, though, it might be appropriate to add that the close-up is also used as an "insert." The insert is a cut-in of a close-up of a letter, a newspaper headline, a sign—any written or printed legend—which it is obligatory to show in large-size detail, for plot requirements.

Unless the insert is to be used at the tag end of a shot, as a transition device to dissolve into another scene, it is always best to cut back from the insert to a re-establishing shot of the full scene in which the material of the insert was only a detail, in order to reorient the audience to the situation which called for the close-up.

The television screen-play writer must be wary with the printed insert. Remember, the small television screen reduces such printing to an almost unreadable size. If a sign is used, be sure it is printed in large type, with only a few words as the legend. Use every dodge you can to avoid showing an insert of a letter, a page of type, a newspaper item, or a telegram. Allow one of the characters to read it, or parts of it. If it is absolutely essential to show it in print, be sure it is brief.

If a telegram is part of the plot, for example, have the person sending the telegram read it over the phone to the telegraph operator, or reverse the process and have the operator read it to the person receiving it.

The insert can also be a close-up shot of any prop which must be shown in full-screen detail for plot purposes. Ordinarily, such inserts are not photographed on the regular sound stages while shooting of the picture is in operation. Instead, they are photographed on "special effects" stages.

Extreme close-ups

At times the writer may find it necessary to particularize even more than the conventional close-up will permit. For example, he may want to indicate a fleeting expression in the eyes, or point up a wart on the nose, or a mystery-story clue, or even show a thumbprint. In such cases, he would resort to the extreme close-up.

This device was used in an amazingly effective manner in the Czech film *Ecstasy*. By means of an extreme close-up of the girl's lips as she entered her lover's cottage, the audience was able to sense the heat of her passions by the manner in which the skin of her upper and lower lips adhered to each other and then separated almost reluctantly.

Care must be taken, however, that such shots be used sparingly. If overused, they will lose their shock value and thus lose dramatic impact. The same injunction should be applied to the use of ordinary close-ups. Their use should be timed, and they should be integrated into the script as a whole so that, with building, the full effect of their dramatic possibilities can be realized. When such *extreme* close-ups are used in television pictures, they should always be followed by a re-establishing larger shot to reorient the audience.

Moving shots

So far, the discussion of camera usage has been confined to static shots, in which the camera holds on a subject which is at varying distances from the camera, to obtain varying effects on the screen.

These static shots, however, can be combined with certain camera movements to obtain even more effective results. But before going into detail about these moving shots, it is necessary to give the following warning, which will be repeated again and again:

The camera should be moved only when there is a definite reason for doing so!

One of the most frequent faults found in live television programs is the overuse of unmotivated pan and dolly shots. This occurs because the basic scenes have not been previsualized by the writers for intrinsic action. With this conception of action lacking, television directors are forced to fall back on the surface action of unmotivated pan and dolly shots. A study of the following material should show how this error can be avoided in television films.

With these words of caution, we shall go on to what is perhaps the meat and substance of camera technique as it pertains to the screen-play writer.

The pan shot

The word "pan" is a contraction of the word "panoramic," which was used in the early days of motion-picture making to describe the swiveled action of the camera, as it was swung slowly from one side to another to obtain a complete view of a distant scenic vista, usually a mountain range or closer foothills.

It is this sidewise motion of the camera, to obtain a continuous, moving, panoramic image, that is now known as a "pan shot."

But the present-day use of the pan shot is not confined strictly to scenic panorama, for which purpose, incidentally, it is still ideally suited. Nor is it confined to any other type of panorama. The pan shot, nowadays, is *any* shot in which the camera moves from one side to another in order to *follow the action* taking place in front of it.

Follow action only. Note well the italicized words: *follow the action.* They tie in with the rule given at the opening of this section. For no pan shot is justified unless there is a definite reason for using it. And one of the most important reasons for using a pan shot is to follow *significant* action. Note now the italicized word *significant.* Not all actions are significant. Their importance depends on the nature of the action and its place in the screen play. But only when the action is *significant* should the pan shot be used.

The pan shot is used considerably in Western pictures to follow the action of cowboys on horseback as they chase each other over the floor of a valley, or as the stagecoach goes hurtling down a narrow mountain road or hangs precipitously over the edges of hairpin turns.

An extraordinarily effective pan shot is the one in which a speeding vehicle advances to the camera, which holds on it until it is almost head on. Then, as the vehicle passes by, the camera is pivoted quickly and follows the speeding vehicle as it continues down the road. The effect here—of catching the vehicle first when it is small, of having it gradually increase in size until soon it assumes full screen proportions as it seemingly hurtles pell-mell into the audience itself, and then of moving with it as it rushes by headlong to decrease gradually in size—is one that can be breath-taking when done well, for it has all of the elements of dramatic build-up interwoven into a continuous flow of violent, moving action.

Exit and entrance pans. The pan shot is also used to follow individual actions, such as entrances or exits from one room into another. It goes without saying that the exit or entrance pan should be used only where such movement is essential to the development of the story. There is no sense in wasting a pan shot on an exit or entrance that does not add to the story's development. It is best, then, simply to cut away from the action and cut to the next scene. But if it is necessary to follow a character from one room to another, then a direct cut would be confusing, because the audience would have been given no indication of the character's intention of leaving the room. Thus, if they see him in one scene standing at the window of the kitchen as a direct cut is made from the scene, only to find him in the next scene entering the living room, the audience would be puzzled by this abrupt "jump cut," as it is called, and the flow of continuity would be considerably impaired. If, however, the cut is made to a scene in which the character at the window does not appear, it is not necessary to pan him away from the window to the door, even though in a succeeding scene he is shown entering the dining room.

Pan motivated movement. The pan shot is also used to follow an actor although he makes neither an exit nor entrance. It can take him across the room or yard, or from the fireplace to the window. But always remember, there must be a definite reason for the movement of the actor to warrant the camera movement. When such pans are used simply to have the camera move, and for no other reason, the illusory sense of movement created will tend to counteract the effect of genuine movement obtained from other shots, in which the camera movement was justified by completely motivated character movement.

That accounts for the failure of Hitchcock's *The Rope* to realize its full potentialities as a great picture. The picture was shot as a series of continuous pan shots, long shots, medium shots, close shots and close-ups, so that cut-ins and cutaways were avoided. This called for an inordinate amount of camera movement, from side to side in pan shots, up and down in tilt shots, up and back in dolly shots, and again from side to side in trucking shots. As a matter of fact, each individual shot was a long trucking shot, with the camera off the tracks.

Hitchcock's purpose in shooting his picture with this radical technique was, perhaps, to obtain a continuous fluidity of movement never before achieved by the camera. And in motion pictures, where the smooth flow of continuity is extremely desirable, such a technique may, in theory, seem promising. But in actual practice, if we are to judge from the results of *The Rope*, it is obvious that in trying to achieve this much desired fluidity, Hitchcock was forced to overwork his camera. He was forced to move it in order to get from one significant detail to another at times when camera movement was completely unjustified because it was unmotivated. The result was that a great deal of the extraordinary camera movement that was legitimate was negated by the camera movement that was superfluous.

In one scene, for example, the camera was forced to dolly in from a medium shot of James Stewart to an extreme close-up. With that done, the camera pulled back again to a medium shot and then panned away from Stewart to additional, continuing action.

In a normally shot picture, Hitchcock would never have dollied in for a close-up and then out at the same time, because he would have been aware of the jerkiness that such camera action creates. Instead, as always, he would have cut away from the close-up to, perhaps, a re-establishing shot, or to a cutaway for a reaction shot of another character. But because he was forced to use unmotivated camera movements, he spoiled what was, in many other respects, a vitally important picture.

Revelation pan. One of the most electrifying uses of the pan comes when it concludes with a startling revelation. The stock example, used in murder-mystery stories, is to have the camera pan slowly across an empty room and then suddenly reach and hold on a corpse. The use of contrast—as between the quiet, static room and the revelation of violent death—is what makes for the dramatic impact. Usually the camera then dollies in to the corpse and holds on a close-up of the blunt instrument, or whatever instrument of death has been used, or on some other significant detail necessary to the development of the plot. This method of capping one dramatic impact (the pan revelation) with still another (the close-up particularization) can have an exceedingly dramatic effect on the audience. Here again the device should be used only sparingly, so as not to weaken its effectiveness.

It is with the pan revelation device that the screen-play writer can assure himself that his camera direction will be followed by the director. No director would dare to discard a fresh approach to the device, for he would realize that, to the average audience, he, and not the writer, would be accredited with its creation. The pan revelation, like the pay-off pan, is another means by which the writer can assert himself creatively.

Pay-off pan. Another type of revelatory pan begins with the camera panning with a person without holding on him completely. Instead, it holds momentarily on some significant detail and permits the person being panned to walk out of the frame, centering the new item of interest for dramatic particularization. To cap this impact, immediately after holding on the new item, the camera often dollies in for a close shot, or a close-up, of what has interrupted the pan. The effect here is of endowing the camera with the human trait of curiosity. And when that curiosity results in a dramatic pay-off, the impact is made even more effective.

A splendid example of this was found in *Miracle on 34th Street* where, after the lawyer has proved in court that Santa Claus does not exist, the audience discovers, by means of a pan, the old gentleman's cane standing in a corner of the room.

Medium to close pan. The pan shot is also an excellent device for taking the audience from the general to the particular, and for connecting the two. Thus the camera can hold on one action in the medium shot, and wind up holding on a close-up of, say, a letter lying on a desk. This method avoids the dollying in, which is a time-consuming device as far as production is concerned.

Reaction pan. The pan can also be used quite effectively to present a collective reaction to a speech or an action. In *The Magnificent Ambersons,* while some dialogue was being conducted, the camera panned from the speakers' heads across the hallway and along the staircase, revealing various eavesdroppers to the conversation.

Subjective pan. Another spectacular use of the pan is to make it appear to be the eyes of one of the characters. When he enters a room, for instance, if he is searching for something, the camera can be panned slowly around the room, as though the camera lens were the character's eyes. This creates the illusion in the audience that the camera is also their eyes.

This effect was perfectly presented in the French picture *The Grand Illusion,* when the prison searchlight, piercing the darkness and falling on the ground in a blazing white pool of light, slowly panned the prison yard, searching out each nook and cranny for the escaped prisoners, as the panning camera followed the light around.

Limit the pan. Don't go overboard in using the pan. Remember this: The pan is not a true representation of the human eye in operation, as it moves from one place to another. For actually, instead of moving smoothly across an expanse of space like the camera's eye, the human eye skips from one point of interest to another. This means that there are a great many details lost to the human eye because of inattention and blurring.

Camera pans tend to slow down tempo. This was obvious in *Lady in the Lake,* where the camera was supposed to be the eye of Robert Montgomery, the detective protagonist. Instead of skipping about the room as the human eye would do, the camera eye always panned slowly from place to place. A plethora of disturbing nonessentials cluttered up the audience's vision and slowed the tempo to a pedestrian crawl, unfortunately quite often in spots where the reverse tempo was desirable. The subjective camera technique is faulty because of this.

Flash pan. The pan can also be used to simulate the human eye in its place-skipping proclivity. When it is essential to show two or more vital actions taking place simultaneously in the same vicinity, the flash pan (also called the "blur pan") can be used as an ideal link. This device is the result of having the camera operator jerk his camera around violently from one action to another, so that the connecting link between the action appears on the screen as a blurred flash. It will be necessary, in order to produce this linkage, to flash-pan *into* the succeeding scene so that, when the two shots are put together, it will appear as though the camera zips from one object in sharp focus to another object also in sharp focus.

Transition flash pan. The flash pan can also be used as a transitional device to connect two shots of actions which are simultaneous in time, but geographically separated. The effect is achieved by flash-panning *away* from the first shot, flash-panning *into* the succeeding shot, and then linking together the two flash pans optically, so that the effect is of a flash pan from one shot into another. This device should be used infrequently in any one film. And it should be used only to indicate simultaneity, to take the place of a direct cut, which indicates continuity of action in time.

The flash pan can also be used as a connecting device for dramatic contrast. In the documentary *The City,* the camera held on a long shot of an old city, then flash-panned across the river to hold on a long shot of a new city. A direct cut here would not have been so effective in pointing up the contrast.

Avoid reverse pan. A final injunction about the use of the pan: *avoid reversing the pan too often in the same shot.* A single pan works enough strain on the audience's eyes without having them jerked to and fro to cover the same territory. The result is a choppiness that destroys the smooth flow of continuity.

The reverse pan should be used only at certain times, and then quite cautiously. If it is absolutely essential that two separate actions in the same vicinity be tied together to indicate simultaneity, contrast, or revelation, the camera can pan from one action to the other and then flash-pan back to the first action again for a revelatory reaction. It can also be used in fight scenes, or in any scenes of violent action in which the contestants shuttle from side to side. In such cases the jerky effect is permissible because it suggests the seesawing results of the fight and matches the filmic tempo with the story tempo.

Although a good director will do it automatically, it is advisable to indicate, whenever making a long pan, that the "CAMERA HOLDS" on various important elements included in the pan shot's purview. This will give the film cutter definite places in which to cut in particularizing close shots or close-ups without being forced to do so in a moving shot—a virtual impossibility. The same applies to any and all moving-camera shots.

The pan shot is more time-consuming than the straight shot because it may require a number of n.g. takes, resulting from the operator's inability to follow the action and hold it centered. For that reason, there should be far fewer of them in a television film screen play than in a screen play for theater presentation. The television script writer should not avoid them completely but resort to them only when they are absolutely necessary.

The tilt shot

In addition to being able to pan horizontally, the camera can also pan perpendicularly, both up and down, in what are termed "tilt shots." Thus, the tilt is an ideal device for catching important falling or rising action.

If it is important to reveal a prop falling from a table to the floor, for instance, to show it rolling under a chair and being hidden, indicate a close shot on the prop on the table, then, "as Joe's arm nudges the brass ring off the table, the CAMERA TILTS DOWN to catch the falling ring." The roll of the ring under the chair may have to be shot separately and cut in, to make certain it will be photographed exactly where it is required.

The tilting-up shot is often used to photograph a person getting up from a chair, or from any sitting position, provided it is necessary to show the action in a continuous flow. When this isn't necessary, the action is often shot in two parts, the first showing the person starting to get up from one angle, and the second showing him completing the action. The entire action, though, is taken in each shot, but the film editor will trim off the tail end of the first shot and the opening frames of the second, and splice together the two shots, thus getting the whole action from two different angles.

The tilt-up shot is also an excellent means of emphasizing height. Tall buildings, high cliffs, anything of imposing height, can be made to appear higher than they actually are simply by placing the camera near the base of the edifice and then tilting it up slowly. This is especially effective when the action taking place on top of the building or cliff is an important story point.

In the German film *Berlin,* the camera emphasized the height of the wall of a bomb-wrecked building up which the boy climbed and from the top of which he fell to his death. The same effect was achieved by Rossellini in his *Germany—Year Zero,* when he emphasized the height of the bomb-wrecked building from which his boy leaped to his death.

The tilt-up can also be used as the tail end of a transition. This device starts in a panning close-up of a person walking. The camera then tilts *down* to a shot of the feet treading along. The shot of these feet is then dissolved through, either to a close shot of the same person's feet, or to another person's feet, depending on which the story line calls for. Then, still panning, the camera starts to tilt *up* from the feet to a close-up of the person walking.

Remember, though, that motion-picture cameras are not confined to straight horizontal or vertical movements. They are designed so as to be able to combine the pan, the tilt-up, and the tilt-down all in one operation. Thus it is possible for the camera operator to pan a subject diagonally, down a flight of stairs, while he tilts down with it to keep it centered, or reverse the process if the subject is going up a flight of stairs. In Hitchcock's *Stage Fright,* the camera opened with a close shot on a man (the camera being on a boom, no doubt), as the man exited from a door, went down stairs, and opened a door. In the meantime the camera, tilted down to his feet in a close-up, traveled down to the door as it opened, and then tilted up to catch a close shot of Marlene Dietrich.

In addition, the vertical axis of the camera can be set *at an angle* to the vertical axis of the subject being photographed. The result is that the image on the film will be shown as being tilted forward or backward, an effect experimented with in many of the German and French *avant-garde* films. It should be used rarely and *only when it actually contributes something definite*. In the British *Brief Encounter,* the grieving heroine was photographed so that she appeared to be leaning forward when the train passed the station in which she was standing, in order to give a visual representation of her intention of throwing herself under the train wheels. Then, when the suicide thoughts subsided, the camera was tilted back to normal.

In the German film *Wozzeck,* a succession of tilted camera shots aided in building up to the climax of Wozzeck's delirium scene. And in Duvivier's *Carnet du Bal,* the sequence with the epileptic doctor was shot with tilted-camera angles to symbolize his lack of equilibrium. The same tilted-camera angles were employed in Eisenstein's *October* when the workers marched up the ramp, to emphasize the weight of their labors.

Dolly shots

The modern motion-picture camera is a flexible and mobile instrument. In addition to being able to pan and tilt simultaneously, it can also "dolly in" or "dolly out"—that is, move in closer to the subject or back away from it at the same time that it is panning and tilting.

What is more, while panning and tilting, the camera can also "dolly"—move along parallel with the subject, keeping the subject centered. This type of dolly shot is called the "traveling" shot. Slower action can be shot with the camera on a regulation dolly carriage. Faster action requires that the camera be placed on a vehicle, the speed of which is equal to the speed of the vehicle or person being photographed.

Trucking shots. Dolly shots, often also called "trucking" shots (or "tracking" shots in England) or described simply as "The CAMERA MOVES IN," or "the CAMERA PULLS AWAY," or "the CAMERA TRUCKS ALONG WITH," are almost always made on a "dolly" (a rubber-wheeled camera carriage) which rolls on a set of aluminum tracks nailed down to the stage floor and sometimes kept rigid by means of wooden-bar "spacers." These precautions are necessary in order to insure absolute rigidity to the camera, which will make for smooth-flowing, jerk-free film images.

In writing screen plays for cheap-budget movie-house pictures, or for television films, the number of dolly shots should be cut to a minimum. They are difficult to set up for lighting, and difficult to shoot, especially if a number of involved camera movements are to be used. They are time-consuming and therefore expensive.

At the same time, however, they are extremely useful in many ways. Some have already been mentioned in discussing other shots. As useful as they may be, though, it is best to explore other possible means of obtaining the same effect before resorting to the dolly shot.

Dolly or cut-in?   Significant detail revelation, for instance, can be achieved by means of a cut-in close-up. Instead of dollying in to show what a character sees, the cut-in close-up can accomplish the same purpose. In some cases, where it is essential to speed up the tempo, the cut-in is preferable. For the dolly in or dolly out are slow, time-consuming devices. The forward movement of a film is always deterred by either. And unless the dolly shot can be fitted into a slow-moving sequence, or can be used to open a sequence that builds to a climax, it should be avoided.

Pullback dolly.   The pullback dolly shot is especially suitable for a certain type of revelation. Where the dolly in can reveal a startling detail in the small, as it were, the pullback dolly shot can reveal startling information in the large. A shot can open with a close-up of something which in itself has no particular significance. But the camera can then pull back and reveal something in the immediate vicinity which can furnish a startling revelation.

In the British picture *The Night Has Eyes,* James Mason is made to believe that he is insane. His housekeeper and houseman dope him, and then arrange to have him awaken in a stupor with his hands wrapped around a freshly killed animal whose neck had been twisted. In the final sequence, his girl friend returns to his cottage at night and, at the gate, sees something startling taking place in the cottage driveway. A direct cut in a close-up to the doorway shows what she sees—a rabbit in somebody's hands with its neck being twisted. The reason for the girl's reaction is slowly revealed to the audience, when the camera pulls back and shows that the hands around the rabbit's neck are not Mason's, as the audience is momentarily led to believe, but those of the housekeeper. In this way, the facts revealed to the audience are that Mason is not mad, but that the housekeeper has been plotting to make him think he is.

The camera could have flash-panned from the girl at the gate to the housekeeper at the doorway. But it would have frittered away the full suspense possibilities of the scene, which were completely realized by the pullback dolly. The cut-in was more advisable too, because a flash pan would have had to be shot a number of times before a satisfactory in-focus and centered take would be possible.

In those shots where it is especially apropos for what is shown in the close-up to be seen in relation to what is revealed in the pullback, the pullback dolly is obligatory. If, however, the relationship is not essential—if contrast, relativity, parallelism, or interrelated reactions are not vital considerations, and if the shock of revelation is the only requirement—then a simple pan can be used instead of the pullback dolly.

The pullback dolly is an excellent device for establishing and re-establishing "place"—that is, for orienting the audience to the exact location in which the action is occurring.

Although there may be any number of track lengths available for a pullback dolly, only a limited amount can be used. For at a certain point the camera, if it is pulled back far enough, will reveal the tracks on the floor. This has been overcome, though, when longer pullbacks were found necessary, by resorting to special "breakaway" tracks, which could be pulled away by ropes before appearing in camera view. It is obvious, however, that such preparation requires time and money and is inadvisable for budget theater or television films.

Transition dolly shot.   One type of transition device uses a close-up of a subject at the tail end of a shot, which is dissolved into a similar subject to open the succeeding shot. For example, a final close-up could show a hand pounding a clay figure. This would be dissolved into a hand pounding bread dough. In order to establish the place and the surrounding details of the scene in which the dough is being pounded, it would be necessary for the camera to pull back from the close-up of the hands to a medium shot showing the person who is pounding the dough, together with certain establishing details of his surroundings. Thus the audience is made aware of complete identification of what is occurring.

Re-establishing dolly shot.   In the same way, if a scene ends on a revelation close-up which is the last of a series of close-ups, and which is not to be dissolved through to the succeeding scene as a transition device, it is essential to reorient the audience to the place in which the close-up occurs, and to the general action, of which the subject in the close-up was only a small detail. It is therefore obligatory for the camera to pull back from the close-up to a medium shot to re-establish the scene with the audience.

"Obligatory" is what is meant, for if the shot is to end a scene, it is best to use a moving device, such as a dolly, which would carry the action forward with the succeeding scene, rather than a static, movement-interrupting device, such as a direct cut. This type of shot is ideal for television film use in which reorientation after a close-up is so vitally important.

Travel vs. pan.   One reason for using a traveling dolly shot instead of a pan is that, in the latter, the subject's size grows progressively smaller or larger, depending on whether the subject is coming to, or going away from, the camera. It may be essential, though, to carry the subject large-size for some time, in order to obtain certain physical details, such as realistic expressions or gestures. Then, again, it may be necessary to record certain lines of speech from the subject while he is in motion, in which case the sound level would have to diminish in direct ratio to the subject's diminution in size.

Therefore, a traveling dolly shot would be required so that the image size and the voice volume would remain constant. Even then, if the movie-house or television picture is to be cheaply produced, it might be possible to avoid the dolly shot simply by resorting to the use of a long focal-length lens pan, providing only a few feet of footage of the action are required, and no sound is to be recorded. For, with a long, focal-length lens pan, it is possible to set up the camera some distance from the subject and still get an enlarged image, because of lens magnification. Sound would not be possible because the sound boom, on which the microphone is installed, would be in camera range. This is definite: If the photographed action requires a considerable amount of footage and if sound is absolutely necessary, then a traveling dolly shot is in order.

Crowd scenes on a city sidewalk, in which a certain character is supposed to be centered by the camera, call for a traveling dolly shot.

Traveling dolly shots are used when photographing action in, or on, a moving vehicle, to catch the expression or action of someone in the vehicle. They are especially needed in such instances as cut-in shots, when vehicle interior shots are made, usually with a process, or rear-projection screen, in order to establish a definite place of action. Even these, though, can be avoided in cheap pictures by using an extreme long shot, or even with a long, focal-length lens. And if the scenery cannot be filmed on location, rear-screen projection can be resorted to to obtain the desired effect.

Chinese dolly. Another combination pullback and pan shot is the Chinese dolly, so called because it is executed with the dolly tracks laid at a slant to the subject being photographed. With this combination it is possible for the camera to start with a front view of the subject and finish with a rear view; it can, for example, look down over the shoulder to see what the subject is reading, or show a reverse angle of what the subject is looking at.

The shot opens with a front view, usually on a close shot. Then, as the dolly is pulled back, the camera continues to hold the subject centered by panning slowly so that, by the time the dolly has reached its end position, the camera has made almost a 180 degree pan. This shot illustrates the fact that rules can be broken. The rule forbidding a 180 degree reverse shot does not apply because the continuousness of the shot subject matter sustains audience orientation.

One of these Chinese dolly shots in a picture—or two, at the most —is all that should be used, because of its unusual nature. The first time this technique is employed the audience will be aware of it. The best use of it is as a revelation device at, or near, the story's climax.

A word of caution for the writer of television films: to avoid television screen distortion when reproducing a television film, indicate in your script that all pans, travel shots, and tilts be performed at a slower speed than is customary in shooting motion pictures for theater showing.

The angles

To write a complete shooting script, the screen-play writer must not only be able to call the shots, but he must, in addition, know all the angles.

A motion-picture camera can show the audience not only *what* to see but also *how* to see it. In the main, it is the angle at which the camera photographs the shot that determines *how* the shot is to be viewed.

At the same time, though, the camera angle is determined by certain factors implicit in the screen play. These factors must be taken into consideration by the writer. For, with them, he is able to add to the general mood of the picture, increase or decrease the tempo, affect the rhythm, and intensify the dramatic impact.

One important rule must be noted here in the use of camera angles: *Always change the camera angle or image size when moving from one shot to another.*

Eye-level angle. One of the angles at which most scenes are viewed in real life is from head-on eye level. To reproduce this effect, the camera should be from four to six feet from the ground. Because it is a normal viewpoint, it is comparatively lacking in dramatic qualities. In spite of this, it is often used as a frame of reference angle in order to serve as a contrast to the other unusual angles.

When building for montage, where it is necessary to have something from which to build, the eye-level angle is ideal. These shots would, of necessity, occur in scenes that serve as transitions between more dramatic scenes. Expository scenes can be shot at eye level. In fact, any shot in which the general premise of mood and dramatic quality are more or less static can be carried by the camera set at eye level.

When the eye-level angle is used in a head-on shot, in which speeding action advances a vehicle or person head on into the camera, the effect can be electrifyingly dramatic— as when a train rushes headlong into the camera, or when a character hurtles into the camera as though lunging for an opponent.

The problems now are: What are the angles to change to, and how can they be best used to suit the purposes of the screen play?

Low angle.   The low angle is a perfect camera position for shots that require extreme dramatic effects. The image caught by the camera in this position is one with figures that loom exaggeratedly large.

When the subject is in a medium shot and is coming into a close shot or close-up, the low angle tends to speed up the action. Thus, in murder-mystery stories, or in stories calling for physical violence, the low-angle shot can be used to good advantage. Under ordinary conditions, the camera is taken off the dolly and set up on a small but sturdy tripod.

At times, though, it may be necessary to obtain action that takes place on the floor and relate it to action occurring at a higher level. Thus, if it were necessary to show a boy feeding a dog under the dining room table and, at the same time, show the byplay of action and reaction between the boy and his parents seated at the table, the entire set would be built on a raised platform, about four feet high. Then, with the camera set at ordinary floor level, and shooting up, the floor action would be shot while the higher-level action continues.

Low-angle shots were used advantageously in Welles's *Citizen Kane.* Deliberate planning of the sets, so that actual ceilings were built in, enabled Welles to use this angle for purposes other than dramatic effect. The central character was depicted as a financial and journalistic titan, who towered above his fellow men. Welles himself, who is short, could hardly tower unless his fellow actors were all shorter than he. It was decided, therefore, to shoot low-angle to get this towering, overbearing effect into his characterization.

Murnau was the forerunner in this use of the low-angle shot. In his *The Last Laugh,* Jannings was shot from an extremely low angle when he was a proud, important doorman. Conversely, when he was dejected, he was photographed from a high angle, to convey the opposite effect.

But it is an expensive job to build complete ceilings into sets. Usually only corners are built in whenever the effect is necessary. The use of complete ceilings cuts out the use of catwalks on which the set lights are fixed. This calls for other means of lighting—hidden lighting, side lighting, and specially devised overhead lighting —all time-consuming to set up and therefore quite expensive. But the results, as are to be noted in *Citizen Kane,* are worth the trouble and money.

Low-angle shooting can be a money-saving device for cheap-budget movie-house pictures and television films. To obviate building sets for exterior close shots, it is the common practice to set the camera low, shooting upward at the subject, *with the sky as a backdrop.* These shots can be made in the studio against a sky "cyc" (cyclorama), or on location, when the background does not match the action being photographed. This device is often resorted to for "pick-up" shots, required by the film editor to fill in certain sections of his cut film after the entire film has been shot.

In shooting special-effects miniature shots, a low-angle close-up can give what is actually a toy life-size proportions and feeling. Moving objects are made even more real by increasing the speed of the camera to thirty-two, forty-eight, or sixty-four frames per second.

High angle. The high-angle shot, conversely to the low-angle shot, reduces the height of the subject by foreshortening, and also slows down the action. In doing this, it subordinates the subject's importance and heightens that of his surroundings.

At the same time, the high angle plays a psychological trick on the audience. It gives them an illusion of godlike transcendence—of enjoying the spectacle of human beings making fools of themselves. Therefore, the action portrayed, which is to take precedence over the characters involved, must be important enough to warrant such treatment.

Although the high-angle shot loses in dramatic values because it de-emphasizes the subject, it should be indicated occasionally in a screen play, to give the film editor material for change-of-viewpoint cutting, and thus furnish him with the means of adding pleasing variety and pacing to shot sequences.

Side angle. Both the high- and low-angle shots have a common deficiency—they tend to flatten out the picture so that it loses third dimensional roundness. This lack, however, can be supplemented by a judicious interweaving of side-angle shots which do possess a third dimensional quality. Not only is the subject well rounded, but he remains in a constant relation to his background and surroundings and gains depth and perspective.

A good side angle can frame two or more subjects or actions so that they can be visible at the same time although actually they are some distance apart.

In addition, with careful framing on the part of the operator, extraneous material can be excluded in a side-angle shot, and only the pertinent, relevant material need be chosen for inclusion in the shot.

The side-angle shot is also invaluable in building. The speed of a subject as it hurtles toward the camera—and thus toward the audience—can be carefully controlled by the angle at which the camera lens photographs the shot. Action is practically stopped by the head-on shot. But as the angle is changed—either to the right or left, but preferably to the right, because it follows the natural left-to-right action of the human eye—the speed of the subject can be increased until it reaches a 180 degree variation from center.

Boom shots.   The high-angle shot can also be achieved by means of a boom. The boom is simply a weight-balanced steel arm. One end can be raised or lowered smoothly, almost at the touch of a finger.

It is possible, with the camera on a boom, to get extreme long high shots that can zoom down into low close shots and even close-ups—shots that start high at one corner of the set and wind up low in the extreme opposite corner.

Thus, with a boom shot, an entire sequence can be photographed all in one shot, using the whole gamut of shots and angles. It was with specially designed mobile booms that Hitchcock got many of his long sequences in *The Rope.*

When the boom shot is to end with an extreme close-up on a critically focused subject—a difficult shot to obtain—directors resort to an excellent subterfuge. They start the shot in the close-up—which can be sharply focused in advance—and reverse the action to finish with the full shot. This scene is then cut into the film in reverse so that the sequence in the finished picture will open with a full shot and end with the desired close-up.

The fluidity achieved with such a mobile camera is obvious. But the boom shot is time-consuming, requires a special boom crew, a vast amount of planning, intricate lighting arrangements, many and long rehearsals, and a number of n.g. takes in order to obtain an acceptable one.

Even in a picture in which the budget can afford the boom (unless it is a musical extravaganza, in which a plethora of boom shots is the accepted mode) it is advisable to keep these shots down to an absolute minimum. One or two, at the most, can supply sufficient visual high spots to serve as toppers for a group of sequences; repetition waters down their effectiveness. In television films, the boom is an unfortunate casualty.

The high spot in the British film *The Girl Was Young* came when the camera, on a boom, searched out the dinner club after the heroine entered to look for the missing drummer. After skimming over the heads of dancers, going on to diners at their tables, and taking in the orchestra, it finally went in for a close-up on the missing drummer. The effect was almost breath-taking; the audience was made to feel with the heroine, to experience the same indecision, the same hopelessness and, finally, the same joy at finding the missing man.

Avoid too many unusual angles. It is with unusual angles that a cameraman can really go to town, photographically speaking. At the same time, a succession of unusual angles can be proportionately stultifying. For, as in all the arts, and in motion-picture work especially, the techniques must never be permitted to become obvious. Unusual camera angles have a way of calling attention to themselves almost stridently, because of their unusual, off-the-beaten-track nature.

The camera angle must not be so unusual in itself as to become an attention focal point. Instead, it should flow smoothly from a previous build-up of camera angles, and just as smoothly flow into a following sequence of camera angles.

There must always be an understandable reason for using an unusual camera angle. The tilted-angle shot in *Brief Encounter* is a case in point. Also, the camera angle must stem out of the mood and nature of the shot and scene. A good camera angle should call attention not to the angle itself, but to the action which it is presenting.

Point-of-view angles.   Camera angle is also invaluable in establishing and directing the audience's point of view. Just as a high overhead angle can endow them with a feeling of transcendence, a low angle can give them the point of view of a child looking up at a much taller person. This effect was successfully achieved in the British film *The Fallen Idol* when the adults were photographed at a low angle—from the boy's viewpoint—in order to stress the difference in size and, hence, the differences in thought process.

Conversely, a high angle shot of the child staring up into the camera can give the audience a sense of the adult's point of view. This effect was also used to advantage in the above-mentioned film. It is with this adjustable point of view that the screen-play writer can subtly incise character identification into the audience, and prepare them, physically at least, for an emotional identification.

Murnau's *Variety* was a forerunner in presenting startling and unusual angles. Previously, in circus pictures, the viewpoint of only the audience had been given. But Murnau shot his scenes from the viewpoint of the performer, so that the audience was enabled to identify itself with the performer by means of extremely distorted camera angles.

He accomplished this because he was aware of the properties of the human eye which automatically compensate for distortion by rectifying it to a permanent eye level. Things viewed from an unnatural angle automatically adjust for normality. Thus, the eye can adjust for foreshortening when one part of a person—his feet, say—is in the foreground while another part is in the background. A camera shot could present an unusual effect by showing enormously large feet in the foreground with a smaller torso behind. The eye, however, automatically adjusts so that no such distortion is present. But distortion is eye-catching, Murnau reasoned, and as a result he shot many of his scenes with deliberately distorted effects, not only to achieve shock, but also to give the shots new meanings.

Change angles.   Finally, the writer should realize that the camera lens should be treated as though it were the eyes of the audience, as far as angles are concerned. Normal eyes scanning any scene see that scene and its various elements from a number of ever changing, self-adjusting points of view. They may start to view a room and see, first, a mirror hanging over a fireplace, from a head-on, eye-level angle. Then, in turning—panning the room, as it were—they may see a rip in the rug from a high angle; and then, because a buzzing sound attracts the ear, the eyes may turn up to the ceiling to watch a fly, in a low angle; and finally, because of the odor of flowers attracting the nose, the eyes may continue to turn, for a side-angle look outside the window, and see a bush of blooming roses.

It is just such variety of angles that the screen-play writer must write into his camera directions. But instead of being literal in his presentation, he must be artistically selective, so as to present the angles as dramatically as possible, with a judicious interlarding of cutaways and cut-ins.

Reverse-angle shots. In re-establishing from a close shot or a close-up it is often more feasible to do so with what is known as a "reverse-angle shot." This requires that the camera be turned 180 degrees and faced in an opposite direction from its original position.

Reverse-angle revelations. Reverse-angle shots can also be revelation shots—that is, they can be used to reveal a startling fact suddenly with dramatic shock.

In the picture *The Show Off,* when the hero refers to his notebook while he taunts his girl with the supposed fact that he is overloaded with dates, a reverse-angle close-up on the notebook reveals an empty page.

In the documentary picture *Passport to Nowhere,* after showing a camp full of war-ravaged DP's, a shot of two boys is introduced, showing them happily playing a game of billiards. This relief from horror, however, is short-lived when the succeeding shot, a reverse angle, reveals that each boy is moving about on only one leg because the other has been amputated.

Dialogue reverse angles. The most commonly used reverse angle shot is the series of intermittent close-ups made of two people conducting a dialogue. Here, a close shot or close-up (depending on the importance of the lines of dialogue) is shot of one person over the right shoulder of the other. This shot is then followed by a close-up or close shot (usually one to match the previous shot) of the other person, shooting over the left shoulder of the first person. These pairs are then continued, being intercut with close two-shots, or medium shots of the pair in conversation, significant close-ups of eyes, mouths, hands, etc., or cutaways to props or reaction shots of others in the vicinity. There may also be a combination of these various shots.

Such reverse angles, with the terseness they engender because of the nervous cutting involved, are ideally suited for scenes which must be presented with a staccato beat. In Wyler's *The Heiress*, for example, the long-running scene between Dr. Sloper and Morris dragged considerably because it was played as a long-running take in a medium shot. Alternate, reverse-angle intercutting could have given this dramatic scene the proper tempo.

It may be enlightening to explain how these reverse angles are shot. Although they will be indicated in the screen play in sequence, actually, on the stage, they will be shot out of sequence. Each person will run through all his lines while the other character feeds him his cue lines. Then the second character will be shot in a close-up for all his lines, while the first person feeds the cues. These are then sent to the film editor, who cuts up the shots and reassembles them alternately, and intercuts with medium shots and cutaways.

Regardless of how the reverse-angle close-ups are shot, the screenplay writer should indicate how he believes they should be edited. He may desire, for example, that certain lines from one character be heard as an overlap—that is, while we see the close-up of the first character, we hear the second character's voice.

Such voice overlaps, however, should be indicated only when it is necessary to show the *reaction* of the first person to what the second person is saying. And if that reaction is highly important to the story—to develop character, to advance the plot, to top a scene that has been deliberately built to a climax—it is advisable to indicate that a close-up be used, so as to exact its full significance.

Reverse-angle action.   Except for the above ruse, though, reverse-angle shots are frowned upon in most studios. The belief is—and often justifiably so—that such shots, necessitating a sudden wrench in point of view, disorient the audience from the locale of the action.

This may be true, especially when the action is static. But when the scene is replete with action—action that is identifiable in itself—locale orientation can be retained. When there are identifiable props in the scene, orientation can also be retained, despite a sudden reversal of camera angle, because the easily recognizable prop would serve as a guidepost to immediate orientation. A medium shot of a person signing a paper could be followed by a reverse-angle close-up, shot over the person's shoulder, of the paper being signed; the paper, the pen, and the signing action would combine to establish identification and orientation.

Cutaways

The close-up, as has been explained, is a shot that focuses the audience's attention on a significant detail of the main action. The cutaway, however, takes the attention from the main action and focuses it on a secondary action that can be related to the main action, seemingly separate from it, or used as a commentary on it as a sort of visual, editorial aside. But no matter what kind it may be, the cutaway must always be related to the main action in some way or other—in paralleling action, in repetitive character movement, in similarity of mood, or in contrasting action, movement, or mood.

Establish cutaways. It is essential, in most cases, that the subject of the cutaway shot be established, either visually or verbally, before the actual cutaway is introduced. This will serve to orient the audience to it so that unnecessary surprise and awkward confusion will be avoided. This can be accomplished by indicating that a full or medium (for television) shot be used, usually in the establishing shot for the scene, which will include the subject of the forthcoming cutaway in the background, and not necessarily in too great prominence.

Related cutaways. Ordinarily, the cutaway shot should be a close shot or, if the subject's facial reaction is important, a close-up. It could also be of some minor action in the same scene, as for example, the reaction of an onlooker hidden in a closet to something he sees going on in the major action outside the closet. Then, again, the scene of the cutaway action could be different from that in the main action. For example, a bored taxi driver could be indicated as waiting at the curb for the people involved in the main action, inside a house, to make up their minds about leaving with the taxi.

In the film *The Mudlark* the director, Jean Negulescu, photographed a reaction cutaway shot of the servants observing the antics of John Brown, who is trying to teach Wheeler how to open his mouth when feeding himself with a spoon. He shot the servants merely staring down amusedly at the boy. A knowing screen-play writer—and especially one who had observed a mother feeding her infant—would have indicated that the servants' mouths would have opened expectantly, unconsciously aping the boy. This would have been a perfectly natural and humorous reaction.

Unrelated cutaways.   When the cutaway is made to an action that is not definitely related to the main action, it is usually on the action of the minor characters in the subplot, in a sort of "in the meantime" position. Thus, while the audience's attention has been concentrated on the main action at the dock, let us say, where the heroine is arriving from Europe, the cutaway—after she is seen embracing her husband—could be to the office of her father-in-law, who may be concocting one of those dastardly schemes inimical in-laws are supposed to inflict on innocent heroines. With this foreshadowing and suspenseful plot line established, the audience's attention could then be returned to the happy lovers at dockside, who are blissfully unconscious of the in-law trouble hovering over them.

It is obvious, then, that the cutaway could be an ideal means of building up suspense. It has been used for this purpose since the beginning of picture making, and is continually resorted to, even today, especially in Westerns and murder mysteries.

Cutaway action-direction.   In these pictures, a series of interlocked cutaways is used to climax a chase. In Westerns, for instance, preceding the inevitable clash between the posse and the cattle rustlers, a sequence of short cutaways is inserted. These show first, a shot of the posse, on horse, thundering from left screen to right, across the frame. Immediately following this shot is one showing the rustlers, on horse, riding hell-bent for leather from right screen to left. Another pair of similar cutaway shots—in different locations,

of course—follows the first pair. These may be changed in the angle
of shooting or in the size of the image. Then, still another pair of
similar cutaway shots is used, the number of pairs depending on
the amount of footage to be allocated to the sequence. The final
scene will cap this series of contrasting screen-direction shots with
a re-establishing shot showing the baddies eventually meeting up
in mortal combat with the goodies.

The same technique of successive cutaway shots can be adapted
to the murder-mystery story in which the murderer stalks his victim.
Here both subjects may be traveling in the same direction—as is
always the case in the chase, in which the chaser catches up with
the chased or loses him—and suspense can be built up with a series
of cutaways, first of the murderer, and then of the prospective
victim.

When indicating such cutaway sequences, it can be of invaluable
aid to the director for the screen-play writer to write in all screen
directions the subjects take—from R (right) to L (left) or from
L to R.

Cutaway comment.   The cutaway can be used in other ways. It is
an ideal vehicle for permitting the writer to comment editorially
on the action. In Pudovkin's picture *End of St. Petersburg,* immediately after a shot showing soldiers fighting and dying in the mud,
came a cutaway showing financiers bidding in the stock market, in
a visual, mordant, and ironic aside.

Humorous comment can be furnished by placing a cutaway of,
say, a cat licking its fur clean, immediately following a girl primp-
ing in front of her mirror. Animals can be used in paralleling action
cutaways in many such ways, dramatically and symbolically, as well
as humorously. In the Czech picture *Ecstasy,* for instance, a number
of cutaways were made to the mating antics of a stallion and a
mare, not only to symbolize the passion of the hero and heroine,
but also to parallel their action in alternating scenes.

Another sexually symbolic cutaway from *Ecstasy* showed an extreme close-up of a flower outside the lovers' cottage, as a drop of
dew splashed from the stamen onto the pistil. The picture was overloaded with so many similar cutaways that much of the symbolism
was lost.

Cutaway to relieve tension. The cutaway can also be used as a means of relieving tension. In the picture *M*, starring Peter Lorre, the tension created by the build-up to Lorre's murder of the little girl was relieved by a cutaway shot of the girl's rubber ball as it rolled from behind the hedge and stopped near by. At the same time, the balloon that Lorre had given the girl was released by her dead hand and floated up to be caught in the telephone wires overhead, which action was also shown in a cutaway shot. That these cutaways were effective is attested to by the fact that in the 1951 remake of the older version most of the effective cutaway shots were duplicated.

In his novel *Portrait of the Artist as a Young Man*, James Joyce used this type of relief perfectly in the scene in which the boy, Stephen, witnesses a violent quarrel between his uncle and aunt. As the aunt gets up to leave, she knocks over her napkin ring which falls to the floor, rolls around, and comes to rest under the boy's chair. By switching the reader's attention from the peak of the quarrel to a seemingly insignificant detail, Joyce was able to relieve what could have been almost unbearable tension.

Carol Reed is a master in the art of cutting away to details that appear to be visual *non sequiturs*. In *The Fallen Idol,* he heightened the psychological drama of the boy's flight by cutting away to a hose spraying the glistening cobblestone street. At another time, he used a ladder leaning against a wall for a similar purpose. This oblique use of significant detail, however, can be dangerously confusing if it is not done at the psychologically correct time, and if it is the least bit out of line with the locale, the action, or the emotional mood of the scene.

Scene-capping cutaways. Cutaways within the scene can serve as perfect scene cappers. Although not strictly a cutaway, the trucking shot in the French picture *Devil in the Flesh* is a good example. It started with the camera on the boy and girl embracing in bed. Then the camera trucked behind the bedstead, so that intermittent glimpses of the amorous pair were seen. Then the camera panned over to the roaring log fire in the fireplace, to symbolize the paralleling action taking place near by and to cap the scene significantly. It was not done in the picture, but a perfect way of coming back to the same scene, after the boy and girl had spent their emotion, would have been with a time lapse dissolved through from the roaring fire to a shot of the same fire in glowing embers. This would be followed by a pan across to the bedstead again, and then a reverse trucking shot across the head of the bed, as was done previously, to end on a shot of the pair lying in the bed, weary but happy.

Lapse-of-time cutaways. Film editors find cutaway shots lifesavers when they are confronted with shots that, because of inept directing, cannot be spliced together satisfactorily.

In cases where, for example, the error results in a so-called "jump cut"—in which continuous action is broken up by a violent jump—a cutaway shot showing an onlooker's reaction, or any other subject, can bridge the jump in the cut. Although this is strictly a director-cutter problem, the screen-play writer can use the cutaway in a somewhat similar manner.

It would be far too time-consuming and boring, for example, to show the entire action of a telephone linesman as he puts on his paraphernalia of tool belt and pole-grappling hooks. The action is too unimportant to be shown in its entirety, and not long enough in time to warrant a dissolve. In such a case, the linesman could be shown starting to don his belt. Then a cutaway to someone watching the act, or to some other scene, could be inserted to cover the time needed by the linesman to finish his preparations, so that when he is next seen he is ready for work.

Such cutaways indicated in the screen play are almost always shot by directors who are aware of the film editor's most common dilemma. When such cutaways are not indicated in the script, the knowing director improvises—with props or minor characters available to him on the set—to photograph for cutaways, not only to provide his film editor with a scene cover in an emergency, but also to be used for build-up purposes.

Indirection

In the following section on time lapses the suggestion is made that the audience be given an opportunity to figure out some things for themselves. It is not necessary to put everything down in black and white to make certain they'll "get it!" In other words, it is psychologically sound to achieve audience acceptance by flattering your audience with the idea that they can be depended upon to make apt deductions by associating certain facts with other facts.

Reaction cutaways. Thus, when writing a murder scene, it is not necessary to show the bullet entering the body in order to indicate it was hit. In the first place, the currently reigning Morals Committee in Hollywood would not permit it. But at the same time, it is possible to indicate what happens in the main action by showing, in a reaction cutaway, what some person's reaction to that action is —by indirection, in other words.

In the picture *Payment Deferred,* for example, indirection was resorted to when Laughton's nephew was being poisoned. The camera lingered on a shot of Laughton, standing across from his nephew and watching him fascinatedly as he drank the poisoned liquor. In addition, a close-up cut-in of Laughton's own liquor glass, quivering in his shaking hands until its contents spilled over the sides of the glass, heightened the power of the shot. At no time was it necessary for the audience to see the nephew going through the throes of poisoning. Instead, they saw an oblique reflection of his suffering in the suffering of the poisoner.

Hitchcock is a master of the indirection shot, which he uses to build suspense. Simply by photographing a cutaway shot of a door swinging gently, he suggests that a trapped person has succeeded in escaping through the door, without actually showing him going through it. This effect was used in *The Maltese Falcon,* when a shot of the open door informed the audience that the trapped killer had escaped while his captors were arguing between themselves.

In the picture *Miracle on 34th Street,* Edmund Gwenn (Santa Claus) is seen showing a little girl how he can handle a wad of bubble gum. A close-up shows him starting to blow up the bubble. Then a cutaway to a close-up of the little girl's face shows her reacting to the bubble she sees being blown up. From her widening eyes, the audience can almost see the bubble increasing in size until finally it is heard to burst with a pop. In the next shot, Gwenn is seen in a close-up trying to remove the bubble gum from his beard. This bit of oblique visualizing by means of an indirection cutaway shot was used not only as a cutaway shot but also, first, because it was not thought advisable to waste footage by showing the entire process of blowing up a balloon; second, because Gwenn was probably unable to blow a bubble balloon; and third, because even if he were capable, the uncertainty of obtaining a large-sized bubble that would burst with a pop would make trying to photograph it a Quixotic adventure. All of these objections were overcome, and the dramatic effect was heightened, simply by resorting to a reaction cutaway that indicated the whole business by indirection.

Cutaway from death.   But it is with murder that indirection finds its most fruitful source of inspiration. Because, according to the Morals Code, the murderer cannot be seen pulling the trigger or slashing the knife in the same scene with the victim, the resources of implication, indirection, and suggestion must be tapped by the creative screen-play writer.

A close-up on curtain rings being torn away from a curtain rod as the murdered victim grabs the curtain on his way down to the floor has become a favorite since its introduction a few years ago. In *The Informer,* where the escaping Sinn Feiner leaped out of the window and was then shot by a British soldier outside, a close-up on the Sinn Feiner's hand, with the nails clawing and scraping on the window ledge, before the body started to fall, was sufficient to suggest that he had been mortally wounded.

Foreshadowing cutaways.   Death can also be suggested by a sort of reverse indirection. That is, instead of implying death by using a cutaway *after* the deed has been perpetrated, it can be suggested *before* it takes place. In Chaplin's *Monsieur Verdoux,* as Chaplin takes his last drink of rum in the death cell, he throws his head far back and displays a long, living expanse of throat pulsing as the rum goes down—the same throat the audience knows is going to be slit soon by Madame Guillotine's razor-edged blade.

The same type of foreshadowing technique can be used to build suspense and heighten dramatic intensity. Cutaway shots to a bridge wrecked by a flood, a loosened wheel, a booby-trap bomb waiting passively, a highway torn up by storm, a rail torn loose from its tie —all intimations of impending disaster, natural or concocted—can be indicated before the accident occurs. These will foreshadow the imminent catastrophe by indirection so that, when the accident does occur, it is quite often unnecessary even to show it taking place. As a matter of fact, in cheap-budget movie-house pictures, and in television films where cost is of the essence, such inexpensive catastrophes, suggested by indirection, are welcome stand-bys. The catastrophe is usually suggested only in sound, while the camera is focused on a subject to get his reaction to the catastrophe which has been previously foreshadowed by indirection. Costly fires can be suggested by this treatment, simply by flickering arc shadows over peoples' faces.

In Chaplin's *A Woman of Paris*, because a real French train was unavailable, or because the budget made building a complete mock-up infeasible, Chaplin shot a sequence on a French depot set without actually showing a train. Instead, he photographed the lights of the train flickering across a close-up of Edna Purviance's face.

A lot of fun can be had with indirection shots. Van Dyke once showed a shot of a dog on a leash about to do his business. Being unable to photograph the real thing, the director took a close-up of the dog's leash tightening in its master's hand, as the hand pulled back. Then the hand remained still until later, after the dog had obviously sprayed a tree, the leash was seen to tauten again, and the master's hand was drawn forward, indicating that the dog was on his way once more.

Time lapses

What are they. One of the most effective devices available to the screen-play writer is the time lapse. It was with this mechanism that early motion pictures were able to break away from the confines of the "four-wall" technique adapted from the stage.

For, with the time lapse, it was possible to leave the immediate scene of action and traverse a period of time essential to the development of the story but not important enough to be completely dramatized.

The early pictures paid little attention to this new device. They had already established the direct cut as indicating a paralleling action or actions immediately following the action of the preceding shot; the dissolve as connecting two shots and indicating a lapse of a certain amount of time; and the fade-out and fade-in as indicating the lapsing of a still longer period of time. But the actual ingredients of the lapse were ignored.

How they are used. Present-day pictures, however, make full use of the potentialities of the time lapse. Quite often, as in matched time lapses, they have made too full use of it, and the technique has jutted out conspicuously, to the detriment of realism. The beginning screen-play writer, especially, succumbs to the innate brilliance of matched time lapses and overloads his script with them.

A time lapse is a filmic device which indicates pictorially a hiatus of seconds, minutes, hours, days, weeks, months, or years.

In the early days of movie making, they were achieved, photographically, in a number of different ways. All were optical effects, performed manually, in the camera first, and later, chemically, in photographic labs. Today most optical effects are created mechanically in machines especially designed for the purpose.

Dissolve time lapse. The dissolve, which is the basis of all pictorial time lapses, is a method of *fading out* the image at the tail end of a shot and then, about halfway between full image and complete fade-out, *fading in* the introductory frames of the succeeding shot, in reverse density from that of the frames in the previous shot. This results in a smooth transition of dark to medium of the last frames of the first shot, blended with medium to dark of the first frames of the succeeding shot.

Dissolves can vary in actual screen time. They can be slow, medium, or quick, depending on the pacing required by the mood or action, as determined by the writer and carried out by the film editor.

Wipe time lapse. Another technical method of achieving this effect is with the use of the wipe. The purpose of both methods, however, is the same—to indicate a lapse of time. When both were first introduced, motion-picture makers went overboard in their use and loaded pictures with dissolves and wipes. But a leveling-out process followed, and today dissolves, matched dissolves, and wipes (especially the last) have been relegated to their proper place and importance.

Time lapses impede action.   Time lapses tend to slow down the forward action of a picture. Actually, action stops when a time lapse is introduced. Because a time lapse is nothing but a symbol—a motion-picture convention accepted by the audience only by force of habit—it veers tangentially away from realism and, thus, away from action continuity.

The ideal motion picture would be one that uses no time lapse whatsoever. Hitchcock attempted just that in *The Rope,* where the length of time consumed in showing the film was identical with the length of time covered by the action of the story. But obviously it would be inadvisable, as far as story diversification is concerned, to write all stories within such strict time limits. Hence the need for time-lapse devices.

Telescope story time.   This fact must be stressed, though: Try to telescope the time limits of the story. A time-sprawling story saps dramatic intensity because time is a vital dramatic factor. It demands time lapses to cover inordinately long periods of time, such as are encountered in most stories of epic proportions.

Long time lapses destroy continuity by breaking up into two separate stories the two sequences joined by the time lapse. When this is repeated a number of times in the same picture, the result is a series of separate stories with damaged coherence and integration.

In the light of the success of such pictures as Maugham's *Quartet* and *Trio,* in which separate and distinct stories with no connective elements of unification were presented as one picture, such advice may seem ill-founded. But these made no pretense of being unified motion pictures. They were frankly presented as separate, short motion pictures to be seen at one sitting, much like a presentation of a group of one-act plays in the theater. It was not necessary to tie up the last story with the opening story, as is essential in the standard motion picture, where the opening sequences must be carefully integrated not only with the closing sequence, but with all the other sequences in the finished picture.

Avoid time-lapse clichés. Because time lapses can be brilliantly effective, and because truly original ones are difficult to come by without resorting to intensive creative thought, the screen-play writer has been guilty of resorting to hoary and time-worn devices.

The oldest and perhaps the most widely used (even today) is the clock. It is the most obvious, because it is directly related to the passage of time. This is especially so when the time lapse to be indicated is a matter of minutes or hours. The simplest use of this device has the clock face faded out at the early time, and then faded in to the later time, the passage of time being indicated by the change in clock hands. Another variant still being used calls for a specially rigged prop clock, manually operated behind a set flat, in which the hands are seen to spin around and then stop at the time at which the lapse ends. Usually a pan is used to get to the clock. Then, if the clock is not in an extreme close-up, the camera will dolly in to one, to be followed by a match dissolve through to the clock face with the new time on it. The same technique is used on wrist watches, desk clocks, wall clocks, and in clock reflections in mirrors. A considerable amount of effort is spent in trying to freshen up what is, at best, a hoary, frayed device.

When the elapsed time is more than a matter of hours, and runs into days and months, the calendar gimmick is resorted to. This ancient wheeze uses an optical effect of leaves of the calendar being torn off in slow motion and floating away until the date required by the story is reached. This sort of calendar art has become so trite that writers have completely run out of refurbishing tricks. To fall back on the calendar is to confess to a paucity of inventiveness.

When the spread of time can be indicated by seasonal changes, Nature is often called into play, with a montage of spring, summer, fall, and winter scenes. These scenes, usually from stock, are often of varying locales. Sometimes though, special production shots are made of a single scene from the picture, and are re-dressed with birds for spring, flowers for summer, leaves blowing in the wind for fall, and boughs covered with snow for winter.

Now this sort of thing has in it the seeds of creative variation. Nature is so varied in all its aspects, and landscapes can be affected in so many ways by Nature, that variations of this time lapse should be possible with not too much thought.

The same can be said of the many other time lapse clichés: the piled-up milk bottles or newspapers left by canny, though undiscerning, vendors; the waves washing interminably against a seashore; the same waves washing away footprints in the sands of time; the roast turkey dissolving through to a gleaming turkey skeleton; the "you can't do this to me!" last line dissolving to "look what they done to me!"; the window darkening from day to night and vice versa; the hourglass with the sands trickling down; the new pair of shoes dissolved through to the same shoes worn out—these and a multitude of variations on the same theme. They were once fresh conceptions invented by adroit writers, which, through overuse, have since bred contempt. They have all had their day in pictures.

Use clichés as springboard.   In avoiding these trite but true devices, however, the screen-play writer should not ignore them completely. Rather, he should use them as springboards suggesting other, fresher versions.

In *On the Town,* for example, time lapses were indicated by superimposing a running light-bulb sign across the bottom of the frame—like the Times Building sign at Times Square in New York—which flashed on the time of day at those intervals where it was necessary to establish it. This superimposure was daring but it was effective because it stemmed from the spirit of the picture's locale. This subject will be discussed shortly.

In the British picture *The Seventh Veil,* the girl's visits to the cabaret were shown to take place over an extended period of time by the simple device of opening each scene in the sequence of cabaret shots with a close-up of a different liquor bottle on the table, beginning with soda pop, then going through "cyder," wine, champagne and, finally, an impish and surprising carafe of water.

In *The House on 92nd St.,* the passing of the girl's stay in jail—a year—was shown by superimposing the shadow of a pendulum swinging across a continual change of newspaper headlines, these shots being interspersed with shots of the girl languishing in her cell.

Integrate time lapse with character.   For time lapses to be most effective, it is absolutely essential that they grow out of the character of the action, the locale, the characters, or all three. It is quite simple, of course, to ignore these and to throw in a time lapse without considering them. But the result will always defeat the purpose of time lapse as a vehicle of transition, for, instead of flowing smoothly from one scene to another, the audience's attention will be broken by the introduction of a foreign element.

An hourglass time lapse in a slum sequence, for instance, would be as out of place as a grandfather clock in a preclock historical sequence. Here, a flickering candle inserted in a beer bottle would be more in keeping with the locale.

This does not mean that the writer should confine himself to a literal interpretation of the injunction. The character in the slum sequence may be in a situation in which he is being inundated with woes that engulf him sporadically, much as would the waves of the ocean. The use of ocean waves as a time lapse would be an entirely legitimate poetic extension, provided, of course, there were some indication in the dialogue or action of the symbolism of the waves.

The most effective type of integrated time lapse can come in a situation in which the manufacture of a certain product is seen to be started and then completed. Here the dissolve can come immediately after the product—say, a model boat—has been begun. The dissolve through would be to the model boat completed. This would avoid the tedious details required to show the various steps taken and, at the same time, would carry forward the action.

Use cutaways for short time lapse.   In certain situations where the time lapse is only a matter of a minute or so, and where the continuing action is not interesting enough to warrant showing it in its entirety, a time-lapse device is inadvisable. Thus, when a longish letter is to be written or read, or when a new costume is to be doffed and another donned, or when a narrow river is to be swum, a more effective filmic device to use would be the cutaway. Here a reaction shot of an onlooker would be intercut immediately after the uninteresting action is begun. Then, when the action has been supposedly completed, off screen, it can be brought back just as it is being completed. This cutaway need not be a reaction shot of someone on the scene. It could be a cutaway to some action—related, of course—in some other locale.

When a time-lapse device is essential to establish the exact period of elapsed time, as when a manufacturing action is to be shown, then it will be necessary, in the shot that shows the finished product, to bring out the exact time in the dialogue, as for example, "You've wasted a whole week on that toy!" from the builder's wife or mother.

This problem of establishing the exact elapsed time is vital to the audience's appreciation of what is going on. When a time lapse occurs, they must always be given to understand exactly how long a period of time "some time later" is.

Dialogue time lapse. The calendar gimmick does it with dates, the clock with clock hands and numerals, and the newspaper headline series with publishing dates or well-known events. But there are many time-lapse devices which do not have these aids. In such cases the exact time must be given in dialogue, either before the time lapse begins, or after it has taken place.

For example, the dialogue can say: "I'll see her after I do the dishes." Now, if we dissolve through from the woman at the kitchen sink to the same woman in the bedroom talking with her sister, the audience will know that the time elapsed was the amount necessary for the woman to have washed her dishes.

Another example: if a character is to travel from New York to Bombay, and if the audience is given some idea as to how that trip is to be made by means of a montage of planes, trains, autos, etc., they will also be given an intimation of the amount of time that has elapsed when they next see the traveler, in Bombay. Some time before the time-lapse montage begins, the character should be permitted to say something on the order of, "I'll be writing you my first letter from Bombay."

Exact time-lapse realism. This business of establishing the exact time in a time lapse can become quite important in creating a sense of realism, or in destroying it entirely. In *Panic*, a French picture, the hero was seen dangling by one hand from the roof of a high building. Following this shot came a close-up of a neighbor telephoning the fire department for help. Then came a dissolve and, immediately on its heels, the arrival of the fire department's hook-and-ladder brigade, clanging fire bells and all.

Because no exact time had been established, it appeared to the audience that the arrival of the hook-and-ladder crew was most fortuitously accelerated—and the result was a loud, collective guffaw at a place where there should have been intense suspense and excitement. To avoid this uncalled-for outburst, it would have been easy to plant the fact, either visually or verbally, that the fire station was close by. In that way, the audience would have been prepared for the hook and ladder's almost immediate entrance, and the undesignated time lapse would have been given a specific period of time.

Transitions

Time lapses constitute only one phase of the problem of motion-picture transitions, a problem which, by the way, concerns itself with the most vital of subjects—continuity.

Continuity with transitions. For one of the most important ingredients of continuity is transition. Without smooth transitions, there would be no continuity. Without adequate transitions there would be no forward flow of movement, no shot, scene, and sequence interlocking, no establishment of shot interrelationships, no pervasive sense of wholeness and completion, no balance and counter-balance between the individual components—in other words, there would be no motion picture.

This is so because of the peculiar nature of the motion picture, which is a compilation of hundreds of pieces of film, each varying from the other in many respects, spliced together so that the result, a motion picture, will depict a story with smooth-flowing, unified, coherent and dramatic continuity.

Shot-to-shot continuity. This continuity between individual shots can be brought about by the judicious use of camera distance and angle, lighting, sound, character action, mood, and dialogue.

From shot to shot, a sustained mood will serve as an efficient carry-over, for example. Matched *lighting* can serve the same purpose. A barred shadow from a Venetian blind can connect a long shot with a medium shot and a close-up, if the same barred shadow is seen on all three. A close-up of a person as he starts to get up from a chair can be cut in as the person reaches a halfway-up position, to be followed by a medium shot of the same person completing the action and continuing with his next piece of business. The *sound* of a typewriter heard in a long shot can be carried over a succeeding medium shot and a close-up to act as a connecting sound link. Direct cuts from person to person can be tied together by means of their lines of *dialogue,* provided the dialogue is written so that each line follows the other in natural sequence—hooked together, in other words—as, for instance, a series of questions and answers. And if the camera distance and angles flow in natural order, or with pleasing symmetry and rhythm—with the traditional long shot, medium shot, and close shot sequence, or with a series of staccato close-ups, or the like—continuity is a natural result.

Sequence transition.   It is the job of transitions, however, to connect each individual *sequence of shots* with its succeeding sequence so as to achieve this all-important flow of continuity.

Strangely, although there is an abundance of raw material for the screen-play writer to work with—both visual and oral—transitions are either neglected completely, so that a break in the continuity ensues, or old, hackneyed clichés are resorted to, such as the chestnuts in the time-lapse transitions on the order of falling calendar leaves and the "you can't do this to me" protest.

It is with the transition that the writer can really create artistically and justify the film makers' belief in their medium as a truly unique art form.

We have already discussed the time-lapse transition, one of the many visual transitions available to the screen-play writer. Suppose, then, we examine the other visual transitions that can be put to use.

Direct-cut transitions.   The simplest, of course, is the direct cut, as, for example, when a character is seen to leave through a door from one angle, and then, by a direct cut, is shown entering an adjoining room on the other side of the door from another angle. That is a perfect transition. But suppose the character is obliged to go through a number of doors or across a number of rooms in order to get to his destination—what then?

Direct cut for suspense.   The handling of this problem would depend on a number of considerations. If, for example, it were nec-

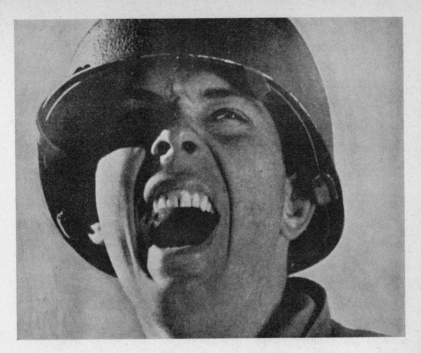

Fig. 1 CLOSE-UP. The dramatizing potentialities of the close-up can be seen in this striking shot. The slight low-angle contributed to the shot's sensational quality.

All photographs Courtesy U.S. Army Signal Corps.

Fig. 2 MEDIUM SHOT. A very pleasing arrangement of the three heads in an effective medium shot.

Fig. 3 CLOSE TWO-SHOT. The same scene as in *Fig.* 2 but with the interest now focused on the two foreground heads. Better filmic composition could have been obtained by cutting out the woman's shoulder. Because this still picture is an enlargement of a single frame, the shoulder remained.

Fig. 4 **CLOSE SHOT.** The same scene as in *Figs.* 2 and 3. Now the interest is concentrated on the central character. All of his expressions are strikingly obvious. In an especially-shot close-shot, the woman's shoulder would have been cut out, to concentrate attention on the big head even more.

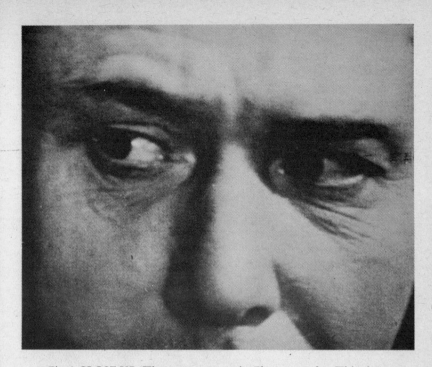

Fig. 5 CLOSE-UP. The same scene as in *Figs.* 2, 3 and 4. This close-up concentrates on the expression in the central character's eyes. This type of close-up is more desirable than the kind which features the eyes alone because of the fact that three heads were seen in the medium shot and two in the close shot. To have followed them with a close-up of the eyes alone would have been confusing because the audience would not be certain which character's eyes were being featured. A close-up of the eyes alone, however, could have followed a close-shot of the single head of *Fig.* 4.

Fig. 6 MEDIUM SHOT. The war poster should have given an indication as to the photographic treatment this shot deserved. Shot from a
low angle—instead of the eye-level angle used in the illustration—with
the figure heads in a big, dramatic close shot, the shot could have been
much more effective than the ordinary, routine shot shown here.

Fig. 7 MEDIUM CLOSE SHOT. What could have been an excellent medium close shot was spoiled by the presence of the cluttered table in the foreground. Actually, the important elements in the shot were the torn up bits of snapshot on the table and in the girl's hands. Were they to have been at the bottom of the frame, alone, the meaning of the shot would have been much clearer.

Fig. 8 MEDIUM LONG SHOT. A fairly good example of the use of a medium long shot. The jerry-built set, however, showing an obviously studio-fabricated staircase and sidewalk spoil the realism. Semi-documentaries, photographed on location, obviate this fault. See *Fig.* 9.

Fig. 9 FULL SHOT. This scene, showing a camera crew photographing a picture on location, shows how only the real thing can make for
absolute realism. It was shot without sound, which was dubbed in later.
Suitable live-sound, dialogue close-ups were also shot later, in the
studio, against studio-built sets duplicating smaller segments of the
real location set.

Fig. 10 MIRROR SHOT. This interesting mirror shot was used in a subjective camera picture in order to show the main character—who was the camera in most cases—to establish his physical lineaments so that the audience could have some idea as to who they were "rooting for."

Fig. 11 LOW-ANGLE SHOT. The imposing stature of the fore-ground cadets is obviously enhanced by the low angle used to photo-graph this shot. The heavy black oblique sections at the top and bottom are part of the basement superstructure used as an excellent foreground framing device.

Fig. 12 HIGH-ANGLE LONG SHOT. This production still demonstrates what can be done with a high-angle shot. It also shows a sound, camera crew in operation. In the picture being photographed, the camera was supposed to represent the main character—seated at the lower left corner—in the subjective camera technique.

essary for plot purposes to establish suspense—if the character were a murderer stalking an unwitting victim—then an ideal means of creating suspense would be to show the murderer going through a number of doors and across a number of rooms and even up or down some creaking stairs—with an occasional cutaway shot to the victim intercut—until the murderer finally arrives at his place of nefarious business.

Wipe transitions. On the other hand, if suspense is unwanted, and if the journey through the various rooms has no particular point in the story, it would be enough merely to show the character entering the first door, and then wipe him into his final destination in the midst of performing the action he is supposed to be doing. If he is picked up entering the room, from the door, immediately after the wipe, it may leave the erroneous impression with the audience that he has gone through only one door in getting to his objective.

Detailed transitions. Remember, it is not always necessary to show *all* the details of a character's going from one place to another in successive scenes. As a matter of fact, only in special cases, when the details of the change of place are essential to the story—to establish a story point, or to sustain a certain mood—is it necessary to go through a step-by-step procedure.

It is not necessary, for example, to show a character leaving a room, going down a long flight of stairs, opening the street door, closing the street door, walking down the stairs to the street, ambling down the street to a subway station, meandering down the stairs of the subway station, riding on a subway train, getting off the train, climbing upstairs to the street, sauntering down the street to his destination, ascending the street stairs to the door, ringing the doorbell, entering, climbing up another flight of stairs, going down the hallway, knocking at a door, opening it, entering through it, and finally advancing to his girl friend to say, "How about a movie tonight, honey?"

Yes, this is an exaggeration. But something like it can be seen too often in a great many motion pictures. Even Hitchcock, who is a master of transition, falters occasionally in this respect, as in the picture *Notorious,* in which he photographed Bergman and

Grant taking an interminable auto drive in Brazil to do their spy-ing. Welles's *Lady From Shanghai* was similarly overloaded with overlong scenic transitions that did nothing but pad low spots in the shooting script.

Detailed transitions for pay-off. Such a detailed excursion, how-ever, has its place occasionally, especially when it pays off in some way or other, as in the Charles Laughton sequence of *If I Had a Million*. There, Laughton, a harassed office clerk who had just re-ceived word of his million-dollar inheritance, is seen to get up from his desk, leave his cubbyhole office, go through a hall, climb a long flight of stairs, cross a hallway, enter a reception room, cross it, enter the president's office, walk up to the president's desk, rasp out a loud Bronx cheer directly at his disconcerted boss, turn, exit, and retrace his victorious journey down the stairs and back to his office.

Cook's tour unnecessary. Ordinarily, though, it is not necessary to go to such extremes in order to create an effective transition. The slightest of visual hooks is usually sufficient to carry the audience attention and orientation from one scene to another. No matter what the IQ of the average audience is supposed to be, they can be depended upon to bridge a minor time gap without resorting to a major Cook's tour.

Dialogue transitions. If there is nothing in a scene that can be used as a transitional hook, the writer can always fall back on dialogue, as was explained in the section on time lapses. The ways of effecting this type of transition are many, and range from the simplest, "Well, I'll be getting along to the office, now" followed by a dissolve and a shot of the character seated in his office, to "I wonder what Stinky's up to?" to be followed by a direct cut to Stinky, at home, spreading glue on his grandfather's toupee.

Match-dissolve transition. Then there is the overworked but highly effective "match dissolve." With this transition device, the action in the closing frames of a shot, usually a close-up, matches the action of the opening frames of the next shot, also usually a close-up. These matching actions are connected by means of an optical dissolve so that, as the closing frames of the first shot fade out, the opening

frames of the succeeding shot fade in, thus linking up the two in
a smooth flow of visual action. Wheels of all sorts are thus interrelated, so that an entire journey across the world can be depicted
simply by dissolving auto wheels, train wheels, plane propellers,
steamship propellers, more train wheels, rickshaw wheels, and so
forth until the character's final destination is reached.

The match dissolve can also be used to interrelate characters
separated by space. In Carol Reed's *Bank Holiday,* as Margaret
Lockwood stared down at the ocean surf on the beach where she
stood, the camera tilted down to her feet to show the sea washing
away the pebbles. A dissolve through to water from the River
Thames, and a tilt-up from it, revealed John Loder, of whose tragic
life Margaret Lockwood had been thinking, standing on the Em-
bankment, also deep in thought.

Motivate match dissolve.   One reason why the match dissolve transition has been so overworked is that, in addition to being visually
satisfying and startling, it can be universally applied. Hands performing a certain task can be dissolved into hands performing
another task; feet running can be dissolved into other feet walking
or running; toast popping up in a toaster can be dissolved through
to a high jumper clearing the bar; ocean waves pounding a rocky
shore can be dissolved through to a person knocking desperately at
a door. The possibilities are limitless. But special attention should
be given by the screen-play writer to avoid the cliché—such as the
wheel match dissolve—and to try for a less obvious, more poetic, more
symbolic transition, something on the order of the last named in
the above examples—of the ocean waves pounding and followed by
the knocking on a door. But he should make certain that the substance of the device stems from the action or the locale. If the ocean-
wave device is used, for instance, be sure the action revolves around
a locale that is near the ocean, so that the physical proximity of the
ocean can be planted beforehand.

Another word of caution regarding the match dissolve—use it
sparingly. To overuse it in one picture is to dissipate its efficacy. A
surfeit of match dissolves will negate their powers of transition,
because they will stand out as technical devices instead of remaining
as anonymous continuity sustainers.

Instead of resorting to a match dissolve, it is often better to use a dissolve from a close shot to a close-up. For example, if it is necessary to dissolve through from a chocolate bar in the hands of a person in one locale to a chocolate bar in the hands of the same person, or another person, in a different locale, the first shot can be a close shot of the person eating the chocolate bar, dissolved into a close-up of the chocolate bar in the succeeding shot with the camera pulling back to a close shot or a medium shot to reveal the new locale. In this way you would be taking advantage of the natural flow from the close shot to the close-up, thus creating an undercurrent of movement in the dissolve.

The term "match dissolve" is given to another type of dissolve transition. This kind adheres strictly to the literal meaning of the phrase in that it consists of dissolving through from one subject to its exact counterpart in another shot. This requires that both subjects be exactly the same in image size and angle and be in exactly the same position in the frame. For the purpose is to establish some sort of paralleling comparison between the two subjects as, for example, dissolving through from a close-up of a rich child to a poor slum kid, or from a tramp to the same man dressed in soup-and-fish. The dissolve serves as a connecting and transitional element.

Sign-insert transitions.   Another visual transition device is almost as old as motion pictures—the sign insert. This is especially useful when the locale of the second half of the dissolve is an institution. Hospitals, laboratories, factories, office buildings, hotels, inns, town-limit boundaries, store fronts, numbered houses—these and hundreds of other similar locales can all furnish the material for a sign transition. They are especially useful in a time-lapse sequence when a character is supposed to be shown making the rounds of advertising offices, for example, in search of a job. Here the entire search can be covered simply by using a dissolve sequence of firm names on office doors, lobby directories, name plates, and so on. The creative screen-play writer could suggest, for example, showing the firm names on stationery or in other likely places.

Stock-shot transition.   Still another means of obtaining a visual transition, one that is also almost as old as motion-picture making, is the "stock shot" scenic view used as a symbol. Paris' Eiffel Tower,

London's Tower Bridge and Trafalgar Square, New York's Times Square—these and thousands of other similar scenes have been used so often in pictures that they establish audience identification the moment they are flashed on the screen.

Title-card transitions. To make doubly certain that this identification identifies, many film makers insist on superimposing a title card over the scenic shot, with the word "London" or "Paris" on it. Just why this should be necessary, especially in such easily identifiable shots, is incomprehensible. At best, title cards are crutches that should have gone out when sound came in. The more creative old-time film producers realized their shortcomings and tried to avoid them, as did Chaplin in his *Woman of Paris*. In present-day picture making, title cards serve only to betray the writer's lack of ingenuity.

Gratuitous title cards. Title cards are especially gratuitous when used to furnish introductory comments just before the picture starts, especially the rolling title card superimposed over a scenic shot from the picture.

In the original script of *Gaslight,* for example, Scene 3 read:
"We SUPERIMPOSE the following words:

PIMLICO SQUARE, LONDON,
1865

The words FADE OUT and we:
CUT TO:"
In the finished picture, however, Scene 2 ended with a dissolve through to a close-up of a sampler being embroidered with the words "Alice Barlow, 1865." Then came a cut to Scene 4 of the original script, of a close-up on the old lady at work on the sampler. Evidently someone realized the static quality of the suggested title card and insisted on the more graphic, more cinematic version instead.

With apt writing, with creative know-how, there is absolutely no reason why the ideas and information usually given in the foreword cannot be made implicit in the picture itself. Such forewords are usually added after the picture has been completed, when doubts begin to beset the producer as to whether certain important points have been overlooked. Had these points been covered originally in the shooting script, the title cards would have been unnecessary. Audiences attend theaters to see pictures, not to read words. One picture shot can depict more than a dozen rolling titles. It is the screen writer's task to make certain that missing information will not have to be covered, as an afterthought, by a foreword.

Fade-out fade-in transition.   A very effective transitional device, that uses the momentary black screen of the fade-out as it reaches its darkest point, can be accomplished by means of camera dollies. If it is necessary, for example, to follow a dock scene with a scene in a shipping office, the transition can be effected by having the camera dolly in to a crate or a barrel, for example, so that the entire frame will be blacked out. The concluding frames of this black image are then dissolved through to the blackness of the opening frames of the succeeding office scene, where the camera may open on, perhaps, an extreme close-up of a character's back, so that the frame is again blacked out. Then either the camera can pull back or the character can move forward, to start the action and reveal the new scene and its occupants.

A somewhat similar transition device was used in *The 39 Steps* during the chase scene, in which Robert Donat was seen to run in a head-on shot into the camera and black it out completely. This was dissolved through to another blackened screen, which turned out to be Donat's back as he ran away from the camera in a tail-end shot, thus exposing the new locale.

This type of transition obviated the use of a number of repetitious "run throughs," which are transition pan or trucking shots of a character, or characters, in a chase sequence, as they crash through dense forest underbrush, stumble through murky slum streets, or run through interminable corridor mazes. Such run-through transitions can be invaluable to connect various chase sequences, but they can become boringly repetitive, hence the need for creative variation.

Run-through transitions.   In the same way, to connect a scene in which someone is seen entering a car, with a succeeding scene in which he is seen arriving at his destination, it is quite often necessary to indicate auto run throughs, in which the car is seen tooling up a road from a number of angles and camera distances, especially when the destination is some distance from the place of leave-taking. Also, if it is essential that suspense be built, such auto run throughs are extremely effective. The same applies to any means of conveyance, especially trains. In scenes where much of the action takes place in the interior of the train, exterior shots of the train hurtling through the night (it's always night in these sequences) are essential to re-establish the fact that the action is taking place on a moving train. They are also invaluable for purposes of transition. It would be impossible to leave the impression with the audience that a certain amount of distance had been covered by the train if all the shots were of train interiors.

Perhaps this might be a good place to explain why most interior train sequences are shot with NIGHT indicated, especially in cheap-budgeted movie-house pictures and television films. DAY shots require that rear-screen projection be used to suggest that there is real scenic landscape whizzing by the train windows. This calls for an involved setup, in which telephone poles and tree shadows must be shown flickering across the faces of the characters, and where grips must shake the mock-up train set to simulate train movement. Most of this can be eliminated, however—especially the rear-screen process shots and the telephone pole and tree flickerings—simply by indicating that the time be night.

Sound-effect transitions. To this point, we have considered only visual transition techniques. There are others which can be used separately, or in combination with the visual. The sound transition devices are, perhaps, the most important of these. One method was suggested in the section devoted to "within the shot" transition techniques. There are many, many others the screen-play writer can use.

The most obvious and therefore most often used is the continuation of the sound of the vehicle being photographed in a series of run throughs, intercut with interior shots, as in the afore-mentioned train sequences. Here the clackety-clack of the wheels and the shriek of the siren can be carried through under both the exterior and interior shots, with the sounds being diminished in volume for the interiors, to indicate they are being muffled by intervening walls.

Dissimilar scene transitions.　The problem in connecting totally dissimilar scenes, however, is not so simple. How, for example, with sound, could a quiet library scene be connected with an immediately following county fair scene? This problem was ideally solved in the British picture *Storm in a Teacup.* The two leads were first seen in the hushed confines of some library stacks, whispering their dialogue. But they were overheard by the typically sensitive though untypically burly librarian, who, upon being disturbed by their talk, boomed out, "Silence in this room," attenuating the last word in a bass but petulant whine. The attenuated "oo" sound of the librarian's bass voice was then carried over, and "segued" (blended) into the loud, bovine "moooo" of a cow in the succeeding scene, which showed the animal penned up in a county fair cattle enclosure. The visual transition was accomplished by dissolving through from a close-up of the bovine librarian to a close-up of the petulant cow.

The screen writer may often find it necessary to cut from a day scene to a night scene. Because the human eye does not immediately adapt to such a sudden change, it is essential to dissolve through slowly, to allow the eye to compensate gradually. The change from night to day, however, does not require a slow dissolve, because the eye can take the quick night-to-day change quite readily.

Night-to-day and day-to-night dissolves should be avoided in television pictures. Technicians monitoring the broadcast film at the television studio will have a difficult time "riding gain" on these quick changes—that is, adjusting their controls to accommodate the varying light densities.

Parallel-sound transitions.　One of the most effective and widely known sound transitions was heard in Hitchcock's *The 39 Steps,* in which the scream of the charlady, when she discovered the dead body, was cross-faded into the shriek of a near-by train siren. Here, the fact was established that the room in which the woman lived adjoined a railroad switchyard. This gave the transition added effectiveness because it became endowed with credibility. Other pictures have adapted this technique so that human shrieks have been segued into such other similar sounds as sea gulls croaking (*The Girl Was Young*) , wild birds fluting, babies crying, factory sirens screeching, musical instruments caterwauling and, in fact, into almost any

mechanical device or living thing that emits a high, piping shriek
or sound.

Exterior scenes can be connected with adjacent interior scenes by
the use of street noises, heard in volume over the exterior scene
and then, in the succeeding interior scene, heard with diminished
volume, the exact volume depending on whether the windows are
open or closed.

Sound and visual transitions.   Sound can also be used in connec-
tion with visual transitions. A dock scene, for example, could be
enhanced with the sounds of distant ship sirens and buoys laid into
the background of the introductory scene, and then carried behind
succeeding shots, to connect them up. Ruttman's first use of the
varied Hamburg dockside sounds, at the opening of his experi-
mental *The Melody of the World,* made for immediate audience
identification. In the same director's *The Sounding Wave,* he introduced the blare of trumpets and the boom of drums at various
intervals in the picture, and even as a background sound, in order
to give the picture the flow of continuity.

Ford, in his *The Informer,* used the sound of the tap-tap-tap of
the blind beggar's cane as a transitional device, even when the beggar was not seen. James Joyce's blind beggar's cane tap-tapping
through his book *Ulysses* may have been Ford's inspiration.

Letter transitions.   Still another sight-sound transition can be effected when a letter is being read by a character. After holding for
a while on him as he starts to read his letter, the voice of the person
who wrote the letter is superimposed, reading the letter he has
written. This is followed by a dissolve to that person, usually in
a close-up, as he gives voice to the written words.

A variation starts with the person writing the letter, cuts to an
extreme close-up of the letter, superimposes the voice of the person
receiving the letter, and then dissolves through to the person who
has received it, reading it.

Simple deviceless transitions.   Finally, scene transitions can be
effected without the use of any definite device, with a simple dissolve
that uses neither the matched visual elements nor the matched
sound elements.

Transition from scene to scene can be accomplished by the sheer impetus of action, from one scene to another, or even from the inexorable forward flow of continuity of previous scenes, provided, of course, that the change from scene to scene is not too sharp. Thus, it would be impossible to bridge a summer scene with a winter scene merely by using a simple dissolve. Nor would it be feasible to connect the bucolic calm of a countryside scene with the frenetic activity of a factory scene, without resorting to some sort of transitional contrivance.

But in the main, there are many scenes that can rely solely on a simple dissolve for transition. In fact, it is suggested that the screenplay writer *strive* to do this. For in overloading a script with transitional devices, the desired effects will be lost completely, and the devices will begin to creak mechanically by the time the picture is half done. But if the devices are interlarded judiciously in the script, *they* will gain from the absence of unnecessary, cluttering, and transition-sapping devices. In addition, the simple dissolve transitions will gain added transition value because of the impetus derived from the devices.

In other words, the transition device can be a most effective tool in the hands of an expert screen-play writer. Misused and overused by an inept muddler, it can defeat the purpose for which it is so ideally suited. Used sparingly but effectively, transitions can make motion pictures move with a flow of uninterrupted continuity.

Montage

In the United States, the word "montage" has an entirely different meaning than in Europe (see page 186). Here it is used to designate a single sequence of quick flash shots used to condense time, or to contrast space.

Montages of this sort are photographed on the production stage, on location, on the special-effects stage, or on all three. The actual splicing with dissolves and superimposures, though, is done in the optical effects department.

There are three general types of montage: 1. the direct-cut

montage 2. the dissolve or wipe montage and 3. the superimposed montage.

Direct-cut montage.   The direct-cut montage is simply a series of quick shots spliced together which, because of their relation in the number of frames used for each, convey a single impression to the audience. It is used when neither a lapse of time nor a geographical and spatial movement is to be indicated.

Thus, in order to impress the audience with the simultaneous group reaction of a number of people to a certain dramatic scene, a montage of a series of staccato, individual close-ups of their reactions can be spliced together to give a sort of sum total, mass reaction.

Where it is necessary to give the impression of fast action taking place in one geographical location and over a short period of time, the direct-cut montage is also suggested. In Kramer's *The Champion,* a series of quick direct cuts, showing gloved fists flying, heads reeling from blows, powerful lunges, and the like, were strung together to give the impression of what took place in an entire prize fight.

Dissolve montage.   The dissolve or wipe montage is used, in the main, to connect a series of action shots to indicate an actual change from place to place and over an extended period of time.

An interrelationship is achieved because, as the frames of the preceding shot fade out, the opening frames of the succeeding shot are blended in.

Using this device, it is possible, for example, to show how a certain character traveled from Chicago to New York by bus, from New York to London by boat, from London to Paris by plane, and from Le Bourget airport, in Paris, by taxi, and then by foot to a bistro in a Montmartre cul-de-sac.

Montages save money.   In modestly budgeted pictures, it is possible to show the characters as actually being in each means of conveyance. In writing such montages for cheap-budget movie-house and television films, however, it is possible to resort to the use of stock shots of vehicular exteriors without showing the character in the conveyances. One or two of the shots may be photographed with the character in a cheaply erected mock-up of a small corner of the plane or train coach, interiors which are often stored on the scene dock.

Historical montage. Montages are frequently used in historical pictures to indicate the passing of a number of historical events, and at times to summarize an entire epoch.

Wipe montage. The wipe montage resorts to wipes instead of dissolves, and usually connects a series of quick shots to indicate the movement of people or vehicles into various localities. Because the nature of the wipe is such that it carries action with it across the frame, it is especially suited to conveying movement from place to place.

Superimposed montage. The superimposed montage is used mostly to present a pictorialized stream of consciousness. An extreme close-up of the subject is photographed first. Then, various quick shots illustrating the thoughts in the subject's mind are photographed separately and spliced together, using either direct cuts or dissolves for connective purposes. These two strips are then printed simultaneously and the result is a double image.

This type of montage is also used to illustrate a geographical change, usually one performed on foot. The character making the journey is photographed first as he walks, runs, or stumbles on a treadmill in front of a black velvet curtain. Here the shot does not necessarily have to be a close-up, but can vary from a close-up to a medium shot. Then the various locale shots are photographed or drawn from stock, spliced, connected with dissolves, and superimposed on the shots of the character in motion.

Time-lapse montage. Montages are the stock in trade as time-lapse devices. They have been used in many traditional ways. One method uses a series of varying newspaper headlines dissolving through each other to cover the time lapse. Another uses calendar leaves falling, or being blown away, in consecutive order. Still another splices together seasonal shots of spring, summer, winter, and fall, each season being identified by the condition of the landscape.

Procedure montage. Montages can be made of mechanical procedures. If a character is manufacturing a certain item, the passage of time required can be indicated by photographing the item in various stages of completion, splicing the strips and connecting them with dissolves.

Date montage. Another type of time-lapse montage uses a sequence of dates that zoom in from a dot to full screen, or in reverse, all performed in the optical effects department.

Symbolic montage. The most creative type of montage is the subjective symbol, used to illustrate a psychological state of mind. The montage used to symbolize Robert Montgomery's becoming unconscious after being hit on the head, in *Lady in the Lake,* was one in which he was seen to be falling through vast space. In *The Snakepit,* the symbolizing of the mental institution as a snakepit was presented with an actual snakepit production scene, with the camera pulling away from the inmates so that, as they waved their hands and arms, they appeared to be a nest of snakes in a deep hole. The montage sequences of ocean waves were apt symbols of the constant wash of the mental aberrations that caused the crack-ups.

Do not overuse montages. Montages are convenient devices. They can serve certain useful purposes. As pure cinema, they have a definite place in motion pictures. But they must not be overused. When too many are found to be necessary, it is because the story line is episodic. Too many gaps in time must be accounted for, and the result is not flowing, continuous action but a series of static visual symbols. The picture *Mission to Moscow* used more than three thousand feet of montage footage because the story line was episodic, because there were too many geographical jumps, and also because location shooting in Moscow was impossible, which made stock montages necessary.

Avoid the hackneyed time-lapse montages, such as those involving pulling calendar leaves and changes of season. If there is a place in screen-play writing for creative imagination, it is in the devising of appropriate effective time-lapse montages. Reject the trite formula that comes first to mind, and try to work out fresh versions. For there is nothing like a newly minted, originally conceived montage to enliven what could be a creaking, dull, technical device.

Opticals

Although the processing of optical effects is a purely mechanical operation, performed automatically by machines especially devised for the purpose, by technicians trained for the job, the screen-play writer should have some knowledge, not only of their use in a script, but also of the manner of their manufacture.

Technically speaking, an optical is a device for connecting shots, scenes, or sequences so as to leave a certain impression with the audience, the exact impression depending on the type of optical used.

Dissolves. The first opticals encountered in a film are normally the lap dissolves which separate the various title cards on which the film credits flashed onto the screen. This series of dissolves always ends with the name of the director on a separate title card, a courtesy which is extended because of a clause in the Screen Directors' Guild contract with the studios. A lap dissolve is a slow fusing of one shot with another, effected by gradually darkening the last frames of the first shot and blending them in with the gradually lightened opening frames of the succeeding shot. The lap dissolve was so named because one shot was said to have been over-lapped onto another. The trend is to elide the word "lap" and to refer to it simply as a dissolve.

Time-lapse dissolve. The dissolve effect is also used to connect two scenes that are separated by a lapse of time. Here, the purpose is to indicate to the audience that some time has gone by between scenes, as distinct from a direct cut, which indicates that the succeeding action seen is concurrent. When the time hiatus is comparatively short—a matter of minutes or hours—the simple dissolve can be used. But when days, weeks, months, and years are involved, it would be more advantageous, in orienting the audience to the exact length of the time lapse, to resort to a montage sequence connected with a series of dissolves.

From six to ten feet of extra film must be shot to furnish the optical department with sufficient footage with which to effect a dissolve. The length of the dissolve depends entirely on the action involved. If a long period of time is to be indicated, a slow dissolve would be suggested by the writer; a shorter space of time would be indicated by a quick dissolve.

Do not dissolve out on one scene and dissolve in to the same scene at the same angle later. The practice is frowned upon. Try to dissolve in on an entirely different scene or angle. If you cannot, dissolve out with a time-lapse dissolve on the order of a close-up of the moving hands of a clock, or night-and-day windows and the like, and you will accomplish your purpose.

Out-of-focus dissolve. There is still another type of dissolve which is used mainly for match dissolves. Instead of diminishing the light content of the last frames of film, they are thrown out of focus first —with a blurred effect—and are then dissolved into the opening frames of the succeeding scene which have been similarly blurred.

This type of blur, by the way, can be used quite effectively in other situations and not necessarily for dissolve purposes. It can be used subjectively—for example, to indicate a blacking out by a wounded or dying character. What he sees—a person hovering over his bed, or a scene (shot usually from his viewpoint, at a low angle) —is blurred out on the screen, thus creating the illusion of what is going on in the character's mind. In *Lady in the Lake* this device was used whenever the detective was conked on the bean, to indicate his journey to nowhere.

Very slow dissolves should not be used in television films. When viewed on a home television screen, such slow dissolves become magnified and tend to slow up the forward flow. They are also misleading in that they may leave the viewer with the mistaken notion that his television set has blanked out.

Wipes. Shorter time intervals can be taken care of with what is known as a "wipe." With this effect, a transition is made by means of having the last frames of the scene pushed off the screen as they are being simultaneously replaced by the first frames of the succeeding scene.

The trend is to avoid the wipe—especially the more complex ones, which will be dealt with later—because it calls attention to itself as a technical device, and thus detracts from the main action. It would be acceptable practice to use a dissolve for time lapses and to resort to the wipe only for purposes of getting a character from one place to another. In this way, if the direction of the wipe—from right to left or from left to right—coincides with the direction of the subject's movement, the wipe will lose most of its obviousness because it will have been integrated into the action of the picture. Thus, if it were necessary to show a person entering a house, without being forced by the exigencies of the plot to show him traversing the number of rooms he will have to cross in reaching his final destination, the use of a wipe to get him, while still in motion, from the door to his destination, would be entirely justified.

Push-off wipes. Another type of wipe used more in commercial and documentary films than in feature pictures is the "push-off" wipe. In this device, which is actually a combination of a wipe on and a wipe off, the first few frames of the scene actually push off the last few frames of the first scene, with an actual line of demarcation being shown, as though a windshield wiper were being drawn perpendicularly across the screen. The trickiness obvious in this effect should militate against its being used in a serious feature picture, and accounts for its having been dropped almost universally after having had a long run in pictures because of its attention-calling novelty.

Special-effect wipes. There are hundreds of variations of this type of wipe available to the picture maker who likes to play with toys. Special-effects technicians can furnish wipes that simulate rain, so that the last frames of the preceding scene are pushed down and off by what appears to be a jagged line of raindrops. In the same way they can supply flame wipes, lightning wipes, smoke wipes, and whirling wipes.

Although, for most purposes, the wipe is virtually proscribed for the feature-film screen play, it has its place in other types of screen play—in educational, business, and training films.

Fade-in, fade-out.   There are two other optical effects used in pictures—the fade-in and the fade-out. Once again the names are amply descriptive of the uses to which they are put. In the fade-in, the *first* few frames of a shot are printed very darkly and become progressively lighter until the standard density is obtained. In the fade-out, the reverse effect is achieved by darkening the *last* few frames of a shot progressively until a black density results.

The fade-in is used in the opening shot of almost every screen play. It says, in effect, "All right—let's start!" It leaves the impression with the audience that they are to be slowly acquainted with an action that does not necessarily begin with the beginning of the film, but has been going on for some time.

The fade-out, on the other hand, is used to suggest to the audience that the sequence of action they have just seen has been brought to a halt, and that a considerable amount of time—plot time, not running time—will elapse before the next action starts.

The next action, however, must always start with a fade-in, in which the blackness of the opening few frames of the first shot in the second sequence are dissolved in with the closing few frames of the last shot of the first sequence. The succeeding frames are then lightened in density until the desired normal lighting is obtained. The word "dissolve," however, need not be indicated. It is enough merely to write in FADE OUT, and then, under it, three or four spaces down, FADE IN.

This fade combination should be used only infrequently in a screen play. For a fade-out definitely stops action. And action picks up again only when the fade-in is fully realized. Overused, it will have a choppy effect and will tend to give the finished picture the unintegrated quality of most pictures that have been adapted from long, time-leaping novels.

Actually, the screen play for movie-house pictures should be designed so that it can fall into three or four definite act separations. And these act separations can be indicated in the script with a fade-out, fade-in combination.

Finally, the screen play and the picture should end with a fade-out in which the action is gradually faded out, to leave the impression with the audience that here is not an abrupt ending to the action they have seen, but rather only an interlude in a series of larger actions which took place before the picture started and which will continue to take place after the picture is over.

The fade-out or fade-in is to be discouraged for television films. In the first place, the television screen cannot picture the complete blackness required by them. Secondly, such blackness on film tends to cause a disturbing edge-flare on the television screen. Finally, long, dark fades on a television screen slow up the action which, in television productions, is highly undesirable because of the need for overriding possible audience boredom with constant movement.

Audiences have become habituated to these opticals as screen conventions. And it is just these conventions that have made motion pictures the distinct art form they have been and can continue to be. Only by using them sensibly, by making certain that technical excellence does not detract from creative art, can the screen-play writer fulfill his obligations to his craft.

At the same time, the writer should realize that these are not inflexible conventions. If they can be supplanted with more inventive substitutes, by all means suggest them.

Special effects

The close-up photograph necessary to the shooting of sign inserts, extreme close-ups of eyes, lips, and other particularizing shots, requires the work of specially trained technicians, and uses specially designed cameras and camera equipment. It would therefore be too time-consuming to try to shoot this type of close-up on regular sound stages during actual production, where a great many people would be tied up while the special effect was being photographed.

Trick effects. In addition to inserts, the special-effects technicians prepare and shoot certain trick sequences. Model sets, for example, are done in special effects. Shipwrecks, train wrecks, volcanic eruptions, the parting of the Dead Sea waters, catastrophes of all sorts, would be too costly and too difficult to reproduce in life size but can be photographed as special effects, often with amazing results.

Special effects are almost invaluable in shooting fantasy films, in which people seem to disappear, or walk through solid walls, and so on.

But special effects is a costly procedure and the screen writer should confer with his producer before indicating them in his script. They should seldom be used in cheap-budget movie-house pictures or in television films where, in addition to an absence of inclement weather, there are seldom any violent catastrophes—unless they can be obtained from stock footage.

Such effects as lightning flashes, storm clouds, moon and cloud combinations, shipwrecks, auto crashes, lava flow, earthquakes, floods, and train wrecks—together with the multitude of other catastrophes with which a story character can be bedeviled—can usually be found in stock film libraries. With clever work, a film editor can intercut them with production shots so that the desired effect can be obtained. Unless you can screen this stock footage, and thus become acquainted with what is available, it is best merely to indicate that stock footage is to be used without going into too much detail as to how it should be intercut with the production shots you write in.

Television films can use a great deal of stock footage to lower production costs. The writer of this type of picture could make himself quite desirable and appreciated were he to acquaint himself with the types and sources of available and appropriate stock footage and indicate them in his screen play.

Camera tricks. The motion-picture camera can be called upon to play any number of tricks for the screen-play writer—tricks that may solve writing problems that would otherwise cause a good idea to be discarded. It is well to assume, then, that the camera—manned, of course, by a highly versatile crew of skilled technicians—can do anything. It practically turned somersaults when it was locked, upside down, to a revolving floor, to record the effect of Fred Astaire's dancing on the ceiling.

The camera can be made to photograph supposed underwater scenes (for budget pictures) simply by sliding a pair of specially lighted gauze screens in front of its lens.

Image distortion can be achieved by pouring a thin film of oil down over a piece of glass placed in front of the lens.

Multiple exposure or process-screen photography can make it

possible for an actor playing twin parts not only to talk with himself but to cross his own image.

"*Matte*" (masking) shots permit a budget-conscious producer to photograph an imposing edifice simply by building the lower part as an actual set while the upper section is painted on a frame of glass placed in front of the lens. More expensively produced "traveling matte" shots call for a highly involved system of matte cut-outs graduated in size to accommodate human action in the scene.

By means of false perspective, an actor can appear to be walking a tightrope, although he actually is walking a plank to the edge of which a rope has been nailed. The camera is placed in such a position as to photograph only the rope without catching the plank.

Things can be made to appear or disappear simply by stopping the camera and then putting in or taking off whatever is involved in the "magical" effect.

In the picture *Beyond Tomorrow,* a ghost was seen to appear and then walk in the midst of a crowd of people. Yes, it was done with mirrors, as is the trick of photographing a single ship so that it becomes a whole fleet of ships which, when photographed with a split screen, could become the fleets of two opposing forces.

These are but a few of the tricks the camera can perform. There are many, many more. But most of them are carefully guarded secrets. Studios do not want competitors to profit from them and they also fear that by informing the general public of them audiences will not accept them as real, and thus lose interest.

Process screen shots

It would be appropriate, at this point, to discuss the manner in which the process (or rear-projection) screen can be integrated into motion picture production, and into screen-play writing considerations.

The process screen is a large, single piece of translucent plastic material, averaging about 12′ x 16′, with brass grommets around its four edges, which are used for lashing the screen onto a huge wooden frame.

A motion-picture scenic shot—or even an action shot—called a "plate," and about two hundred feet long to avoid repeated rewinds for additional takes—is projected on the rear of this screen. In front of it, actors play their parts on a set that is integrated with the scene being projected on the screen. The speed of the plate projection machine is interlocked with the speed of the camera, so that the flickering in the projected picture will be compensated for in the camera, frame by frame.

The result, which a camera in front of the screen records, is a composite of live action, enacted in the foreground, and a film image, projected on the screen in the background.

It should be obvious, then, that with this extremely valuable device, it is possible to photograph, say, a Hollywood actor against an action background that is authentically British, or African, or one that shows any locale of which a sufficiently long plate is available.

The Berlin scenes in *Foreign Affair* were photographed against process-screen plates, as were the Holy Land backgrounds for *Samson and Delilah,* Naples, Venice, and Florence backgrounds for *September Affair,* Persian and Italian Tyrol backgrounds for *Under My Skin* and Tyrolean backgrounds for the skiing shots for *Tell It to the Judge.*

The process screen can also supply, in addition to scenic exteriors, interior backgrounds for shots photographed in the interior of a sound stage. Thus, for example, to avoid taking out a sound crew and equipment to shoot subjects in the interior of a taxicab as it cruises up a downtown street, it is possible to place a mock-up, manually shaken taxicab in front of a process screen, and then rear-project a downtown street-scene plate on the process screen. Shadows of passing trees or telephone poles are flickered across the faces of the actors by a revolving cyclodrum, off scene; or lights are flashed on intermittently to simulate passing street lamps. After dubbing in typical downtown street sounds, together with the sounds of a running auto, the result is a shot that could give the impression of having been photographed outdoors, dialogue and all.

Process-screen photography is not cheaply produced. A special crew of technicians is required to operate the projector. Interlocking of the projector with the camera is a difficult job, sometimes calling for hours of meticulous preparation. Lighting the set in the foreground so that it matches the density of the lighting in the background filmed image is a tricky proposition—as is the avoidance of shadows cast by the foreground players on the background screen. All of which means that more takes are required in process-screen work than in standard studio shooting. Complete correlation must be made between the live action and the projected screen action. For example, if the rear screen depicts a winding road, it is necessary for the live action actor, at the wheel of a car, to simulate manipulating his wheel so that it will match exactly the curve in the road showing on the screen.

But despite the costs involved in shooting, process-screen shooting is infinitely cheaper than it would be to transport a camera crew, actors, and essential material for location shooting.

The screen-play writer, then, should constantly keep in mind the advantages of process-screen shooting. He should acquaint himself with the plates available for use. Of course, such oft-used subjects as "Paris," "London," "Times Square," and the like are obviously on hand. But a working knowledge of the plate library can furnish the writer with ideas for less hackneyed backgrounds that can add variety to what would otherwise be a flat-dimensioned, studio-set picture.

As far as television films are concerned, rear-screen projection must remain only a dream tool. Not until the cost of rear-screen projection is brought down sufficiently to warrant its inclusion in an extremely low budget will this device be available to television screen-play writers.

Studios are loath to divulge the nature and extent of their stock-shot film libraries because they do not like to let the general public in on the know, for fear of disillusioning them, because actors' unions feel such shots deprive their members of jobs and travel opportunities, and because they are obligated to lend or sell them to other studios. But as a screen-play writer on the lot, you should be able to wangle a look at the catalogue. There you will find them listed not only according to subject, but according to eye-level and pace as well.

What is more, you can integrate the process-screen plate with the story line, as was done in *Foreign Correspondent*. There, while the interior of a car was being photographed as it supposedly traveled along a London street, Van Meers, one of the characters, looked out of the window, saw some pigeons—on the process screen, of course—which were also seen by the audience, and commented, "Oh! look at the birds."

WRITING THE SCREEN PLAY

SECTION

Writing the screen play

Now, with all the preliminaries covered, the screen-play writer should be able to begin to work on the shooting script. He must understand, though, that this will not be the *final* shooting script. After he has completed it, the brains and hands of many will pick it apart, elide, telescope, reject, suggest, elaborate—in fact, almost rewrite the entire script for him at numerous conferences. The director, for example, will have made his suggestions after reading the treatment. Certain of his objections will be based on the claim that he cannot shoot the scene as indicated, and he will suggest changes. The producer will expect his ideas to be included. The front-office superiors will all have definite notions which are to be incorporated into the shooting script.

The master-scene screen play

Quite often, however, the writer may not even be permitted to write a shooting script. He may be assigned to do a "master-scene" script. He will not be required to write in camera shots and angles. What will be expected of him is simply a completed treatment. Where, in the treatment, he merely indicated that certain dialogue be spoken, now, in the master-scene script, he will write in all the dialogue. Where the treatment merely suggests, in a literary style, the action to be taken, this time the writer will indicate the same action, but in screen-play form.

Scene I for instance would be written as follows:

FADE IN
EXT. ENTRANCE MERIWETHER HOSP.—DAY

1. A cab is parked at the curb. A nurse is handing a bundled-up baby to its mother and father, MR. and MRS. MEADE, sitting in the cab. They are a typically American young couple, both somewhat fearful and still dazed at their new parental status.

> NURSE
> (with finality)
> There you are, Mrs. Meade.

> MRS. MEADE
> (fearfully)
> Will the ride hurt him, nurse?

> NURSE
> (smiling reassuringly)
> He'll live through it, I'm sure.

> MR. MEADE
> (hesitantly)
> I can hold him, dear.

> MRS. MEADE
> He's not heavy, darling.

> MR. MEADE
> Thanks for everything, nurse.

He slips a bill into the nurse's hand.

> NURSE
> Thank *you!*

The nurse straightens up from the cab, slams the door shut, and grins.

> NURSE
> He's all yours now! Watch out for kidnapers! 'Bye!

The cab pulls away. The nurse watches it for a moment, sighs, and shrugs her shoulders. Then she turns to the hospital entrance, and walks to it, passing the sign on the hospital wall reading MERI-WETHER HOSPITAL, as she disappears into the entrance.

That is a master scene. No camera angles have been indicated. Only a scene description, character action, and the accompanying dialogue have been attended to.

The next scene will be in the hospital room of Jane Bedell, the heroine. The writer will continue with the same method. Only the dialogue conducted between Jane and the nurse—whom we have seen in Scene I—will be written, together with the manner in which it is to be spoken, and the actions of both characters.

The above Scene I may not have been included in the original example treatment. It is the screen writer's prerogative to deviate from the treatment which is, after all, only a blueprint for the screen play. For instance, after making a number of starts, he may decide to begin with an episode that would set the scene (the maternity hospital) and a new-baby situation (to serve as a contrast to the new-baby situation of the main story line) and to plant the baby kidnaping motif, to be developed later.

The opening scene can then deal with minor characters only, in the same situation (the new baby) in which our major characters will soon be seen.

Working in this fashion, with master scenes, the writer will simply fill in the undetailed segments of the treatment, using as much of the treatment's material as is feasible. If the treatment has been well thought out and properly developed, these changes should be of small consequence.

The finished master-scene screen play will then be gone over by the producer and various supervisors, for suggested changes and elisions. The writer will make most of them and resubmit the script. More suggestions will result in more changes until finally a finished script, acceptable to all, will result.

When the final-final screen play is "OK for production," it is mimeographed. Copies are distributed to the heads of every department that will be involved in estimating the costs, designing the sets, hiring the actors, and so forth. The director will also receive his copy.

With the master-scene script as a blueprint, the director will then lay out his camera angles and shots, and correct the action directions to suit whatever exigencies may have come up, usually those brought about by changed set plans, or through differences between the writer's set conception and the finished set as designed by the art department, developed by the drafting department, and executed by the construction department.

The average director would rather work from such a master-scene script. He considers it an encroachment on his directorial preserves for the average writer to direct him as to how to shoot his picture. Even when he gets a shooting script, with all the shots and angles already written in, the director will assert his prerogative of substituting his own camera setups.

But at the same time, if he is given a camera setup that will get the shot across effectively, the knowing director will not be averse to using it. For he realizes that, to the average movie-goer, it is supposed to be the director who is responsible for the finished product, and not the writer.

It is the director who is usually credited in reviews with having succeeded in "contributing splendid interpretive bits of acting," "fashioning marvelous transitions," "contributing a splendid coordination of sound with action," "arranging for a not too obtrusive musical background," and so on.

The fact of the matter is that the director is actually what his name implies—a director, and no more. He is a director of other craftsmen's talents. He tells the cameraman what camera angle he wants, as he visualizes it himself or as the writer has indicated it in the script. The cameraman, then, does the job of getting the camera set up, the lighting properly adjusted, and so on. It is the film cutter who, with the help of the director, will put the finished picture together; the music composer who will write the musical score; and the actors who, with the directive comments of the director, will actually speak the lines and perform the actions. The director will direct the various craftsmen in their jobs for the purpose of making a finished picture that will be unified in all of its varied elements.

That is why what the audience sees on the screen is not always the result of the director's creative ability. Given a screen writer who knows his craft—one who can visualize as well as verbalize, who can create the appropriate visual symbols and then translate them into revelatory dialogue and action, who is cognizant of all the techniques of screen-play writing—the director can receive a shooting script, with camera directions, which he cannot help following.

The shooting script

At the same time, the knowing screen writer can write his camera directions, actions, and dialogue so that the director will be forced to shoot just what the screen writer has indicated in the way he has indicated it. In many respects, a professionally written screen play can be, to all intents and purposes, a predirected screen play.

FADE IN

EXT. ENTRANCE MERIWETHER HOSP.—DAY

1. MED. SHOT on a cab parked at the curb. A nurse is handing a bundled-up baby to its mother and father in the cab.

> NURSE
> There you are, Mrs. Meade.

INT. CAB—DAY

2. MED. SHOT on nurse, standing outside cab, as she hands the baby to Mrs. Meade, shooting past MR. and MRS. MEADE, a typically American young married couple who are still somewhat dazed and fearful of their new parental status.

> MRS. MEADE
> (fearfully)
> Will the ride hurt him, nurse?

> NURSE
> (smiling)
> He'll live through it, I'm sure.

                              MR. MEADE
                              (hesitantly)
                        I can hold him, dear.

                              MRS. MEADE
                    Oh! he's not heavy at all, darling.

EXT.—CAB AT CURB—DAY

3. MED. SHOT on nurse as we see Mr. Meade slip a bill into
    her hand.

                              MR. MEADE
                    Thanks for everything, nurse.

The nurse slams the cab door shut and grins.

                              NURSE
                          Thank you.
The nurse straightens up.

                        He's all yours now. Watch out for
                        kidnapers! 'Bye.

4. EXT.—CAB AT CURB—DAY

REVERSE ANGLE

The cab pulls away and out of the frame. The nurse stares after
it for a moment, sighs, shrugs her shoulders, turns to the hospital entrance and walks to it, the CAMERA TRUCKING IN
to her, as she passes the sign on the hospital wall reading
MERIWETHER HOSPITAL. As she disappears in the entrance, the CAMERA CONTINUES TO GO IN for an EXT.
CLOSE-UP on the sign.

                                        DISSOLVE

By holding on the nurse and then trucking in with her to the
hospital entrance, instead of panning out with the cab, we can indicate that the succeeding action will continue with the nurse, and
not with those in the cab. Were the latter to be necessary, we would
pan out with the cab, holding on it for a while, and then cut directly into the cab interior. As it is now, we will cut into the hospital interior, on the nurse again, as she enters Jane's room.
Since little time will elapse between the time we last see the nurse

at the hospital entrance and when we next pick her up, a quick dissolve from the close-up on the sign to, perhaps, a close-up on Jane's room number, is in order. However, if it were necessary to indicate a lapse of considerable time, we could tilt the camera down to the nurse's feet as she walks into the hospital, and then dissolve through to her feet walking into Jane's room.

When the above shooting-script scene is shot, the director will shoot the cab exterior from one camera setup, and the cab interior from another setup. The film editor will then intercut the exterior shots with the interior shot, as indicated in the script, unless he and the director have other plans. Then again, the director may decide to shoot a few close-ups of the baby in the nurse's arms, or of the anxious parents in the cab. If these are available to the film editor, he may decide to intercut some of the close-ups into the other shots. In this case, though, because the close-ups would not necessarily reveal details that are important enough to require spot-lighted revelation, it would be doubtful that the director would cover himself with extra close-ups. That is why they were not suggested in the shooting script.

The foregoing discussion should give further indication as to the qualifications necessary to the screen-play writer and his use of motion-picture techniques.

In the previous sections, we dealt largely with things literary and with things technical. The idea, the synopsis, the treatment, and even the master-scene screen play, were simply literary exercises that could well have been written by any competent writer with a specialized knowledge of dramatics—as it pertains to the motion picture—and with a flair for visualization in addition to verbalization.

But the writing of a shooting script calls into play a number of specialized skills—skills that often are not within the province of the ordinary writer.

Granted the screen writer should have the psychological insight to develop character; a sense of story so as to be able to involve his characters in and extricate them from various situations; the plot faculty to juggle these situations so that they tell a well-ordered story; the ability to dramatize these situations so that they can present impact; together with the various other literary aptitudes necessary to the equipment of the experienced writer.

In addition, as a qualified screen-play writer, he must know the possibilities and the limitations of the motion-picture camera.

At the same time, he should know quite a bit about acting and its problems, so as to be able to write the necessary action descriptions.

What is more, he should know something of opticals—the manner in which they are made so that he may know how they can best be used.

Then, he must have a considerable knowledge of sound-track devices and techniques, and be able to co-ordinate sight with sound.

He will be at a considerable advantage if he has, in addition, a working knowledge, at least, of film cutting, set designing, and musical background accompaniments.

The screen writer who possesses all of this knowledge is the ideal. Ordinarily, he would soon be able to step out of the screen-play writer class, and become a writer-director, a director, or even a producer. But it stands to reason that the more specialized knowledge the writer has of those elements that go into the making of a motion picture, the more qualified he would be for writing screen plays.

The problem is how to obtain that knowledge. Courses in screen-play writing at colleges and universities attempt to teach it but with varying success because, obviously, they can teach only the theories. The best place to learn the *practical* fundamentals is at a motion-picture studio. But studios rarely open their doors to beginners. A few of them, sporadically, have tried to institute a system of using junior writers, in which inexperienced screen-play writers (though they may have had a great deal of writing experience in other media) are taken in hand by an experienced supervisor, and put through a course. For the most part, though, studios seldom use inexperienced screen writers—which puts the ordinary writer more or less on the horns of a dilemma. Quite often, however, because a writer's book or play has been purchased by a studio, and an arrangement made whereby the author "goes with the deal" to work on the screen play, he is paired off with an experienced collaborator whose job it is to supply the technical details of the screen play.

At other times, if a collaborator is not furnished, the novitiate screen-play writer is given a cubbyhole office, a typewriter, and a sheaf of clean white paper, and is told to get to work on his treatment and, eventually, his screen play.

Then, by a process that borders on osmosis, if the writer is experienced in research, he manages to garner a heap of information regarding the screen writer's craft from other screen writers, from assistant directors, from producers, even from secretaries who often know more about screen-play writing than many writers for whom they are working. Also, he will obtain a pile of old scripts and pore over them for clues. Then he will arrange for screening of finished pictures, often of those made from the scripts he has already read. Gradually, by an extensive series of trial and error attempts, some of the fundamentals of his newly chosen craft may begin to seep in.

He will try to buttress his findings by going onto a shooting stage to watch pictures being shot. If he is genuinely concerned with learning, he will ask questions of the director—provided he finds one who is sympathetic and co-operative—the cameraman, the assistant director, and even of the grips, whose knowledge of picture making, though circumscribed by the limits of their own craft, often exceeds that of a great many who are supposedly more experienced in matters cinematic.

By observing the many rehearsals necessary before a take is made, and the many retakes before an OK take is shot, the learner should be able to get an idea of some of the dialogue faults to avoid. He should be able to learn a little about camera angles and, particularly, he should become aware of the patent advantage of *showing* a scene in *action,* rather than of telling it in dialogue.

If he is personable enough, and willing enough, and happens on a camera crew that is co-operative, he may even be permitted to squint through the camera "finder," which is a sort of square telescope with a ground glass viewer at one end, that will enable him to see just what the picture frame will contain, and thus discover the possibilities and limitations of the motion-picture frame, as it is affected by varying distances and lenses in order to make a close-up, a medium shot, or a long shot.

What, then, are the *practical* details of screen-play writing techniques? From now on, we shall explore and examine all aspects, define them, give examples, and try to fit them into a pattern which, when completed, should provide the basis for learning the fundamentals of the art of screen-play writing.

In the beginning was . . .?

Where to begin? How to begin? These questions have plagued all writers. But the screen-play writer has problems which other writers never encounter and which put the answers to the plaguy questions in an entirely different category.

Because a motion picture flashes by continuously, without stop— as contrasted to the printed story, which can be reread for clarification of missed or misinterpreted points—the order in which its varied elements are shown is highly important.

What should be shown first, for example? Should it be an atmospheric scene designed to set the mood of the picture? Or should it be an action scene revealing character? Should these introductory scenes be of a merely expository nature, a sort of static introduction, as it were, to the action to follow, or should they be those in which the audience is thrown into the story, without preliminary preparations?

Actually, there is no set rule to govern the choice of a film's opening. Each picture calls for individual treatment. Certain stories may lend themselves only to certain types of opening, while others would be best handled with completely contrasting types.

Open with a bang?   Generally speaking, though, it is standard Hollywood practice to leap into the story feet-first, without expository preliminaries. This sets the pace for the picture, which must then move along quickly. "Open with a bang!" in other words, is the oft-spoken injunction of Hollywood producers.

Wyler's *The Letter* really opens with a bang when, after establishing the locale—a plantation in Asia—with a long-running pan shot, a pistol shot suddenly punctuates the scene and a man is seen running down some bungalow stairs followed by Bette Davis, who continues to pump bullets into her lover's body.

Opening with a bang—either aurally or visually—is definitely essential to the television film, in which audience interest should be instantaneously aroused the moment after the opening commercial has been given. The station change-over dial is too readily available to the televiewer to risk losing his patronage. For ordinarily, it is the opening few seconds of the television film that induce the televiewer to continue viewing or send him off on a wave-length journey to more promising programs.

Opening with a bang, however, despite its attention-getting virtue of movement, has its drawbacks, drawbacks which European— and, especially, British—pictures have overcome simply by opening *without* a bang.

For opening with a bang can militate against building. It is necessary to keep up the opening pace throughout, to sustain interest. It is necessary, in order to build, that the pace be continually quickened so as to reach a satisfactory climax. Unfortunately, this is a difficult procedure. Such paces are seldom sustained. And the results are sagging scenes and sequences that make for disinterest and dissatisfaction.

Open slowly? British pictures have been criticized—by Americans—as being pedestrian and lacking in action. The reason is that British screen-play writers and directors deliberately pace their pictures—especially in the opening scenes—to a slower tempo. And they do it in the belief that, although action is a *vital* requirement in motion pictures, it is not to be used to the detriment of other requirements, which are just as, and sometimes even more, vital.

Opening to build. It is obvious from their pictures that the British believe the gradual—and therefore natural—development of character is vitally important. So they begin their pictures with an over-all visual exposition of the milieu in which the action will take place, as was done in *It Always Rains on Sunday*. That done, they go in from the general to the more specific, by showing the people who will be involved in the action as they go through their normal workaday lives. From this they become more specific, and single out the protagonists and antagonists, so as to set them up in their proper relation to each other, and to the story line.

Only when these expository preliminaries have been attended to do they begin to get into the action itself. But, even then they do not leap into the action with a bang. Instead, they build to it slowly—again, naturally—piling incident upon incident, scene upon scene, until the vital action is reached. That done, the pace is quickened. But not too fast. The fast tempo is left until the end of the picture, where it properly belongs, using the most effective building techniques. For interspersed with the action are bits of comedy and crisis relief—sometimes seemingly unrelated to the story line—as were the idle cricket-talk scenes interposed in Hitchcock's exciting *The Lady Vanishes*. Also interspersed are seemingly incongruous bits of character development.

This character development is not confined to the principals only. For the British believe that minor characters should not be slighted. They are seldom introduced with a single characterizing line of dialogue, on the order of "Gee! my feet are killing me!" from a salesgirl; or "I hate driving cabs!" from a philosophical cab driver. Instead, they linger a little longer on the character, so as to round him out sufficiently, to make certain he fits in with the well-rounded character development of the principal characters. In *The 39 Steps*, for instance, the minor characters of the Scottish farmer and his young wife were not only fully developed, but their dramatic story was injected into the main story line.

The reason for this emphasis on minor character development is that the British believe that both elements must be completely integrated if they are to be presented successfully. In art, the background must be integrated with the foreground, to give suitable and esthetically satisfactory prominence to the foreground material. If the background material is slighted, the foreground material will suffer. In the same way, the British believe that if the principal characters and their story line are not backed up with well-rounded characters involved in a subplot, then the main story line will not be presented in its proper perspective.

This method, however, does not always result in felicitous pictures. Sometimes there is an almost robot-like adherence to the tenets of building. Too often a scene is designed to build with the traditional medium shot, close shot, close-up, medium shot, long shot progression. Then it comes to a crisis, with the same process starting all over again in succeeding scenes. Because of this, a mechanical sameness is bound to appear. Moreover, this defect tends to make the good sequences stand out from the bad. That is why so many otherwise excellent British films invariably contain sequences that are quite inept.

It is because we have been conditioned by the swifter paced American films that most of us find British films pedestrian. But the success of so many excellent British films has changed the situation somewhat. Our audiences are seeing more and more British films. And the more they see, the more will they enjoy the slower paced but more realistic British pictures, and the more opportunities will there be for the screen writer to present the screen play that opens more leisurely, with more characterization and, certainly, more effectively.

This brings up another subject—one of particular interest to television screen-play writers. Until recently, most of the better foreign films were shown at movie theaters that specialized in them. They were called "sure seaters" because a certain segment of movie-goers attended them faithfully every week. This segment, however, was quite small compared to the millions who studiously avoided foreign films, and it has remained fairly constant in size so that, even today, few foreign films achieve the box-office success of many less deserving Hollywood products.

Television films can change that because they go directly to the audience, whereas the audience must go to the theater for a non-television film. Television allows the audience to view its wares, to sample its entertainment, for no extra charge. This means that, from now on, millions who would never have crossed the street to see a foreign film or a more intelligently written home-grown product with a more limited appeal than the usual Hollywood fare will have them delivered into their homes. Thus, by making accessible to a vast new audience those pictures that have heretofore been shunned, the norm of good taste and appreciation can be tremendously increased. The television film writer has in his craft a potential for improving the American standard of visual entertainment.

Building

In addition to having a sense of the visual, the screen-play writer must possess a film sense. A creative film sense demands of the writer that he be able to tell his story in strictly visual terms, by writing in little segments of life, so as to present a complete mosaic.

The filmic sense.   In other words, the screen-play writer can, if he has a filmic sense, give a feeling of life to what are ostensibly dead images on the screen, regardless of the fact that they are apparently in motion. At the same time, he should be able to convey the impression that this life is artistically created and so has an esthetic entity of its own.

The Russian director Kuleshov proved that he could photograph a series of entirely disconnected shots and, after assembling them, present a completely different and entirely whole scene. In the order of assembling, he spliced together shots of:

1. A young man walking from left to right
2. A young woman walking from right to left
3. Both meeting and shaking hands, as the man points to something off scene
4. An immense white building fronted with a broad flight of steps
5. The young man and woman ascending the steps

Regardless of the fact that each of these shots was photographed in a different place and at different times, when they were assembled the over-all impression was that the action was continuous in time and spatially at the same locale.

The Russians have tried many experiments of this sort, building up scenes out of disconnected shots. At one time they assembled shots of the hands, feet, eyes, and heads of a number of different women and, after assembling them, gave the impression that they were all cut-in shots of one woman. At another time, they took some quiet close-ups of an actor and intercut them with three different kinds of cutaway shots:

1. A shot of a bowl of soup the actor was supposed to be looking down at

2. A shot of a woman lying dead in a coffin

3. A shot of a little girl playing with a Teddy bear

Although the reaction close-up shots of the man were all the same, the audience reaction to each of the different cutaways was such that they associated their own responses with those of the actor.

The Russians also tried an interesting experiment in juggling varying shots. When the following three shots were assembled in 1, 2, 3 order,

1. shot of a man smiling,

2. shot of a revolver pointing,

3. and a shot of the same man looking frightened,

the effect was that of having the man frightened by someone holding a gun and ready to shoot. But when the sequence was juggled, so that the order of shots was 3, 2, 1, he was changed from a coward into a brave man!

Build dramatically. Thus, it can be seen that a picture can be endowed with predetermined meaning and with the smooth flow of continuity if each shot is built up dramatically in the scene, if each scene is built up dramatically in the sequence, and if each sequence is built up dramatically in the entire picture.

In the shot, this building of dramatic effect is created by character action and dialogue, as they are presented by an appropriate use of camera distance, angle, and movement. These separate elements have been discussed in their various sections.

In building the shots within the scene, however, it is essential to be conversant with certain other techniques. These facts must be remembered first:

1. If the story is to move forward, each shot and scene should add to the forward movement.

2. As the story progresses, every situation and event must be presented more interestingly and more attractively.

3. The characters of the people in the story must grow—either for better or for worse; but some growth must be evident to carry forward an integrated sense of movement which will tie in with the flow of filmic continuity.

4. The emotions of all the people involved must grow in intensity, so that the decisions they are forced to make will, in themselves, become more important to themselves and hence to the story.

Use cause and effect. To accomplish these necessary adjuncts to filmic movement, an important physical law must be applied: the law of *cause and effect.* First, the *cause* of the situation must be presented, to be followed shortly afterward by the *effect* it produces.

In the picture *Return of Rusty,* for instance, the little refugee boy, Loddy, is still devil-ridden with his memories of the war. In order to dramatize this, the writers prepared a scene as follows:

INT.—LIVING ROOM—DAY

FULL SHOT of room as Loddy paces the floor distractedly, on the *qui vive.*

EXT.—STREET—DAY

LONG SHOT on newsboy pedaling his bicycle up the street.

INT.—LIVING ROOM

MED. SHOT on Loddy as he seats himself at piano and disinterestedly plays one-finger, obviously at a breaking point.

EXT.—STREET—DAY

MED. LONG SHOT on newsboy pedaling up the street. He stops at house next door to Loddy's house and throws a folded newspaper, which lands with a thud on the porch.

INT.—LIVING ROOM—DAY

CLOSE SHOT on Loddy as he stops playing and listens intently to the sound of newspaper thud o.s. (off scene), in distance. Suddenly the sound of the newspaper thud is heard close up. Loddy's eyes widen. Then his head falls to the piano keys with a discordant bang. He starts to cry and, slowly, his body sags as he crawls under the piano and covers his head with his arms, as though trying to protect himself from an imagined missile.

From this it can be seen that cause and effect were taken into consideration in building the scene to pay off with the boy's terror. It should be observed that it was not necessary to show again the newsboy plopping the newspaper on the porch outside of Loddy's living room, because that action had already been established in the previous shot. Then, by suggestion, and by using only the *sound* of the newspaper's thud off scene, the action was suggested instead of being repeated, the suggestion heightening the action by indirection rather than by actual action.

Build with details.   In the same way, and for the same purpose of building the shots within the scene for the most dramatic impact, scenes should be built up with significant details.

A catastrophe scene, for instance, could be built up so as to develop it to its fullest interest and understanding and to its peak of dramatic intensity. This is done with cut-ins and cutaways; with reaction shots of spectators in close-up; with pan shots of whatever moving vehicles would be racing to the scene; with shots of suffering; with action shots of valiant rescues; and with shots of the smoke and flames, or of the flooding waters, or of whatever the catastrophe may be.

Remember this—first try to build interest and understanding for the audience. Then go into the main line of the story. In Carol Reed's picture *The Third Man,* in order to build to the startling shock of showing the porter being carted out dead to a sidewalk ambulance—and also to reveal this fact slowly to Cotten and his girl friend, who are approaching the scene—Reed inserted a series of shots of various people looking anxiously out of high windows at what is going on in the street below, together with shots of other people running out of doors and houses. So that when the pair finally come up to the scene of the ambulance, the audience interest and curiosity have been so piqued that the revelation of the fact that the porter is dead comes with an immense dramatic impact.

Build-up between scenes and between sequences is achieved by means of suitable transition devices. Only with an effective build-up is it possible to present a picture that follows the most important dictum of motion-picture rite—*make it move!*

Building the components

You may have observed a peculiar repetition occurring throughout the preceding material—an insistence on "flowing continuity" and on "making certain that a shot flows smoothly out of the previous shot and into the succeeding shot." You will note them even more frequently in the following material.

Build for continuity.   The repetitions were done purposely. For it is only with this smooth-flowing, moving quality that motion pictures can achieve stature, and it is because of a lack of it that they become abysmal failures.

This building of shots, scenes, and sequences is what contributes to make up the motion-picture shooting script. In Europe—and especially in Russia—this process of assemblage is called "montage."

The European conception of montage sees its techniques as being applied not to an individual sequence, as is done in Hollywood, but to the picture as a whole. It recognizes the fact that uninspired, orthodox film editing, as performed in most American pictures, is vacuously mechanical. It also believes that the application of true montage principles to film editing—and to screen-play writing, if much of the editing is suggested in the screen play by the writer—requires creative filmic imagination.

Therefore an attempt will be made here to apply the methods of European montage to the creation of a shooting screen play, so that a finished picture, closer to the original concepts of the screen-play writer, will result.

The European principles of montage are also applied in Hollywood, but under varying classifications, and with considerably varying results. The basic reason for the varying results is to be found in the different audiences. But the fact remains that European audiences attend and appreciate American films, while many European films—and especially in the past few years—have become quite popular with American audiences.

Organize for flow.   In writing the shooting screen play, and to make use of all the components already discussed, it is necessary to organize the filmic material so that it flows smoothly and continuously and results in a picture that is unified, coherent, and entertaining.

Organize for scene length.   It is necessary that this organization be done, not only from shot to shot, but from scene to scene and from sequence to sequence. In this organization, certain adjustments must be made to achieve maximum results. Attention must be paid to the length of the shot, the scene, and the sequence so that the tempo required by the story line will be captured successfully.

Organize for rhythm.   Not only must the length of the shots and scenes and sequences be considered by the screen writer but, in addition, he must arrange them so that the action flows rhythmically —and not in a dull, deadly straight line—within the shot, within the scene, and within the sequence.

Organize for interrelationships.   Although a motion picture consists of short, separate bits of film spliced together, there must be a definite relationship with the other bits written into each bit. In other words, each shot within a scene must conform to certain building principles, and each scene within a sequence must conform to the same principles, so that each sequence within the picture as a whole will present a conglomerate mass effect of the same basic building principles.

What are these basic principles?

1. The fact that *motion* is the prime consideration in a motion picture demands that there be a continuous *sequence* of filmic images moving in orderly progression from beginning to end, in a coherent, unified flow.

2. Although this continuous flow should connote and depict action, it is not necessary that actual physical motion from place to place be shown to achieve it. The effect of motion can be obtained by contrast—by, for instance, *opposing* one quality to another quality so that, by opposing, a sense of action is suggested rather than effected.

3. In the same way, motion can be implied, when not actually depicted, simply by *repeating* certain qualities, the sense of action resulting from the mere repetition of those qualities.

Image size

Progression in image size.   The primary rule of cinematic photography is to shoot all scenes from the long, medium, and close distances. This is to allow the film editor enough cinematic material with which to splice the picture together, by using the first basic principle of orderly progression.

The same progression can be obtained by reversing the order as is often necessary—in going from close through medium to long shot.

Opposition in image size.   When the latter series is followed by, or follows, a series of the former, the second principle—contrast—can be achieved. Or, by opposing a close shot and a succeeding long shot, or the reverse, the same effect of opposition will result.

Repetition of image size.   The third principle—repetition of shots —can be achieved by indicating a series of close-ups or medium shots. When such a series is put in juxtaposition to a contrasting series—as a close-up series followed immediately by a series of long shots—then opposition results and the second principle is achieved.

Image angle

Progression in image angle.   These same principles can be followed in regard to the other aspects of film making. The angles, for example, can be varied to follow the three principles. They can achieve sequential continuity by using a series of angles, each greater than the other, or a series each smaller than the other. Low, front, and side angles—or in reverse order—can make up another series of angles.

Opposition in image angle.   The second principle of contrast results from following a radically low-angle shot with a radically high-angle shot, or vice versa. Contrast can also be achieved by following a shot photographed from one side, by another photographed from a change of as much as 180 degrees in angle.

Repetition in image angle.   Although practice insists that the angle be changed in each successive shot, a change in camera distance permits the use of similar angles to achieve the repetitive principle.

The same three principles should be applied to camera move-

ment, so that the tempo of the individual shots can be integrated
into the over-all tempo of the picture.

Camera movement

In addition, the *direction* of camera movement should receive similar montage considerations.

Progression in camera movement. Sequential continuity can be
obtained by having successive shots contain action that moves from
right to left, or vice versa. Or the actions can be tilted up on successive shots, or tilted down. Successive camera pans, or trucking
shots, should also be made in the same direction to effect the desired
result.

Opposition in camera movement. The principle of contrast should
be applied in the direction of camera movement by indicating that
successive shots be reversed. A pan or trucking shot from right to
left, for example, can be followed by a pan or trucking shot from
left to right. A tilt-up can be followed by a tilt-down.

Repetition in camera movement. The repetitive principle would
require that the direction of a pan, a trucking shot, or a tilt be
repeated in successive shots.

This principle is used quite often in opticals, when a series of
numerals indicating year dates zooms in from a dot to large size to
suggest a lapse of time.

Tempo

The tempo of a shot can also be regulated by these three principles.
This requires that the screen writer time his action and dialogue
so as to be able to estimate correctly the approximate film footage
that will be required to cover them. A good stop watch, therefore,

can become part of the screen-play writer's equipment, especially one that indicates the film footage together with the elapsed time.

Progressive tempo. Sequential progression can then be attained by writing in a series of successive shots that are of similar length—for example, a series of three or four shots, each of which runs about six feet long.

Opposing tempo. Contrast, obviously, can result from writing in a series of shots that vary considerably in length—the first shot of two feet, followed by one of six feet, which is followed by one of three feet, and then winding up the scene with a shot running thirty or forty feet.

Repetitive tempo. Repetition, of course, would simply require repeating the length of the shots—as a series of two-foot exterior close-ups (a favorite of the Russian Eisenstein, by the way).

Build with a purpose. This fact, though, must be emphasized: *These principles must be applied not arbitrarily, but methodically.*

A series of slow pans, for example, should not be indicated only because a pattern of sequential progression is desired, but primarily because it is necessary to induce a suspenseful mood.

In the same way, the organization of shot lengths to obtain results from the application of the repetitive principle should not be done solely to achieve these results. The primary reason for using a series of short-length close-ups, for instance, would be to stimulate a sense of excitement; the reason for using a series of long-length long shots would be, primarily, to suggest a sense of relaxation.

All the elements of each shot must be so organized that the same three principles can be applied to the shots within a scene, and the scenes within a sequence, so that the sequences themselves can be organized, using the same three basic principles.

Build for rhythm. The sum total of this organization would result in a pattern of rhythm that would be most felicitous to the finished picture. It would be most felicitous because, contrary to the manner in which most screen plays are written, directed, and produced, the desired rhythm would have been deliberately and consciously written into the screen play.

Tempo and rhythm

There has been a great deal of loose talk thrown around about the factors of tempo and rhythm. Both are subjects of an evanescent nature, and have never been postulated, clarified, or standardized. More often than not, the terms are erroneously used interchangeably. Like the word "showmanship," which theatrical entrepreneurs love to bandy about, "tempo" and "rhythm" are resorted to when the speaker intends to be as vague as possible, to avoid having his idea backfire on him. If he says, "There are fifty frames in every foot of film," his ignorance can be thrown into his face simply by referring to any standard book on the subject. But he can take refuge in generalization by saying, "It's the tempo of that scene I don't like," and rest assured that nobody can contradict him.

Tempo is one thing, as has been shown. Rhythm is still another. Both are indispensable to the fashioning of a screen play and to the eventual making of the resultant picture.

Tempo is timing. Tempo is—as its accepted meaning should indicate—timing. It is governed by the length of time—and hence the number of frames or feet—a shot, a scene, and a sequence should require in order to present an idea or mood as well as possible.

Certain mood effects can be achieved by certain timing factors. The illusion of excitement in short-time shots is enhanced, naturally, by short sections of film, by quick camera movements, by character movement, by short spurts of dialogue and the like.

Conversely, a sense of calm can be obtained with longer-length shots, with static or slow camera movements, and so on.

If the tempi in all the shots are so integrated that the combined tempi can, in turn, be integrated within the sequence, and so that the combined tempi of the sequences can be integrated into a complete picture, the over-all tempo of the picture can be regulated so that what finally emerges is exactly what the screen writer put into the screen play, and what he intended to produce.

Rhythm is flow. Rhythm, on the other hand, is a modulated flow of filmic and sound patterns that results from following certain basic principles.

This rhythm can be made intrinsic to the screen play by the writer—by judiciously manipulating the shots, the angles, the camera movement, the character movement, and the length within the individual shots to conform with the three principles of progression, contrast, and repetition. At the same time, if the scenes within the sequence, and the sequences within the picture, are similarly treated to follow the three principles, the result should be a screen play that will have that elusive quality of rhythm.

Practically all the factors involved in the use of montage now fall within the province of the director and the film editor. This is so, not because they are natural to those offices, but because the screen-play writer has been universally considered as an inoffensive and necessary contributor to the making of motion pictures. As a result, his work has been shorn of many creative details that should ordinarily have come within his province, but which have been relegated to the director and the film editor.

There is no reason why the screen-play writer cannot, and should not, regain these creative duties. Certainly his creative background should furnish him with the necessary esthetic wherewithal. That he can perform these duties has been amply demonstrated by the success of those pictures that were made by writer-directors. But even if the writer is unable to direct his own pictures, he can make certain that his creative ideas are followed by the director and the film cutter.

Write in detail. Dialogue, for instance, can be written so that it would be impossible to shoot it in any way other than the one indicated in the screen play. In the same way, camera angles, camera movement, and character action can be dictated by the writer so that the director will be forced to shoot them in the manner indicated in the script. The length of the individual shot, which has never been considered within the screen-play writer's domain, has always been, first the director's job, and then the film editor's. But the screen-play writer, as the prime mover, can dictate. He can, simply by writing in complete detail the necessary action, and by writing in detail all dialogue and all character reactions and directions. He can dictate by timing all the action and the dialogue, with a stop watch, to make certain that the length of the finished shot will conform with as little variation as possible to the length he feels necessary to the shot. This, in turn, he knows should conform to the inner patterns of pacing, timing, and rhythm that he has tried to work into the shots within the scene, the scenes within the sequence, and the sequences within the finished picture.

There is no reason why this cannot be accomplished by the screen-play writer. It demands knowledge, experience, and the know-how of filmic techniques. But these can all be learned. And if to this knowledge are added the ingredients of esthetic discernment and artistic integrity, the quality of the finished picture will be enhanced tremendously.

Directors often find themselves in a similar predicament. For any number of reasons, they may discover that they are directing a picture in which their ideas are at odds with those of the writer, the producer, or the film editor. In such cases, the director photographs his shots so that they can be cut in only one way—his way. One method at his disposal is to shoot the individual shots with little or insufficient overlap, in picture or in sound. Without overlaps—which are the tag ends and beginnings of each shot, both in picture and in sound, that can be matched perfectly to continuing action or sound in a preceding or succeeding shot—the film cutter is forced to splice the bits of film in the order in which the director originally shot them, without being able to intercut from long shots to closer shots in the way and at the time he, the film editor, feels necessary. By neglecting to shoot cutaways, the director makes certain that his long-running shots will run as long as he deems necessary. These methods of assuring themselves of having their finished pictures cut in their own way are termed by directors "cutting in the can." They practice them consistently.

There is nothing to prevent the screen-play writer from "directing and cutting in the script." To yield more and more to producing only the bare bones of a picture, with a master-scene screen play, is tantamount, for the screen-play writer, to relinquishing his inalienable esthetic rights. If he is to fulfill all the potentialities of his creativity, he must add the sinews and flesh and surface patinas, so that the finished product is his as he originally created it.

Only in this way can the screen-play writer negate the destructive influence of "too many cooks," now rife in the motion-picture industry. Only in this way can the screen-play writer assert his individuality, assure himself of proper delineation of his work, establish himself firmly in a manner which truly befits him and his craft.

Dialogue writing

As with all the other elements that go into the making of a motion picture screen play, motion-picture dialogue must move. If it pauses to digress, even a trifle, it stops the all-important flow of continuity so vital to the successful unreeling of a motion picture.

Continuity with dialogue.   Motion-picture dialogue must also possess, to an unusual degree, the important filmic quality of continuity. It must flow continuously from line to line, from speech to speech. Fortunately the continuity is aided, in the motion picture, by visual movement, character movement, and film cutting. The screen-play writer must always be prepared to take advantage of these aids. What is more important, he must never err in his dialogue, so as to negate the movement these aids furnish.

Visual more important than verbal.   This important fact must always be kept in mind: *The visual must always take precedence over the verbal.*

The most common error in a beginner's screen play is usually to be found in his resorting to dialogue to give essential facts, when the same facts could have been given visually, and thus more graphically. One of the chief purposes of film dialogue is to give only those facts that cannot be portrayed by action.

For example, it would not be necessary to have one of the characters ask of another, "Are you hurt?" when it would be possible to show, by means of a close-up on a bruise, or of blood, that such was the case.

The screen-play writer should always keep in mind August Thomas' dictum about dialogue: "A line must advance the story, develop character, or get a laugh."

Film dialogue can be used to establish the facts of the past in order to bring the audience up to date.

Film dialogue can be used to describe locale.

It can also tell of the movements of various characters not in the scene.

And at the same time, it can present the theme of the story.

Film dialogue also possesses the important function of characterizing the people in the story. For speech is revelatory. In one line, it can furnish a character's education, social status, occupation, country or state of origin, temperament, and emotional condition.

Education. The diction to be used for each character must vary with each character. One of the most difficult tasks of the screen-play writer is to be able to divorce his own tricks of diction from those of the character whose speech he is setting down. That done, he must write their speeches so that his ditchdigger uses only those words that would be within his educational scope, while the college professor would do likewise.

Occupation. Also, the speech must be made identifiable with the character's chief occupation. Because the garage mechanic, for example, would be continually working with things mechanical, and would be talking largely with people in his own occupation, his speech would be larded with the jargon of his trade. Even his similes would stem from it. He would say, for instance, "That guy's as stubborn as a frozen wing nut!"

Care must be taken, though, to make certain that his allusion will be understood by an audience that is not generally conversant with automotive speech. Introduction of the word "stubborn" in the above example would give the uncomprehending a clue to the otherwise foreign simile.

Care should also be taken not to inject too many strange and technical expressions into the speech. One or two, in the character's opening lines, to establish his occupation, and a few following and interspersed through his succeeding lines are sufficient. The balance of his similes could be the usual clichés, to be found in the speech of all people. Source material for various occupations can be found in a good slang dictionary.

Emotion. All speech is affected by the character's emotional condition. When composed, he speaks normally; when angry, he speaks quickly, in sharp, short, jerky sentences; when happy, he speaks rapidly; when sad, he speaks slowly and hesitantly.

Tempo. A person's innate character is mirrored in the tempo of his speech. The stubborn bite off each word with clipped determination; the meek meander along with faltering "uh's" and "ah's" and interjected "ands"; the pedantic use long-winded sentences; the strong-willed speak with determination; the aged speak slowly, contemplatively; the young gush out their thoughts like a spring freshet; poetic folk use high-flown tropes; the dull and unimaginative resort continually to clichés.

Verbal clichés

The use of clichés in a screen play can make for excellent characterization. But at the same time, they can be harmful, when used indiscriminately.

Avoid the bon mot. For most of us speak, as well as write, in verbal clichés—even those who decry the cliché in writing. Talking is not writing. Conversation can be creative, but only for a limited few. The art of the brilliant conversational bon mot is not commonly practiced. And one is led to suspect that even in those who are accredited with its mastery the supposedly freshly concocted verbal tidbit was actually pretty well predigested before it was sprung on the listener, as was the case with Oscar Wilde's brilliant quips.

You have only to eavesdrop on the conversation of the people around you—sophisticates included—to realize that the average person does not talk in original, brilliant aphorisms, smart wisecracks, or topical jokes. Instead, he confines his sparkling repartee to outlandish puns and, more often, to hoary clichés. It sometimes requires hours and hours of labored writing for a writer to evolve one tag-gag for a character. How, then, can it be expected of an average person—even one who has a flair for humor—to drip quips at the flip of a lip?

Use clichés to characterize. At the same time, people do not use a continual procession of clichés in their speech. Some characters, perhaps, may be developed who are addicted to them, strictly for comedy effect. Frank Sullivan's "The Cliché Expert" in the *New Yorker* is a perfect example of the fun to be had at the expense of a cliché addict. But even here, it would be out of place for a screen writer to use a consistent stream of clichés, as does Mr. Sullivan's cliché expert, despite the fact that some people may talk almost exclusively in clichés. He must only lightly season his character's speech with clichés or lose the credibility of the character in an indigestible welter of words.

Gags choke up character. Which brings up the matter of the overly gagged-up dialogue used currently in screen writing for almost every type of picture, from the brittle, social comedy (where much of it can be used legitimately), through the Western (where adaptations of old saws and homilies may, perhaps, be suitable), to the small-town, small-boy story (where, certainly, as little as possible of the smart gag would be warranted).

It is one thing to entertain an audience with jokes—and lose character credibility—but an entirely different matter to inject an occasional quip into the dialogue without endangering the character's status as a living, breathing entity.

One of the most prevalent faults in screen writing is to be found in the lack of characterization. This is so especially in the gagged-up script. Characters in these become robots, lacking the individuality necessary to real people, because all are pallid reflections of the writer's own psyche—a condition brought about by the uncontrolled and often superfluous spreading of the gag and the gagged cliché.

Clichés for comedy. The gagged verbal cliché is a device that may be used for comedy effect—but again, sparingly. Here the cliché is used as a hook from which the gag is hung. Quotation clichés are ideal for this purpose. "The early worm catches the fish," used to hurry a lagging character to a fishing trip, or "a rat in burro's clothing, huh!" used when a supposed rat in a basement turns out to be a burro. These are possible—if somewhat corny—twists to clichéd quotations. But used unsparingly in a script, they would become completely gratuitous.

The conclusions, then, regarding the use of verbal clichés are: they can be used, but not overdone, to create effects. They can, for instance, be inserted to build a humorous character who is addicted to them; to add naturalness to the dialogue of ordinary folk; or to serve as springboards for gags, witty repartee, and topical patter. But the writer must always keep in mind that, at best, clichés are crutches, jaded short cuts. He must compromise, use moderation, resort to clichés only for rounding out character, but with the selectivity necessary to the creative craftsman in all the graphic arts.

Dialects

Another potent method of rounding out character is with the use of dialects. Until recently, the screen-play writer was only someone who happened to be around to string together a few choice words into a script. But his emergence as an absolutely essential starting point for a picture and his belated acceptance as a required entity have given him the importance he justly deserves. Yet, if he neglects his duty as a recorder of accurate speech—speech that is as much a part of the character portrayal as diction, physical defects, etc.—the writer neglects his duty as a writer.

For dialect speech is an important adjunct to character delineation. It is more than a half-baked medium for slapstick comedy. As Garson Kanin has put it, "There is tenderness and beauty and pathos in the attempts of newcomers to express themselves in our tongue." Authentic dialect speech can spot a character instantly, unequivocally, in the milieu from which he stems. It can clothe an otherwise uninteresting character with a distinctive and colorful personality. It can give three-dimensional qualities to what would ordinarily be a paper-flat character conception. It is as revelatory as make-up, as picturesque as costume, as characteristic as gestures, as identifiable as physical disabilities, and as dramatically effective as facial expressions. Without a writer to give him the words, the actor is a gesturing, posturing mute. His art depends on what the writer tells him he should say. And if the words are deficient in character identification, then the actor's performance suffers because of it, the character he portrays does not achieve its inherent promise, and the entire dramatic structure is irrevocably weakened.

To just what extent does the average screen writer furnish the

actor with dialect lines? A great many scripts solve the dialect problem simply by ignoring it. No indication is given by the writer, who
should know as much of the manner of speech as its content. The
result is a characterization either entirely lacking in identifying
personality or only barely suggesting it because of the limitations of
an actor working with sufficient knowledge but inadequate tools.

In one way it is quite understandable why the writer studiously
avoids the use of dialects. Its study is specialized. It calls for an
immense amount of work, of research, of classification, and of adaptation. But because it is a puissant though neglected writing tool,
its study should be cultivated assiduously. In fact, each dialect is
a study in itself, for each dialect has its unique variants from the
"standard" form of speech.

That is why, in a limited section such as this must be, it would
be impossible to give a complete course of study in dialects for
screen-play writing. The subject is too vast, the available material
far too extensive, to be presented in capsule form. But it is possible
to give directions and suggestions that may help the interested
writer so that in time he can become proficient in the correct use of
authentic dialect speech.

The only comprehensive books to be found on the subject are
Manual of Foreign Dialects and *Manual of American Dialects.**
They should furnish the writer with an excellent guide for the use
of foreign and American dialects.

For treatment of the speech variants between American English
and British English, especially on the subject of idioms, Mencken's
The American Language is highly recommended. But it is not
enough merely to choose isolated words from Mencken's lists and
imagine you can pop them into an Englishman's mouth and expect
him to sound off like Lord Cholmondeley (pronounced Chumley)
or 'Arry 'Awkins. Many English writers have done just this in supplying supposed American idioms for their American characters,
with disastrous results and many an English writer has writhed at
an American writer's laughable admixtures of supposed British idioms and expressions with bald-faced Americanisms.

The use of only a minimum amount of dialect would be a good
working compromise. The dropped "h" in cockney, the "d" and "t"
substitutes for "th" in German, "y" substitute for "j" in Swedish,

* Written by Lewis and Marguerite Herman and published by Prentice-Hall.

the aspirate "uh" ending to final consonants (correctly used) in Italian, the dropped final, glottal-stopped "t" in Scottish—these are a few that may be used in foreign dialects. In American dialects, the dropped final "r" in Southern, Eastern, and Negro speech is valid, together with the dropped "g" in the "ing" ending words, as in "fightin'" and "doin'." An occasional dropped "l," as in "he'p" in the Southern dialect, together with a few other such helpful hints to the actor, can be used provided they do not detract from the understanding of the word's meaning. But dialect stress should be made on the use of localisms and idiomatic expressions.

There is an invaluable source of American idioms in the files of the magazines *American Speech* and *Dialect Notes*. They contain classified lists of idiomatic expressions, region by region, together with, in many instances, treatises on the manner of pronunciation. A course of study devoted to a careful, annotated survey of these magazines could be invaluable to the writer who is serious enough about his craft to strive for perfection.

But most important of all, the writer must develop, in addition to his traditional photographic eye, a dictographic ear. He must listen carefully to all foreign-speaking people and to all American-dialect speaking individuals, and record their oddities of expression. His notebook should have sections devoted to speech as well as costume, to local Americanisms as well as characteristic mannerisms. He must realize that, in speech, he has a powerful and effective means of delineating articulate mankind.

Foreign language dialogue

This discussion of the use of dialects in dialogue brings up another important speech problem. Since the motion picture found its tongue, the screen writer has been plagued with the ever recurrent problem: How should the speech of foreign-language speaking characters be treated for the most esthetically satisfying results? How, for example, should two Parisian gendarmes be made to converse—in their native French tongue, in a French-English dialect, or in straight English?

This problem has been made particularly urgent today, because of the emergence of a type of picture using a deliberately internationally slanted theme, with a story line enacted by players of mixed national stocks, who speak a variety of languages. Recent examples of this sort of picture include *The Search, Four in a Jeep, The Last Chance* and *Marie-Louise*. Earlier films in this genre were *Grand Illusion, Friendship, No Man's Land,* and *Jewels of the Crown*. All are European films.

In *The Last Chance,* more than eleven separate languages and dialects were spoken, including straight British, British with a Scottish accent, American, Italian, German (various dialects), Swiss, Yiddish, French, and Serbian.

Faced with such multilingual characters and beleaguered by the categorical imperatives of the average Hollywood producer, the average Hollywood writer would have thrown out individual characterization for the easier-to-write, easier-to-sell straight English dialogue. But the Swiss producers and screen writers of *The Last Chance* were more courageous than their Hollywood brethren. They chose the more difficult way. And the result was a better picture than could have been produced in Hollywood.

For it cannot be argued that the picture was not artistically enhanced by the fact that its characters were made real through the medium of real speech. No phony, labored dialects marred the characterizations. There was no stretching of audience credulity, by forcing English words from obviously unEnglish tongues. The Frenchmen looked like Frenchmen, acted like Frenchmen, reacted like Frenchmen and, what was most important, talked like Frenchmen. And the same could be said of all the other national characters. They were truly representative of their milieus.

But at the same time, *The Last Chance*—and the other international pictures—suffered because of their reliance on multilingual speech. They were hampered from achieving maximum success because of a basic shortcoming—few people in any audience are sufficiently conversant with all the languages used in the pictures. So subtitles translating the foreign dialogue were resorted to.

At best, this method of conveying meaning is an inadequate makeshift. It distracts the audience's visual attention from the action to the flow of a disconcerting, badly printed, ludicrously translated stream of words. Of necessity, much of the action is lost, even in momentary chunks, while the visual attention is being diverted from the actors to the subtitles. Also, the painfully written and rewritten lines, in their original language, would be completely ignored by the subtitle translator, who is forced to compress a long speech into just enough letters to fit into an exactly spaced subtitle segment. Lou Holtz's story of the fellow who translated a character's prolix spate of foreign verbiage into a monosyllabic English, "No," may be apocryphal, but its counterpart can be viewed time and again in many subtitled foreign films. What is even worse, entire speeches are often completely ignored because of the whims of a lazy translator or the immutability of censorship, so that long stretches of film flicker by unmeaningly.

Obviously, then, the printed subtitle is out of the question if perfection is to be achieved, if the inherent virtue of the finished picture is to be realized. Attempts have been made at "lip syncing" (dubbing in actual voices) using translated versions of the foreign speech. This seems to be the general practice for Hollywood pictures distributed in foreign countries.

This method, too, is patently unsatisfactory. A character written around the unique and established vocal antics of an actor such as, say, Jack Oakie, could hardly be projected by the dubbed voice of the so-so, but French, Henri Duval. The words would be there, perhaps, but the characterization would remain with Oakie in Hollywood.

Again, lip synchronization is a virtual impossibility because of the divergent movements of the lips which, let us say, utter an English vowel sound while being shaped for an Italian lip consonant. Such subterfuges are futile because they militate against the success of matching the vocal sounds with the lip movements, which has accounted for the perfection of the talking picture. It was the lack of synchronization that prevented the talking picture from emerging long before it actually did, and it was only after a method was devised that made for perfect synchronization that the talking picture arrived. "Out-of-sync" talking pictures defeat the happy amalgam of sight and sound—they stutter.

How then can this language barrier be overcome? How is it possible to retain the unquestioned virtues of foreign speech and still convey sufficient meaning to a nonunderstanding audience without detracting from the picture's visual message and without emasculating the screen writer's labors?

It is with human actions and reactions that the screen writer can partially solve the vexing problem of foreign speech. The clue to the former can be found in Shakespeare's *Hamlet* in his injunction to the players: "Suit the action to the word—the word to the action."

For it is possible to write dialogue so that, although the words may be gibberish to the audience, the accompanying actions of the actor may present a revealing clue to the content of the words. Thus, if the gist of the character's words is that he is stifling because of the heat in the room, if his "business" is such that he unloosens his collar, indicates by his expressions that he is stifling, and then goes to the window and throws it wide open, then the meaning of his foreign speech should become obvious even to the most undiscerning. This example, of course, is an oversimplification. But if such business is written in by the screen writer it can aid considerably in elucidating foreign speech.

Further speech clarification may be gained in the written-in business, especially that of a character's reactions. This method can be even more revelatory than the actions themselves. The content of a foreign-language speech can be easily deduced from the reaction to it of another character. Told that he should make certain that a trunk can go through a doorway, a German porter can demonstrate the content of the German lines simply by going through the motions of measuring the width of the doorway with his hands and then measuring the width of the trunk in similar fashion. A simple nod of the head to indicate the job can be done, and the foreign speech becomes crystal clear.

More emphasis should be put on the use of pantomime in the actions of characters who use foreign speech. Many scripts are too wordy because pantomime is seldom indicated by the writer. Before talking pictures arrived, pantomime was a prime requisite in every script. Murnau's *Last Laugh* was presented without a single title card, both relying entirely on pantomime. Chaplin reached his zenith in acting strictly with pantomime and his sound pictures have not added a whit to his stature. Pantomime is acting on an international status. It can be understood by the Hottentot, the Ainu, and the supposedly more civilized Man of the Western World.

It can convey more emotion than a word. It could obviate the language lack were more of it to be written into a foreign-language script.

But the most effective means of making the foreign language intelligible lies in the actual writing of the dialogue itself; which is where the role of the special writer must emerge. With only a bare, working knowledge of the foreign language to be used, he can inject certain words into the foreign speech that could be easily understood by most people.

The English word "chocolate," for example, has a similar-sounding counterpart in almost every European language.

This does not mean that the writer should insert the word "chocolate" into a script simply because it has international understanding. It is used here only as an example of thousands of other words with similar universal pronunciation, words such as: "hotel," "impossible," "information," "monument," "minute," "moment," "national," "permission," "photograph," "police," "profession," "restaurant," "secretary," "service," "study," "telegram," "telephone," "theater," "tobacco," and "uniform." The word "address" can be found in a recognizable form in languages ranging from French (*l'addresse*) through Dutch (*het adres*) to the Turkish (*adres*).

Also, there are words common to many languages which, although they may not be similar in spelling, still retain similar meanings, as with the exclamation "Stop!" In French, the word generally used is *halte*, which is similar enough to the English word "halt" for anyone conversant with the English language to understand. And the French verb *stopper* makes the English "stop" understandable to a Frenchman. Other languages use the following words: *alto* (Spanish) ; *halt* (German) ; *stoppen* (Dutch) ; *stopp* (Swedish) ; *stop* (Danish) ; *stopp* (Norwegian); *stok* (Lithuanian) and *haltu* (Esperanto) .

This knowledge can be used so that, instead of writing a character's foreign language line to read "Where does he live?", in which the verb "live" has few recognizable counterparts, the line would be changed to "What's his address?" Thus, despite the fact that most of the audience would be ignorant of the foreign words "What's his," all would be aware of the word "address" and, from it, understand the implication of the entire line.

These are a few of the methods with which the language problem in screen-play writing can be overcome. Others may suggest themselves to many. With them, and with industry, research, and increased knowledge, there is no reason why, in the future, the foreign-language speaking characters in scripts should not be endowed with naturalness and realism, through the gift of tongues.

The dialogue hook

Suppose now, we get into the more practical aspects of dialogue writing, with the purpose of presenting a script that will result in a smooth-flowing picture.

Pictorial continuity can be aided considerably by a smooth flow in dialogue continuity. It can also be interfered with if continuity is lacking in the dialogue.

The basic principle, of course, is to make certain that there is a continuous progression of cumulative ideas that make up the story itself, of which the dialogue is only a part. This should take care of dialogue continuity, and of transitions between shots, between scenes, and between sequences.

But there is to be considered, also, the important element of connective continuity between lines in the shot. For individual speeches can be written so that they will be tied together in a smooth, continuous flow of verbal movement.

The device for achieving this smooth flow is the "dialogue hook." Actually, it is simply a method that uses the closing words of a line of dialogue as a hook, to connect with the opening words of the succeeding line of dialogue from another character.

Single word repetition.   The repetition of a single word can be used to hook into a previous speech, as in:

DAN

Well—I gotta go now.
Good-by, Dora.

DORA

Good-by?

DAN
Yes. There's no sense for us to kick
each other around like this.

DORA
What about *love?*

DAN
What *about* love?

Line repetition.   In the foregoing example, still another type of
hook can be seen in action—the repeated entire speech, but with a
different word emphasized, to indicate a difference in meaning.

At the same time, it illustrates another kind of dialogue hook—
the question that is answered with another question, without including a reply to the original question.

The repeated words need not come at the end of a line. They
can be repeated in the body of the speech, as in this example:

HANK
Maybe he's come to ask for help.

VINNY
He's come to ask for *something.* We
can be sure of that.

Let us see how the dialogue hook operates in practice, with repetition first.

FRANK
What's all this about?

TONY
About you, Frank.

Notice that, in the first speech, the closing word was "about." Notice also that in the succeeding speech, the word "about" was repeated as the initial word, causing it to be tied in with the preceding
line of speech.

Another example uses progression to tie together a series of speeches.

> TONY
> We can take in the Riviera, Sue, and ...

> SUE
> (interrupting)
> And Cannes, and Paris and ...

> TONY
> (interrupting)
> The whole works, yes!

The order of progression, in the above example, obviously carries the ear from speech to speech, so that the effect is one of continuation.

Still another example:

> CY
> He must be a tough guy!

> STU
> Yeah! a very tough guy!

The simplest, most often-used example can be found in the question and answer form.

> HAYNES
> Why did you do it?

> STRINE
> I don't know why—I just did it,
> that's all.

A question naturally calls for an answer. Therefore, the audience's ears have been conditioned to expect one and, in almost a reflex action, subconsciously move forward with the question, and without stopping to wait for the answer, flow into its comprehension.

When the question is followed by another question which calls for still another answer, the effect is that of pyramiding the hook device, as in:

> BESS
> Are you really upset about me?

> KARL
> No! why should I be?

> BESS
> Well—I just thought you would—a
> little, at least.

An ideal place to use the dialogue hook can come with groping, unfinished speech, as in:

> HELENE
> (groping)
> It's hard to explain, mother, it's . . .
> well . . .

> MOTHER
> (with a smile)
> The measles?

> HELENE
> (still groping)
> Oh, no, mother! It's . . . oh . . .

> MOTHER
> It's love, dear. I know all the symptoms.

A line of speech that is in agreement, or in disagreement, with a preceding line, will serve ideally as a dialogue hook, as in:

> BLACKY
> I was a damn fool, sheriff!

SHERIFF
Right the first time. You're getting
smart, Blacky.

BLACKY
You're wrong there. I'm not smart—
I'm just a dope, a lucky dope.

In the foregoing example, both types of hook were used, and the
hooking effect can be readily observed.

The hook can also be a combination of various hooking elements.
Let us take the following dialogue as an example:

SERGEANT
What took you so long?

PRIVATE
Stopped over at the mess tent for
some rations, Sarge. You know about
an army's traveling on its stomach.
Napoleon said it.

SERGEANT
So what?

PRIVATE
I say, if you travel on your stomach,
then feed it.

SERGEANT
And *I* say, if you don't stop feeding
your stomach, you'll soon be traveling on your back—in a hearse.

Questions, answers, repetitions, cumulations, progressions, and
developments have all been incorporated as hooks in the above example, so that the lines flow into each other and out of each other
from speech to speech.

The deliberate interruption can also be used as a hook, as in:

> ELLEN
> I know, but . . .

> TOM
> (interrupting savagely)
> I don't want to talk about it!

> ELLEN
> But you've got to understand that . . .

> TOM
> (interrupting again)
> Oh! I understand—everything and I . . .

> ELLEN
> You're a stubborn mule! I'm through.

Despite the fact that an interruption—and especially the double interruption of the previous example—breaks up the flow of speech, it is effective as a hook because its suddenness, coupled with an immediate flow of speech from the interrupter, serves to pick up the flow before it actually comes to a full stop and, at the same time, couples the two speeches together.

Finally, there is a more subtle means of hooking together speeches. This makes use of ideas rather than words. It calls for the planting of *ideas*, their development, their building, and their capping, all within the compass of a number of speeches. Although it is inadvisable to do so, an idea development, from speech to speech, can be hooked together without resorting to actual dialogue hooks. But if there is an idea linkage, cemented together with dialogue hooks, the result would be that smooth flow of verbal continuity so essential to a motion picture.

Speech length

It can be stated dogmatically that there is almost no place in motion-picture dialogue for long speeches. A long speech impedes action. Short speeches increase it. Since action is the prime requisite of every filmic element, the short speech, in the main, should be adhered to.

That does not mean, however, that the dialogue should consist of short, curt, pithy one-word and one-line speeches throughout. Nor should the short speeches be written solely with words of one syllable. But the preponderance of lines should be worded economically, and should be as pithy as possible unless, of course, the character of the person talking is one who is being portrayed as verbose.

Long speeches can be used, but not to describe events and situations that could otherwise be told in action. Rather, they should be used mostly to describe emotional states, thoughts, and other material that cannot be portrayed by action.

Ingrid Bergman was given a thirteen-minute peroration in Hitchcock's *Under Capricorn*. As usual, this long speech was part of the picture's climax. And to prevent the story action from bogging down to an inevitable stop, action was simulated by camera movement, character movement, change of image size, change of angle, reaction cutaway shots from onlookers, and the like, all of which tended to give some sort of continuous movement to what was, at best, a tour de force.

Speech length regulates tempo. The tempo of the picture as a whole can be regulated by the length of the individual speeches. Thus, in scenes that require a quickened tempo, the speeches must be short, the lines incisive, the words choppy, and the rejoinders immediate and sharp.

Conversely, for scenes designed for a slower pace, the speeches should be longer, the lines more leisurely, and the words less concise than in the faster paced shots.

Stream of consciousness

At certain times in a screen play, it may be necessary to supplant spoken dialogue with unspoken thoughts. The most effective method of depicting thought processes in motion pictures is by means of pictorial action. A person's thoughts can be determined to a great extent by the manner in which he acts. But there is still another, more specific technique for presenting a character's inner thoughts. It makes use of what is known as "inner monologue" or "stream of consciousness."

From Shakespeare's day to the Victorian era, this inner monologue was given in the form of soliloquy "asides." That is, all stage action was stopped to permit the inner monologist to turn his head from the other characters and give verbal vent to his thoughts.

Today such crudities have been mercifully junked. Instead, dependence is put on the pictorial action that is the *result* of causative thought. But, at certain times, spoken inner thoughts have been portrayed as such, while all action stops, and the character, in close-up, meditates on his mental woes. O'Neill's stage play *Strange Interlude* was one long series of such interior monologues. The technique was carried over into the screen play. The result was a picture that was as jerky as a horse's fly-pestered haunch. When the characters were "acting" it moved, but when they "thought" it stopped completely.

Use stream of consciousness sparingly.   The best advice regarding the inner monologue is this—don't use it. But if you must, use it correctly. Use it as James Joyce did in his book *Ulysses*. Study his techniques in giving the thought processes of Leopold Bloom and Stephen Dedalus. Make especial note of his broken speeches.

The Russian director Eisenstein foresaw great possibilities for motion pictures in Joyce's interior monologue devices. But he was aware of the fact that, unless skill and aptitude were used in portraying these rambling inner monologues, the result would be nothing more than an action-stopping, theatrical soliloquy.

Memory recall thoughts.   There are certain times, however, when a memory recall may be injected into a script with excellent effects. If a certain graphic phrase or sentence is to be remembered by the character, it may be given—usually through an electronic filter—as a sort of off-stage voice. A character may have been gibed by another character, with a remark such as "You're weak. You'll never do it!" Some time later, when the gibed character is about to do what he had been told he could never do, the memory recall of the giber's voice, through filter, mockingly calling out, "You're weak! You'll never do it! You're weak! You'll never do it!" can be inserted to represent the character's thoughts, and can be used by him as an incentive, or a deterrent, either to do or not to do what he is about to do.

Monologue

Another device that should be discarded by pictures is the exterior monologue. When the character is alone, the monologue is, at best, an anachronism that should have gone out with high-button shoes. It stops action, it is unrealistic, it offers gratuitously information that could just as well have been presented pictorially and, therefore, more effectively.

The monologue may have some legitimacy when used as a long speech in reply to another character's cue line, and when that character is still on scene. In *Brief Encounter,* the unfaithful wife's verbal maunderings somehow retain reality, because they are supposed to show that she is trying to imagine how she is going to tell her husband the story of her brief encounter with love. But this is a device that can be used only rarely.

Motivate monologue. If you must use a monologue, be sure that it is well motivated. The monologue can gain credence from the fact that it is being spoken as a fervent prayer, for example. A number of other similar situations present themselves: a child can give a monologue to her doll; a grandmother to her sleeping grandchild; a man to his dog; a girl to her image in the mirror. But whatever the situation, it must be one that enhances the monologue with at least an aura of credibility and audience acceptance. Unmotivated monologues are entirely unrealistic, and since realism is one of the prime requisites of motion-picture dialogue, unmotivated monologues deserve to be allowed to rest in peace, together with many other outmoded theatrical trappings of the past.

Dialogue realism

What is realistic dialogue? Obviously it should consist of words used by real people, reacting to real situations, in a manner that creates sympathy between the characters and the audience, so that they will be accepted by the audience as being true to real life.

But the screen-play writer cannot write dialogue that is absolutely true to life and expect it to accomplish his purposes. For were he to reproduce the actual speech of average people, the result would be a hodge-podge of halting, half-finished, verbiage. Dialogue would meander down inconsequential bypaths, lose audience interest, and, certainly stray dangerously from the strict but necessary injunction that every word of dialogue must contribute something to the character or plot development to warrant its use.

Realism compromise. Hence the screen-play writer must compromise with what is actual realism in order to achieve an *effect* of realism that will carry the story forward, develop character, and retain audience interest.

Dialogue selectivity. Once again, this can be accomplished only by creative selectivity. It is absolutely necessary that the screen-play writer possess the ability to eliminate all nonessentials of speech, to highlight only those elements that move the story, actuate the characters, or entertain the audience—to write dialogue, in other words, that does not *present* actual speech, but rather *represents* it, realistically and dramatically.

Dialogue ungrammatical. To do this, the writer must always keep in mind the fact that people do not always talk with grammatical precision, even if they are college professors who teach courses in advanced English.

The normal grammatical word order in the English language has the subject come first, the predicate next, and the modifier following. "He walked away."

In the average *colloquial* speech, however, the word order varies considerably from the grammatical norm. Modifying phrases that would normally come at the end of a sentence are often used as sentence beginnings. "That paper—over there, I mean—bring it to me, will you?"

Use dialogue tags. Colloquial speech is full of little tags and verbal formulas. A study of Joyce's *Ulysses*—in the interior monologue

—should be quite fruitful in supplying any number of these inverted tags and formulas to the screen-play writer who conscientiously desires to write realistic dialogue as it is spoken by real people.

For it is only with realistic dialogue that the actor, through the screen-play writer, can hope to establish contact with his audience, so that what he says will give them the effect of having been spoken by him for the first time, instead of having been memorized and rehearsed time and again. It is only solid, realistic dialogue writing that can furnish a sense of immediacy to what is being said.

Overtones.   Although the screen-play writer should be vitally concerned with realism in his dialogue, he must consider other dialogue requirements which should accomplish their purpose without detracting from realism. One of these important considerations is the matter of dialogue overtones.

In music, overtones are those residual higher tones that continue after a certain, complex tone has been sounded. In dialogue, overtones are those residual ideas that are connoted, or suggested, by a statement not directly describing the overtone ideas. Thus even the most vacuous of remarks can be charged with a significance that is not immediately recognizable in a line of speech.

For example, take the simple word "no." Stated plainly, it implies what it means—a retort in the negative. But this word may have many derivative overtones. "No," in reply to a startling statement would imply disbelief. In an unsure reply to a question, the "no" would be given an overtone of halting dubiousness. "No," in reply to a question calling for a strong negative answer, would be given with emphatic crispness.

In the sentence, the same principle applies. The statement, "Well, I think I'll leave," could be applied to dozens of varying situations but with varying overtones. Consider the long-hair music aficionado, who is being bored at a be-bop concert. His manner of saying, "Well, I think I'll leave," would vary considerably from the manner in which it would be spoken by a man who suddenly sees his girl's husband enter a room in which the husband's head had just been gayly festooned with horns. Consider, also, the difference in overtones in the same line spoken by an escaped convict who is surrounded by the police, and is about to take another French leave. And how would that same line be spoken by a dubious but willing girl who has been invited to take a drive into the country with a noted rake?

Dialogue directions. The only way for the screen-play writer to be sure that the proper overtones result from an actor's reading of his line is to indicate his meaning with an interpretive direction. Thus, in the first example, the line would be written out, "Well, I think I'll leave," but added to it, in parentheses, would be the direction (bored). The second example would necessitate that (sheepishly) be included after the line, the third (harshly), and the fourth (dubiously).

Many actors and directors resent these intrusions into their interpretive bailiwick on the part of the screen writer. But unfortunately there are many actors who require these interpretive signposts. And if the screen-play writer wants to insure that his lines will receive the interpretation he feels they require, he should see that his intention is always made crystal clear to the actors. The good actor —the actor who respects his craft and the ability of the writer—will accept these directions, at least at their face value. If they give him even a minute clue to interpretation, he will be grateful to the writer for having supplied it.

Avoid gratuitous directions. There are many instances, however, when such interpretive suggestions (and that is all they should be) are unnecessary. Certainly it would be completely redundant (and insulting to the actor) to tag the statement "You're a damned liar!" with an (angrily) direction. Where the meaning is explicit, and where the manner of interpretation is obvious from the sense of the words, these interpretive suggestions should be avoided. But where there is any doubt regarding the manner of interpretation— where, in other words, there can be varying overtones—then, by all means, state specifically the interpretation you feel the lines require.

Although it is not mandatory, it is best to keep these interpretive directions as uniform as possible. The participial adverb is the most feasible, for it can be tied in with the same grammatical construction in which action directions are couched.

Indirection

A very effective technique for dialogue economies can be found in the device of indirection. This device has a double result: it can economize in dialogue on the one hand, and at the same time it can flatter the audience by permitting them to reach certain conclusions independently. In addition, the shock value of indirection is intellectually stimulating and, therefore, entertaining.

In *My Favorite Wife,* for example, as Ellen takes a shower, her mother, in a close-up, and obviously looking at her daughter's nude body off scene, is made to say, "My! Ellen! you're all brown!" This, in addition to having the afore-mentioned results, gave the audience a titillating picture of Ellen in the nude, without actually showing her in that censorable condition.

This sort of dialogue indirection can be used quite effectively, especially in those situations where a shot of what is being discussed is a pictorial impossibility. But once again, it cannot be used indiscriminately. It is a device which, when used judiciously, can have positive effects but which, when overused, would be deleterious to the effect desired.

Dialogue punctuation

A very important consideration in the writing of screen-play dialogue is the insertion of proper punctuation marks. This may appear to be information of the most elemental nature. But punctuation, in dialogue especially, has a definite purpose. It can give the actor a positive indication of the writer's ideas about the dialogue interpretation. At the same time, it can furnish him with the writer's suggestions for pacing.

An example of how a change in meaning can be effected with a change in comma placement should prove how important dialogue punctuation can be. Take the well-known sentence, "Woman, without her, man is a beast." Were the second comma to be shifted over one word, so that the line read, "Woman, without her man, is a beast," the meaning would be entirely different.

Reading punctuation vs. acting punctuation.   This fact must be understood and used in dialogue writing: an actor's conception of punctuation differs considerably from the ordinary reader's conception. The actor uses punctuation as signposts for sight reading. He uses punctuation to give him an idea as to where and how he should breathe. He paces his interpretation according to the punctuation given him.

For that reason, some sort of punctuation system must be devised by the screen-play writer, and then strictly adhered to, so that consistency can be maintained throughout.

The following system has been found completely workable and sufficient in variety to give the actor the necessary clues:

The period should be used to indicate a complete stop.

The comma, on the other hand, should signify only a breath stop, a one-count pause between phrases or between cataloguing words.

A longer pause should be indicated by a dash or, if desirable, by a series of three dots.

Three dots should be used to terminate a broken speech, one that is left dangling in mid-air.

One injunction: When writing a speech that is to be faded out and then segued into either a sound effect or another speech, make certain to give the sound department sufficient wordage so that an effective coupling can be made.

The underlined word, to indicate emphasis, should be used sparingly, and only when there may be some doubt as to the exact word to be accented for emphasis. See italicized words on page 206, in DIALOGUE HOOKS, for an example in which underlining for emphasis was essential.

The usual punctuation marks for exclamations and questions should be used.

All other punctuation marks—colons, semicolons, dash series, and so on—should be avoided.

Interjections

A very important device for imparting realism to dialogue is the interjection. Few people begin their speeches without some sort of interjection, on the order of "well," "so," "oh," and so on. That is because real people are not so quick-witted as they are represented in the average screen play. Replies to questions, comebacks, quips, and the like, do not come to their lips immediately. As a result, they begin to answer by using an interjection, which gives them time enough to think up an answer. Eventually they fall into the habit of resorting to it, even when it is not necessary, so that it becomes an identifying tag. Such tags can be used for character identification in dialogue. But they must not be permitted to intrude too often, or the effect will be lost in ludicrousness.

As a matter of fact, screen-play writers themselves are prone to fall into these same faults of interjection repetitions, especially with the word "well." Care should be taken that all of the writer's unnecessary "wells" and "ohs" are deleted from the dialogue when polishing and revising the script.

Dialogue revision

Once the dialogue has been completely written, the writer should drop the script for a while. He should disassociate himself from it, so as to rid his mind of all its elements. The purpose here is to achieve an attitude of objectivity about his own work. For the writer is prone to fall into certain patterns of writing. Unless these patterns are broken, he will find, when the time comes for script revisions, that he is unable to throw off the patterns and, thus, is incapable of revision.

This done, he should then begin to read his dialogue aloud. He should do this with one hand cupped to his ear, as actors do, so as to hear himself better. If possible, he should read—acting as best he knows how—into a recording machine, shot by shot. Then, on the playback, he should listen intently for the following dialogue faults.

Superfluity. First draft screen plays are usually replete with superfluous verbiage. Trim off every word that does not add something —character, story, or entertainment—to the picture. If you know that a joke was added only for a laugh and also that it holds up the action, use the blue pencil. Out with it! The screen-play writer must be ruthless with his own work. The small voice of conscience, some-how, will operate whenever a wrong word or phrase is used, or when a joke is inserted where it should not be. Mark these places with an "x," or with a colored pencil, so that when the time comes for revision you will know exactly where the objectionable spots are. A second reading of them will almost always convince you that your original reaction was the true one.

Repetition.   Carelessly repeated words are, perhaps, the most fre-quent of dialogue errors. An attempt should be made to eliminate repetition, especially when the repeated words or phrases are close to each other. In the following example,

JOE:
I'll *say* she is!

FRANK:
Say! where'd she go?

the repetition of "say" is awkward. Its complete elimination would do no harm to the dialogue. Watch, also, for the unwarranted repe-tition of names. This is a common failing in most writers of dialogue and should be checked for constantly. However, be sure to identify new characters by their names, in the dialogue, at their entrances.

Repetition, of course, is welcome when it is used designedly for dialogue-hook purposes.

Length.   Check for speech length. No matter how important its contents may have appeared at first, any long speech can be trimmed down without destroying the meaning. Make certain that these long speeches will be given pictorial pace with visual action, with camera and character movement, with changes in image size and angle, with reaction cutaways and the like. Break up most long speeches with interjections, questions, or any of the devices mentioned under DIALOGUE HOOKS on pages 205–210.

Rhyming.   Words that rhyme with other words in the same speech, have a tendency to creep into dialogue. These should be rewritten so that the rhyme is broken. Rhyming words call unnecessary atten-tion to themselves, and thus dissipate audience attention.

Singsong. The same objection applies to the accidental use of a too regular, singsong beat in dialogue lines. The regularity of the beat should be broken, so that the attention-getting words will not lose out to an extraneous element.

Alliteration. Alliterative tongue twisters are to be avoided in dialogue lines. They can become severe hazards to actors, who often fluff them, thus necessitating additional shot-takes. Eventually they will be changed by the actor himself, by the director, or by the dialogue director. It is to your best interests, and to the interests of your work, that you make these changes yourself and thus be assured that the substitutions will not be made ineptly.

Telephone dialogue

There has never been a directive regarding the use of telephone conversations in pictures, and the manner in which they are to be written into screen plays and, eventually, shot.

Judging from the procedures now used, telephone conversations are written, directed, and edited according to the whims of the three craftsmen involved. In one picture a number of treatments may be used: (1) a conversation in which we see and hear only one of the telephone pair conversing, usually the person on whom the camera is focused; (2) a cutaway from the person making the call the instant contact is made with the one being called, and then holding the camera and sound only on the second person's questions and answers; (3) a conversation in which we hear the person seen on the screen, talking with the person on the other end of the wire, without hearing what the unseen person says; (4) the same as number three, above, but with the voice of the person at the other end of the wire being heard through a telephonic filter; (5) a cutaway shot to the person at the other end of the line, in which we hear and see him talking, and hear but do not see the person who made the call originally, through a telephonic filter; (6) a conversation in which we see and hear the people at both ends of the wire, by means of direct alternate cuts from one to the other; and (7) a conversation in which we see and hear both parties on the screen at the same time, by means of a split-screen camera technique.

When several of these methods are used in the same picture, the result can become rather confusing. Even if the audience does not react confusedly, an element that could add to the over-all effect of unity and coherence is being deliberately neglected.

The better screen writer does not gloss over such details. He knows that *every* element in his picture must contribute something to the over-all effect, and that any element that can contribute something to that over-all effect should not be ignored. He knows that a motion picture is the result of pasting together film clips containing thousands of such details, some of which may appear completely insignificant in themselves. He knows that if he gives the proper attention to all these details, he stands a chance of adding a better screen credit to his list.

It is details such as these which, if misused, make for vague dissatisfactions in audiences. Quite often, after seeing a picture, audiences are unable to put their fingers on exactly what it was that made the picture unsatisfactory.

This vagueness, though, is not the result of a subtle intangible. It is rooted in errors brought about by an indifference to seemingly minor details. The reasons for dissatisfaction are unrecognizable to an audience because they are not sufficiently cognizant of the technical faults to be able to recognize them as such. Obvious and glaring mistakes are often easily identified, but what the audience believes are intangibles are actually minor details ineptly handled.

Use consistent phone dialogue. The screen writer, then, should decide what method of telephone dialogue he would like to see used in his picture. Having done that, he should adhere to that method *consistently* throughout the picture. The director, then, must shoot the shots the way the script is written, particularly if the dialogue is so germane to the action that it can be shot in no other way. And the film editor, in the same way, having been supplied with certain obligatory shots, can do nothing but cut them in the way the director shot them, which was also the way the script writer indicated.

The choice of methods, insofar as the writer is concerned, depends on the importance of the dialogue, and the effect he would like to achieve on the audience.

For instance, in a mystery story it may be necessary to withhold an important clue from the audience. This clue is to come from one of the parties to the telephone conversation. Only one of the people then can be shown at the phone—the detective, let us say. But the carrier of the clue, to whom he is talking, will not be shown, nor will his clue-carrying dialogue be heard on the sound track.

Replies to questions put by the person calling on the phone may not be of sufficient importance to the story to warrant hearing. This may be in a situation in which the character calling on the phone does so only to get out of camera emphasis range, so that the camera can accentuate some other aspect of the scene; or in a situation in which a person is making a series of calls to various places, when it is not important to see or hear the person making the replies. In the situation where a series of calls are made, if the last call brings forth an important story point, then it would be a good idea to let the audience see and hear both sides of the conversation.

If the replies are important, but if the person making them is unimportant to the story—as would be the case, for instance, were one of the characters to call a railroad station for information regarding trains—then we need only see and hear the person making the call, and we need only hear the voice of the person at the other end of the wire through a telephonic filter.

But in situations in which both people taking part in the phone conversation are important to the story—and particularly if what they say is pertinent to the story-line development—then both participants should be seen and heard, by means of a series of alternating direct shots.

This can be done in two ways, each method depending on the degree of importance of the character, and of what he says. If, for instance, it is necessary to show the *reaction* of a telephone conversation participant to what he hears, then, by all means, he should be both seen and heard simultaneously. But if the reaction is not too essential, the scene can be written and played so that, by means of alternating direct cuts, we see one person on the phone, hear his question, and then hear the reply by way of a telephonic filter, without its being necessary to cut away, visually, to the person making the answers. Then, when we do cut away to him, we can repeat the process by having the audience see and hear him answering the questions, and, at the same time, by having them hear only the person putting the questions, by way of a telephonic filter.

Only when it is absolutely necessary that the audience see and hear the combined *reactions* of both participants in the telephone conversations should the split-screen device be used. For, at best, this is a camera trick that has no legitimate place in a realistic story. Quick, alternating cutaways from party to party, without resorting to the use of the telephonic filter, can almost accomplish the effect desired. And when a quickened pacing is called for, the alternating series of short-clip cutaways is far more effective than the split screen.

Thus, only by alternating shots as described above, can a unified pattern of shots be achieved that will be both credible and esthetically pleasing, as far as the general pattern of the picture is concerned.

Dialogue cutaways

A situation may occur in a screen play where it will be necessary to cut away from the scene of action to another scene, to show what is taking place there.

This is a device that can be used in a number of instances. For example, the dialogue information may be repetitive. That is to say, a character may have to detail to a newcomer certain happenings which the audience has already seen. To avoid awkward and boring repetition, it is advisable to have the repetition start—only to identify it—and then have it cut off sharply as the action is cut away to something happening somewhere else.

Then again, the story line may make it advisable to switch action locales, in order to avoid being forced to tell the audience of some plot point which might destroy suspense. Thus, before the crook, whom the detective has just collared, can tell the audience that the head crook is to be found at the docks, in order to keep this information from the audience and to sustain suspense, the scene would be switched just at the point where the crook is about to divulge the whereabouts of his chief. Then, perhaps, we could cut to the chief, at his hide-out, going about some of his nefarious business. Then, when we cut back to the detective and his singing captive, we could find them in a car on their way to the docks.

There are a number of other places in which the cutaway can be used, and they were treated in the section CUTAWAYS. But here we are dealing only with what should happen to the dialogue in a cutaway.

For example, if the cutaway is made at a certain point in the dialogue, where in the dialogue should the cutback to the original scene be picked up? Should allowances be made to cover a lapse of time? Or should the dialogue pick up immediately where it was severed for the cutaway?

Here again the answer can be made by the director or the film editor. Ordinarily the director would shoot the entire scene at one time. The film editor would insert the cutaway and then, in his cutback, pick up with the dialogue at his discretion. But the screen writer can more or less force the hands of both the director and the film editor by writing in the dialogue so that it cannot be shot or edited in any way other than the one indicated in the script.

The answer to the problem of cutaway dialogue is to be found in the fact that although the audience accepts the convention that while one action is going on a direct cut can be made to another action which is supposed to be going on simultaneously, a certain amount of time will have elapsed during the presentation of that simultaneous action. The audience then will retain—in addition to a feeling of simultaneity—an actual knowledge that some time has gone by.

Now, to compensate for that knowledge so that it will mesh with the feeling of simultaneity, it is good practice not to pick up with dialogue in the cutback at the exact point where it was previously broken off. Instead, it is advisable to leave the audience with the impression that enough dialogue and time have elapsed to cover the cutaway.

For in spite of the accepted convention, time does not stand still. And the audience will be left with the false impression that the original scene has been frozen in time to allow for the cutaway, if the cutback picks up at the exact point at which it broke off.

To make sure, then, that the director will not shoot the entire dialogue, and thus supply the film editor with enough footage to make this mistake, *do not furnish the director with the dialogue which you want dropped during the lapse of time.*

Write only enough dialogue to cover the story line in the original scene. Cut it off at the point you feel is appropriate. Then write the cutaway scene—dialogue and action. That done, cut back to the original scene, but do not pick up the dialogue at the point at which you cut it. Instead, time the action and dialogue of the cutaway scene, determine the amount of both that would have taken place in that time, and then start the dialogue in the cutback scene so as to allow for that timed hiatus. In that way, the director can shoot only what action and dialogue you have given him.

This is not possible, however, if you are writing your screen play in master scenes. Here the director will shoot the entire scene. The film editor, in turn, can throw in a cutaway scene without worrying about the time lapse.

Writing character action

Because motion pictures are basically a medium for movement, the screen-play writer is confronted with a double problem: that of furnishing verbal descriptions of *character* actions and movement and, in addition, of *camera* actions and movement. The latter function, as has been explained, has been considerably curtailed for the writer. The camera is a machine that, somehow, does not exist as far as the average screen-play writer is concerned. Fortunately, the task of describing character actions has been retained by him. Although, gradually—because of exigencies developed by stage-set demands, and, therefore, unknown to the writer when he began to work on his script—even these character directions have been tampered with and deviated from.

Nevertheless, by and large, the screen-play writer still retains the prerogative of furnishing character-movement descriptions. And until some unassailable substitute can be devised by the higher-ups, he will continue to do so.

Many directors, though, resent the writer's action directions, with the charge that they tend to confuse their own conception of the action required. But at the same time, a majority of the directors are grateful—albeit not vocally—for whatever action descriptions are furnished by the writer. And the more explicit those directions, the more grateful they feel.

Describe action thoroughly. The screen-play writer, then, should write out in as much detail as possible every physical action and reaction of every character in the shot. No matter how insignificant or how obvious that action may appear to be at first glance, it must be written into the script. Just as it is the rare director who can handle crowds—such as De Mille and Mamoulian—so it is the rare screen-play writer who can furnish the detailed action directions necessary to the judicious movement of a number of people in the same shot.

Describe actions exactly. These character actions must be more than quantitative—they must be qualitative as well. Not only must they describe all the actions, they must describe them exactly. It is not enough simply to indicate that "Joe crosses to Willa." Joe crosses in a certain way that is characteristic of him, and of him only, at that particular moment, and it may change the very next moment because of a shift in circumstances. Joe may "amble nonchalantly across to Willa," or he may "cross quickly, confidently to Willa." But at no time should he simply cross.

For in the screen play the adjective and adverb are vital and effective tools of the writer. They are the most expressive means of conveying to the actor, through the director, what the writer has in mind for that character. Explicitness is the key word.

This explicitness, however, must be accomplished economically. In fiction writing, the writer can be as discursive and prolix as he desires. He can afford to characterize action by the use of similes, tropes, and poetic comparisons. But in screen-play writing, the purpose of description is not to give reading pleasure, but rather to impart information. Therefore, all directions must be absolutely direct.

Joe does not cross to Willa, "like a wounded bird," or "as though he were frightened by the specter of the consequences." On the other hand, it may be necessary to use similes when there is no word to describe the action exactly. Thus, it would be better to say, "he crosses to Willa as though he were treading on eggs," rather than "He crosses to Willa with caution."

The point is that the physical screen play is not primarily a medium of expression. Its basic purpose is to convey information from the writer to the actor which the actor can use in interpreting his role. The writer, then, should use every device at his command to convey that information as clearly and as briefly as possible. The wisecrack, if it must be used, should be reserved for the treatment or the dialogue. But the character action should be all business.

Act it out. Just as the writer should read his dialogue aloud in order to determine how it may sound, so should he go through the gestures and movements he writes in for his characters, and determine how they may appear visually. In this way he can discover which movements are extraneous, which are missing, and which are overdone, and adjust his directions accordingly.

Present-tense directions. These directions, like the treatment, should be written in the present tense, as though the writer were describing an action that is actually taking place.

Other than the factor of suggesting immediacy, and because it has become standardized practice, the present tense should be universally applied both to the action and the reaction descriptions. Actual action descriptions should be written into the body of the directions section (see section under FORMAT). But the reaction directions should be written in parentheses, under the name of the character speaking, and immediately before his speech begins, as in:

JOE
(grinning sardonically)
That's what you think, Willa.

Participial present. These directions should be written in participial form. This should be done not only for the sake of consistency, but also because it is more economical, verbally, to say, "smiling" rather than "he smiles" or "Joe smiles" or "Joe begins to smile." Here again, though, the participial should receive a qualitative adverb indicating the exact way in which the reaction is to be made. Merely to say "grinning" would leave the actor bewildered as to the exact interpretation he is to give. He could grin "ironically," "grimly," "wanly," "warmly," "disparagingly," in fact, in almost as many ways as there are adverbs. Once again, explicitness is the key word.

These dialogue directions and reactions should not include directions for physical body movement—crosses, arm movements, and so on. These belong in the body of the directions section. A general rule to follow is this: (1) Descriptions of movements of the body above the neck should be given under the character-name heading; (2) descriptions of movements of the body below the neck are to be given in the body of the directions sections.

When a number of above-the-neck directions are to be given in one speech, the format to follow is this:

> JOE
> (grinning sardonically)
> That's what you think, Willa.
> (the grin dissolving to a
> frown of curiosity)
> But *do* you? How do I know *what*
> you think?
> (the frown slowly changing
> to an expression of cunning)
> I know how to make sure, though.
> Yes, I know how.

When it is necessary to combine an above-the-neck direction with a below-the-neck one, the format changes, so that it would be presented as follows:

> WILLA
> (fearfully cringing)
> What are you going to do, Joe?

She backs away, her hands brought up to her breast, as though ready to push him away.

> (continuing, her fear
> mounting)

> Joe! don't! Don't look at me that
> way!
> (her eyes close and her
> mouth gapes as she emits
> an anguished sigh)
> Oh, no! no!

The above rules are admittedly not in general practice. As a matter of fact, screen-play writers use no fixed rules. But they are presented here only in the interests of uniformity and consistency.

Used universally—as are script formats—the actor and director could realize at a glance what are bodily action directions, and what are facial expression reactions.

Another rule could be to confine the action directions written under the character-name heading to facial expression descriptions, and speech quality descriptions only, and to put all other action descriptions in the body of the directions section. At no time, though, should a character's bodily action, such as walking, crossing, falling, etc., be written anywhere but in the body of the directions section. Whichever rule is followed, it should be done consistently, so that uniformity and, thus, instant clarity will result.

Action before speech. Because the audience's eyes are quicker than their ears, it is essential that actions and gestures be indicated before the lines of speech. Thus, if it were necessary to show a girl slapping a man's face, the directions would be written as follows:

> WILLA slaps Joe's face.
>> WILLA
> That's what I think of you, Joe
> Hazlitt!

Delayed reactions. At certain times—especially after an important plot revelation has been made, either visually or verbally—it is more effective to delay the effect after the cause has been exposed, by inserting some sort of dilatory action. Instead of indicating that the character respond to the revelation immediately—either vocally or by physical reaction—prepare the audience for it; "milk" the effect, in other words, by furnishing the character with some routine activity, either one which the revelation interrupted or a completely new one. When his capping "effect" speech is given, simply have him stop what he is doing and then give the speech.

This was done beautifully in *The 39 Steps* when the head spy revealed his identity to Donat by holding up his hand and exposing his little finger, amputated at the second joint. Donat's initial reaction to this was to continue sipping his cup of tea. Then his eyes widened, and his lips parted, to express his sudden bewilderment.

This technique adapts the effective comedy "double-take" device to the dramatic. Like its prototype, it should be used only sparingly —at dramatic high spots—to be most effective.

Exits and entrances.   Character exits and entrances do not necessarily have to be made into a room from a door. To conserve time
by telescoping—provided, of course, the door entrance is not vital to
the suspense or to other script requirements—such exits and entrances can be effected on a close-up of another character or a set
prop. After establishing the opening of a door with a sound effect
(to which the person in close-up can react), the character can be
shown entering the shot from the direction of the door, off scene,
or exiting from it in the direction of the door off scene. Anything of
this sort that can compress and telescope action, so that only the
vital action remains, contributes toward the all-important requirement of the forward flow of continuity.

Crossing actions.   When an action direction indicates that a character is to cross from one place to another, the screen-play writer must
consider certain results. If by crossing he leaves another character
off center in the frame composition, and if the camera is not to pan
the crossing character, then some compensation must be made in
order to frame the remaining character, and thus retain a pleasing
composition. Hence, it is necessary (although seldom practiced) to
do one of two things: (1) indicate that the camera re-center the
remaining character with a slight pan adjustment, or (2) suggest
that the remaining character "dress the stage," as it is termed in the
theater, and center himself at a predetermined spot marked for him
on the floor.

Action for children.   Action directions for child actors—especially
extremely young ones—require special consideration. The average
child actor, no matter how effective his mimicry may be, is woefully
deficient in matters of physical movement. Unless they are shot candid, and not candied, their inexperience and lack of stage presence
becomes magnified when they are given physical movements.
   The acting of Jackie Coogan in Chaplin's *The Kid;* of the tow-
headed boy in *The Fallen Idol;* of the brown-eyed Italian boy in
Bicycle Thief; of the ragamuffins in the Russian *Bezshprzhniki*—
these were all shot by directors who knew how to handle children.
They realized that children *act* when they are told to. But when
they are caught off guard—when they are directed by indirection, by
being given something to do which is not necessarily in line with

the script's action, but which is comparable to it in terms of a child-hood experience—then children can turn in exquisite, fresh, and tremendously effective performances. This, though, is part of the director's function.

Consider children's limitations.   The screen-play writer, however, can make the director's task easier, by considering the limitations of most child actors. Simplicity should be the rule. The directions should be written in simple, understandable terms. The expression changes should not be those resulting from deep-seated, complex compulsions, but rather from those within the scope of a child's ability and understanding. Simple similes may be used, but only those that are in the sphere of a child's experience. He should not be given too much "business" but, at the same time, some sort of prop should be provided for him—something to keep him occupied and to detract his attention from the fact that he is acting.

Animal action directions.   There are similar rules to follow when writing in action directions for animals. Most animal actions are shot either by indirection or *ad lib*. The dog that is supposed to run out of the shot to its screen master actually runs to its real master, who is holding a dog biscuit for it off scene. The dog that tugs at the little boy's coat to warn him of danger knows nothing of what he is doing, and accomplishes its action only after arduous training by its master. So do not call for tricks that would require a long period of time to teach. Indicate only the simplest of actions for animals.

Completely avoid calling for expressions and expression changes. This may sound like unnecessary advice, but one producer is known to have written into a script, "The dog looks up appealingly at its master. Then it turns its head as if to tell him it wants to leave. Then it looks up and tears come from its eyes."

Animals must be tricked into performing. Their work, at best, is spotty, despite the seeming ease with which they accomplish their tricks on the screen. Those effortless tricks, however, are the result of hours of back-breaking labor and expert film editing. The act of photographing one dog's rising on its hind legs and putting its front legs on a boy's shoulders consumed four hours of shooting time.

The screen-play writer should acquaint himself with the standard tricks a normal animal can do, and then improvise. Dogs can swim, for instance, but most of them cannot swim across a wide river, as they are supposed to do in many sequences. The trick here is to indicate a shot of the dog entering the water, another one of it swimming in the water, and a third of it climbing out of the river onto the bank. When cut together, with various cutaways, to rapids roaring dangerously near by, and to the villain taking pot shots at the dog from off shore, the cut sequence can give the desired effect.

Most animals are well dieted before they are brought onto the set to work. Therefore they will hop on chairs, hop off them, scratch at doors, push in doors, look coyly from behind trees, look up appealingly—do anything within reason and within their physical and mental capabilities, to get a bite of food. A close-up shot, for example, of a dog looking up appealingly at its real master, who is holding out a hunk of meat, could be used as a cutaway shot in a love scene, as though to imply that the dog seems to be eyeing the smooching pair with eye-watering desire. Indirection is the answer, and it is indirection on which the screen-play writer should rely, in the main, when writing in action directions for animals.

Budget writing

Now that we have gone into the vital elements of the material on screen-writing technique, it may be apropos, here, to expatiate on the problem of budget writing, which makes it essential for the screen writer, for example, to confine his "time" directions to only DAY or NIGHT.

Ordinarily, in the more extravagant days of Hollywood, when writing screen plays for major productions in the larger studios, the screen writer was not required to concern himself with the cost involved in producing the sets, actors, and props necessary to the picture. The trend, though, has been to economize; hence the following material could be applied even to the writing of screen plays for the larger studios, as well as for the up-budgeted movie-house pictures and television films.

Budgets are usually touched upon in the initial story conferences between the writer and his producer, so that the screen writer can obtain some idea as to how far he can go in calling for expensive sets, a large cast of main-character actors, costly props, and so on.

But when the writer is working on a low-budget picture, he must adjust himself to the amount that can be spent and must write against the limited budget.

"B" picture weather.   For example, no "B" picture or television film can boast of a rain or snow effect. To build the complicated equipment on the sound stage necessary to creating a single rain sequence involves the laying down of tar-paper foundations, pitch-calked seams, built-up gutters, and an elaborate sprinkler system to produce the rain effect—together with the plumbing layout necessary to drain off the accumulated rain water.

This does not mean, however, that the effect of a rain sequence cannot be achieved at all. Ingenious dodges are available to circumvent the exorbitant costs. The effect of rain can be obtained cheaply, for instance, by indicating that the scene is an interior. Then a pipe can be adjusted across the tops of the windows so that the audience get the *effect* of an exterior rain. Sound effects of rain can be added to the track to get a more realistic effect. And before actors enter the scene from the outside, they can be liberally besprinkled with water from a watering can. Which is about all the rain you can expect to get into a cheap picture, where "it's always fair weather."

Visit the back lot.   As for sets, if the screen writer is working at a studio, he should make occasional trips to the back lot and to the scene dock to learn what permanent interior sets and street sets are available, so that he can write them into his script.

Consider re-dressing.   He should also make provisions in his screen play to "re-dress" certain interior sets, if at all possible. Thus, simply by switching a window flat with a door flat, by changing wall-papers, by changing curtains, or by adding or removing Venetian blinds, and by changing furniture, an entirely new interior set can be obtained cheaply. Screen writers, especially those writing television films, can aid in this saving by not writing in actions that call for unusual interior set features.

Consider corners. Scenes should be indicated that could be shot in tight medium shots, using corners of sets already erected which require little re-dressing. Such savings can be effected especially where telephone close-ups are indicated.

Avoid staircases. Staircases should be avoided—they are costly to erect. Staircases in hallways should not be suggested, for it is often necessary to tear out the floor of the sound stage in order to obtain the effect of stairs going down.

Library shots. The screen writer should also acquaint himself with the available library of stock footage. It is comparatively much cheaper to indicate a stock-footage full shot of a busy street scene to establish the locale, and then to go in for a tight medium shot, studio-built detail of one of the store fronts, near which the action can be played.

Limit location shots. If location shots are absolutely essential, write the locale directions so that it will not be necessary to travel too far. It is a costly job to transport actors, camera crew, grips, props, electrical equipment, power booster "jennies" (generators), food, and the multitude of other supplies required in location shooting. If at all possible, try to write the scenes so that they can be shot silent, without the need for sound equipment. If dialogue is an essential requirement, investigate the possibility of shooting the dialogue silent and then lip syncing (dubbing in) the dialogue, or of recording the dialogue on tape.

"Cheat" the actors. If this cannot be done, then it will be obligatory for the screen writer to "cheat" in the manner of actor placements. The screen play should suggest that certain lines be given while the actor's back is to the camera, which is on the face of the person who is being spoken to, only to obtain his reaction to the lines being spoken. If he has a reply, it should be short and succinct to permit easy lip syncing.

Arrange also for some of the dialogue to be spoken at greater camera distances than is ordinarily required, so that the actor's lip movements will not be too noticeable. At the same time, write in reaction close-ups on the faces of people, or on things, with only the *voice* of another character heard as dialogue. Then cut away immediately to the person speaking, for the last few words of his lines which can be lip-synced in. And, as the camera is on him for a reaction shot, indicate again the *voice* of the other person replying to what has been previously said.

These are artful dodges that cannot be indulged in consecutively. But, thrown together, they can be assembled by the film editor so that the illusion of a sound sequence can be easily simulated. It may seem that they lie strictly within the province of the producer, director, and the film editor, but the screen-play writer can contribute a great deal if he is aware of the need for, and the technique of, these money-saving devices.

Limit the cast.   The screen writer should also be chary with the size of his cast when writing for budget pictures. Motion-picture actors come high, especially when they are in the upper brackets. The stars are usually hired on contract, but the minor characters often work by the day. Try not to spread out the appearances of these minor actors so that they are in too many scenes. Try to write them so that when the script is broken down, they can appear before the camera in as few days as possible.

A story is told of one shoestring producer who was producing a fifteen-part Western serial. He decided he could add to the box-office potential by using the name of a then current Western favorite who eventually agreed to work on a per diem basis, but at a fantastically high rate. The producer hired the star and ordered his writer to turn out a story involving a masked rider. Then, after shooting the masked rider—a cheap-salaried actor of the same build as the star—for fifteen episodes, the star's services were used for only one day, to shoot the final unmasking scene.

Extras for crowd scenes also add to the cost of a picture. The shots can be written so that the number of extras, together with the amount of time they work, can be reduced to a minimum. Few scenes should be written in which all the extras are to be shown at the same time. If it is necessary, use the scenes only as establishing shots—then cut in to the crowd for medium shots and close-ups, which will cut down on the cost for extras.

Large crowd shots should be particularly avoided in television films—not only because they are costly, and because they must be photographed from a long shot to include the entire crowd—but because such crowded scenes appear on a small television screen as a milling mass of indeterminate characters. Also, in crowd scenes, give no dialogue lines to people in the mob, or identity of the speaker will be lost.

Try not to give extras any lines to read. Only a single word from them and their rate of pay almost doubles. Instead, resort to pantomime. Depend on recorded sound effects for crowd noises which can give you the effect of a large crowd in the background, while you indicate a tight medium shot on a small segment of the crowd.

A story is told of another shoestring producer who was doing a picture in which he had to show armies of Union and Confederate soldiers. He simulated the effect simply by having a dozen extras in Union uniforms run past the cameras in a close shot, then change their uniforms and run past the camera again as Confederates.

In spite of the proverb, the camera *can* lie, and the screen writer can contribute significantly to the reduction of expenses.

The fact that a picture is cheaply made does not presuppose that it will be of poor quality. Some of Hollywood's best pictures were produced at vastly cheaper cost than most of its extravaganzas. Von Sternberg considered *Salvation Hunters* his most sincere work, yet he produced it independently, at a total cost of $4800! Such pictures as *The Informer,* and *Cat People,* termed "sleepers" by the trade, were cheap-budgeted pictures that were both artistic and box-office successes. The European producers are able to turn out masterpieces at costs far below those in Hollywood.

It must also be kept in mind that it is quite possible to go overboard in keeping the budget low, so that instead of having a picture that is cheap only in price, you have one that is cheap in quality as well. In the television film *Back to Zero,* a few feet of stock footage showing crocodiles disporting supposedly in the Zambesi River opened the picture. The rest of the film was shot on what amounted to one set. Never did the camera go outside the Boss' hut, not even when he stood at the window, looked out at a fire, and commented upon it. It may have been too costly to build a fire set, or to dig up some stock fire footage to match the locale. But the fire could have been easily indicated by indirection, merely by flickering a few flame shadows on the faces of those watching through the window. A little creative imagination, at minor cost, could have improved a picture which was at best nothing more than a filmed live television drama.

More important than low budgets and tricks to surmount financial obstacles, are talent, sincerity, honesty, and a genuine desire to make adult, intelligent, and moving motion pictures.

The verbal clichés

One of the things which makes for a dull, formula script turned out on the assembly line of B pictures, shaky A's and, even A's themselves is the direct result of lazy thinking and lazy writing. It is the conventionalized verbal cliché, like "came the dawn," that has become so stale that it often elicits a laugh from many audiences.

The most trite of all these expressions undoubtedly is, "Don't worry, everything is going to be all right." This line has been heard in almost every motion picture produced. Following is a list of other such clichés which, were they to be conveniently forgotten by screen writers, would make for screen plays that would have some semblance of fresh, creative writing.

"You mean. . . ." the fearfully asked, half-spoken question that usually precedes the revelation that that is precisely what the character did mean. It is usually something horrible or startling.

"But my son was always such a good boy" invariably spoken by the grieving mother of a homicidal maniac.

"The lights are going out all over Europe" a horrible favorite during World Wars I and II, spoken as the hero and heroine gaze sorrowfully, hand in hand, through a darkened window, and the sound of bombs and planes is heard in the background.

"Oh! It's beautiful!" the invariable reaction of a girl when she first views a gift, usually an engagement ring.

"Why, you look as if you've seen a ghost!" spoken to a character who has just been frightened by any one of a dozen of terrifying experiences.

"That's *our* song they're playing" always spoken by the heroine to the hero, over a checkered tablecloth in an Italian spaghetti joint, as "their" song is heard in the background played by a one-hundred-piece orchestra.

"No, don't look back. I want to remember you like this," spoken by a leave-taking lover as the object of his sorrow lingers tearfully behind.

"Hold me close, darling! Closer! Closer! Don't ever let me go!" which is self-explanatory.

"Why, you're . . . you're trembling!" spoken by the young lad as he holds the girl's arms close, and gazes down into her tear-rimmed eyes.

"There's only one doctor who can save him—and he's in Vienna!" spoken sadly over the bed of a child who lies dying of a rare disease.

"I've been blind—blind, I tell you!"

"Follow that car, driver!"

"That can mean only one thing—bombers!"

"Hold the presses! I've got a scoop that'll blow the lid off the whole town!"

"He had a fighting heart!"

"I'm comin' out and I'm comin' out shootin'!"

"We're through, washed up, finished—you hear me!"

"Yes, I killed him! Sure I did! And I'm glad! You hear me—I'm glad!"

"He's . . . he's lost the will to live!"

"You're back and that's all that matters now!"

"I know—I've been blind to you all my life."

"She's been living a lie all her life!"

Going to pieces.   The young, inexperienced pilot, miner, GI etc., goes to pieces under the stress and strain of his job. Usually the strong sergeant or foreman slaps the young man on the cheek with a rough but rousing, "Pull yourself together, man!"

Surprise names.   Historical film-stories are particularly guilty of overusing the cliché in which the name of a now famous person is mentioned casually when that person enters the scene as a youth. If the picture is a pre-Civil War epic, and a gawky youth is seen splitting rails, the topper will always be, "He'll never git nowheres, he won't, that there Abe Linkern!" The varieties are endless.

Surprise place names. The same trick has been overworked with place names. The most spectacular, because of its brooding irony, was the shot in Coward's *Cavalcade,* in which the two lovers stand at the deck rail of a steamship, discussing their future happiness. When they walk away, we see they are standing in front of a life-saver, on which is printed the grim, prophetic legend: *Titanic.*

These are but a few of the hundreds that could be culled from Hollywood's products. They are all old, time-worn, hackneyed, hoary. Avoid them.

Prop clichés

Avoid, also, the prop clichés which pop up periodically in picture after picture—clichés which employ, as a gimmick, some inanimate object, such as a handkerchief, usually in the scene where the girl, suddenly brought to tears, draws a big white, manly handkerchief from the breast pocket of the boy's jacket, and wistfully blots out her big glycerine tears.

The pajamas. The little girl who is forced to remain overnight in the great big man's apartment, decks herself out comically in his oversized striped pajamas, with the leg ends dragging and the sleeve ends dangling.

Long underwear. Conversely, if a man appears in a set of baggy, drop-seat long underwear, it is thought almost certain to get a laugh. It has in the past, and it may now. But it is the kind of bur-lesque writing that a writer can hardly be proud of, even when it is a sure laugh-getter. It is much like laughing at the antics of a half-wit.

The buy-off. The stern rich father of the boy enters the chorus girl's cubbyhole, draws a checkbook and pen from his pocket and grunts out, "All right! how much?"

Cigarettes. A cigarette is the most often used prop in the motion-picture business. This is so because many young actors and actresses have not yet learned what to do with their hands while acting. A director, therefore, is forced to give them a cigarette to make sure their hands do not hang stiffly at their sides, or wave fatuously and ineffectually in the air. Too often, though, the young lady smoker never has a match to light her cigarette, which act is always performed by someone who eyes her steadily, the exact manner depending on the nature of the scene.

Other cigarette oldies include the use of an ash tray full of cigarette stubs to indicate a time lapse; the gangster who punctuates his decision for violent action by rubbing out his cigarette in an ash tray (a cigar is usually restricted to the use of brokers, business men, and other more genteel menaces). And let us not forget the grilling scene, in which, after offering the grillee a cigarette, the griller comments, casually and pointedly, "Nervous?"

Props have also been overworked as symbols, especially dolls which fall to the floor from the lifeless hands of a dead child. Candles flicker out when death occurs; flowers wilt after a death takes place; a canary languishes in a cage, to symbolize its mistress' state of bondage, and then flutters out when she is freed; trees bud, flower, wilt, and are then covered with snow, to indicate a lapse of time; a pan must always be filled with hot water when the country doctor arrives to complete an accouchement. The magical bubble of chemicals in a group of variegated but useless chemical retorts and flasks, in almost every laboratory scene; the close-up of chorus girls' legs tripping down the circular backstage staircase; the rocks which are always thrown by outraged disbelievers through the windows of the scientist's laboratory, in scientific-discovery films; the spinning auto wheel dissolved into a spinning train wheel or propeller, to indicate a time lapse; and the horn-rimmed spectacles that always adorn starlets to indicate they are ugly when young, or not so charming when working as the hero's secretary, so that, always, in the love scene, he takes off her glasses and says, "There, you look better this way!" These are only a few of the hundreds of prop clichés resorted to by writers with lazy cerebrums and active memories.

The answer may be in restraining the screen writer from attending the movies, to avoid absorbing these banal clichés. The story told of Alfred Hitchcock is that he once said to an executive producer that he never viewed any finished motion picture. To which the reply was, "But where do you get all your ideas, then?"

On learning from seeing

Of course, the screen writer should attend motion pictures, if only to keep up with the current practices and techniques of motion-picture making. If you should not come away from a picture loaded with a cargo of outmoded film clichés, what should you, as a screen writer, learn?

Your own picture. If you are seeing a picturization of your own screen play, and if you are genuinely interested in improving your abilities, you should pay special attention to a number of elements.

First, you should listen carefully to the dialogue for false notes. Is it verbose? What lines or words could have been eliminated without befogging meaning, to pep up the pacing? Is there word repetition or word rhyming? Do the lines flow? Are some of the speeches too long? Are they revelatory of character?

At the same time look for story holes. Is there anything unexplained? Are all the story threads tied together at the end of the picture? Do any characters drop out suddenly, without explanation?

If you cannot note all these things at one screening, see the picture again. Or obtain a print of the picture and run it through a number of times, looking for other errors.

Now, notice if the exits and entrances were smoothly manipulated. The opticals? Are they presented as you wrote them in the script? If not, try to determine why the change was made necessary.

The scenes dropped, if any—were they justified? Try to visualize the same sequence with the dropped scene included. Would it have enhanced the sequence? Try to reason out why it has been dropped.

Added scenes—do they improve the sequence and the picture? Were shots dropped which might have been obscure in your script?

The running gag—did you permit it to run just a mite too long? Did you pay it off? Try to analyze the audience reaction at the pay-off. Was it worthwhile?

Try, if possible, to observe audience reactions to the high spots of the picture. They will cough in those parts that lag and drag. There will be complete silence where their attention is being held.

Clock your laughs in audience reactions. Did the big laugh really pay off with a boffo roar? What happened? Did you arrange for a few lines of dead dialogue to follow the big laugh, knowing they would be covered up completely? Do your laughs build in the audience's reaction as you tried to build them in the script?

Observe the director's interpretations of your shots. How did he improve on them? How did he fall down? Were the actors' directions that you gave followed? If so, could they have been improved? If not, try to determine why the changes were made, and how the improvement succeeded.

In the cutting, take special notice of the pacing achieved by the film editor. Had you suggested the cuts? Were they followed? If not, why, and how was the continuity improved? Were the cutaways you had suggested photographed, and inserted where you had indicated? What about the reverse shots? Are they all in? If so, what is the effect? If not, how was the visualization of your script improved?

Not your own picture. Accept this: Once you become a professional screen writer, you will be spoiled for enjoying pictures *per se*. For to be entertained by a motion picture, it is necessary that you be receptive to the effects of the picture as a whole, and not to the breakdown of the picture's individual elements.

As a screen writer, you will follow the technique of handling and presenting the material, rather than the material itself. You will find yourself mumbling, "Close shot, pan to table, dolly in to close-up," and the like, disagreeing violently with some things, admiring others, and making mental notes of certain effects you intend to use in future screen plays.

This is legitimate. We learn how to write, after all, by reading the classics—even by reading literature that is not as good as the classics; in other words, by learning from others' successes and mistakes. There is no reason, then, why you should not be able to improve your screen writing by viewing the results of others.

But do not take away the wrong things. Do not be affected by the trite, the mediocre. Know what the verbal and visual clichés are so that when you recognize them you can reject them instantly.

You need not reject them *in toto*, however. That there is nothing in the world that is actually new is a truism that cannot be too often mentioned. What is thought to be new and startling is simply an adaptation of something old—perhaps something trite—but it is the *revitalizing* of the old into what appears to be the new, that makes for originality, just as in Shakespeare's adaptations of the old of Holinshed.

So, in seeing the clichéd devices in pictures, remember them, not as you saw them, but rather as you think you can refurbish them for future use. For example, if you see a candle being gradually decreased in size to indicate a passage of time, do not remember the candle only. Try to analyze the device the candle represented—the gradual wearing down of anything. This should open an investigation of a vast store of possibilities: soles wearing thin, a piece of chalk diminishing in size, a cigarette burning down, a container's water level gradually lowering, the effect of wind blowing up or dying down—these are some of the valid extensions that could be made from the original springboard. To cite still another truism: It isn't *what* you do as much as it is *how* you do it that is important.

Use the same method in relation to all aspects of the film. Use the plot of the story line as a springboard for other plots. This does not mean that you should simply use the "switcheroo" method, which takes the same plot pattern but reverses and juggles characters and character relationships. Your manipulation should be more than that. It should include the creation of an entirely different story line, with different characters, who are to be involved in different situations. The idea obtained from the film should be used only in the nature of a pump-priming device, and nothing more.

In other words, you should be stimulated to legitimate and creative *variations* on the themes presented in films. It is legitimate for any composer to create variations on a Bach fugue. In the same way, it should be perfectly fair for you to create your own variations without suffering reprehensive accusations or qualms.

One of the themes of De Sica's *Bicycle Thief* emerged in Maggiorani's grim reply to the police official's question, "Did anyone witness the accident?" It was "People saw it, sure—but *nobody* cared." Nobody cared about the tragic consequences on a little man's little life of the theft of his bicycle.

The same theme is evident in a story of an entirely different nature, *Death of a Salesman,* in which the wife complains bitterly and urgently that "Attention must be paid." Yes, attention must be paid to the crisis in the life of the little man who was her husband, and who lived such a little life. For "nobody cared" about him.

So, similarity of themes should not be a drawback to using them as springboards for your own work. Given a theme, a writer should be able to create any number of completely dissimilar stories— stories that can stand on their own feet without suffering comparison with other stories using the same theme.

Props

The screen-play writer has still another powerful tool at his disposal with which to obtain action and character development. It is the physical prop—some inanimate object introduced into the story and developed as the story continues. The standard props for all Westerns, for example, are the horse and gun.

Props for pantomime.   The prop is especially adaptable to pantomime, and to the comedy scene. Chaplin's success was built in part on his remarkably telling use of props. All of his pictures offer excellent examples. The fantastic gear-laden machine in *Modern Times* in which Chaplin became stuck was nothing but an immense prop; as were the wrenches with which he chased around the woman with the buttons on her dress. The swallowed whistle which sounded when he belched, in *City Lights;* the toy dog which he suspected of having done its business in his straw skimmer in *The Cure;* the candle floating on the waters of the flooded dugout, in *Shoulder Arms;* the street lamp in *Easy Street;* his bamboo cane, his mustache, his derby, his oversized, patched shoes, and his ragged morning coat —these are all props which Chaplin used to their fullest.

Frank Capra's comic genius flowers with the props he introduces and develops. His "hat" business in *The Awful Truth,* combined with the business of the dog's uncovering it at embarrassing moments, was a howling success. The same business, with a dog pulling up the fringe in the workroom, in *My Favorite Wife,* was still funny, although it was derivative.

The phone-booth props in *My Favorite Wife* were excellently done. In the hotel sequence, as the wife paged her husband from one booth, her husband answered from another booth in the same row. He tells her he is in the airport of another city. He explains away the sound of the booth's electric fan by saying it is an airplane propeller. Then, when he walks out of the booth, he meets her emerging from her booth, and the result is electrifying.

Character props. Props can also be used to identify and develop character. In Welles's *Citizen Kane* a number of effective props were used—the sled "Rosebud," to symbolize the main character's early childhood, and the jigsaw puzzle, used to characterize him as one who likes to put disjointed things together. This was further developed by the business of having him buy an old European castle and arrange to have it torn apart, shipped to America and, piece by piece, put together again.

Props for actor ease. But the prop has still another use, which accounts for its being introduced, *ad lib,* while the screen play is being shot. Many motion-picture actors and actresses—especially those distaff pretties whose chief claim to acting is a beautiful body, and those stony-faced actors whose gamut of reactions is limited to one stock expression—either stand stiffly while delivering their lines, fidget nervously with their hands, or make stylized, ineffectual gestures. It is then that the distraught director throws a pencil, a handkerchief, a matchbox—anything handy—at them, to give them something to do with their hands. The incessant tossing of coins by gangsters, as introduced by George Raft, must have been one director's ingenious answer to this vexing problem.

Write in props. But such props, when introduced on the spur of the moment, cannot become an integral part of the actual story and, therefore, adaptable for dramatic development. Props of all kinds should be introduced early in the story, developed as the story continues and, where possible, paid off at the end of the picture—a sort of pictorial gimmick, as it were.

Props for child actors. Props should be written in especially when child actors are to be used. Given a prop to work with—a doll, a ball, a toy gun, a dog—anything to take their minds off the fact that they are acting—most child actors can turn in a fairly credible performance. One director who was having difficulty getting his boy actor to perform naturally gave him a small branch of leaves to play with as he spoke his lines. The effect was almost magical—the boy's stiff unnaturalness disappeared and he became the boy he was trying to portray.

The success of the old-time *Our Gang* comedies can be attributed to the fact that all the kids were given mechanical props to work with. They became so absorbed in the workings of the props that they forgot they were actors, and became kids playing naturally with toys.

Props for suspense.   Props have a legitimate place in situations that are not necessarily comic. Hitchcock uses them continually for purposes of suspense. The tea-package label in *The Lady Vanishes;* the rope in *The Rope;* the countless missing letters and papers in practically all his pictures; the bagful of dynamite in *The Time Bomb;* the gun firing directly into the camera in *Spellbound*—these and innumerable other props are Hitchcock's stock in trade for introducing and developing the suspense at which he is so facile.

Props as symbols.   Props have a way of turning into symbols. Most of the props in *The Informer*—the reward poster, the blind man's cane, the silver Judas coins, the bundle of notes pushed by the officer's cane—these also became effective symbols. But the prop need not do such double duty, although an apt combination can be put to better use than a single-purpose prop.

Props come in handy.   The screen-play writer should try to write such props into his script, even when he cannot see any immediate need or use for them. The perceptive director can usually be depended on to use a good furnishing prop, either as a hand prop, as an image frame, or as a compositional element. The miniature equine statues in *Ecstasy,* doubtlessly put on the set to dress it up, were seized upon by the director and used to symbolize the animal passions being portrayed. The wide interstices of the headboard of the bed in *Devil in the Flesh* made for a dramatic trucking shot of the lovers in the bed. Architectural details are used—fireplaces, door details (the church door iron ring tugged at by a passing youngster in a picture whose name has been forgotten), exterior and interior staircases (as, for example, the staircase in Carol Reed's *The Fallen Idol*), archways—these are details the knowing director gratefully adopts. Mamoulian invariably brings his roving camera to rest on an architectural detail. Such details can be written in by the screen-play writer, and thus more completely integrated into the story line and movement.

Done with mirrors.   One of the most useful set props in motion-picture making is the ordinary mirror. A great many filmic effects can be devised and executed with it. Mirrors, for example, can be used in time-lapse dissolves. In the British picture *It Always Rains on Sunday,* many of the time lapses were effected by dissolving through from one mirror image to another. Mirror reflections of Robert Montgomery were used in *Lady in the Lake* to furnish the audience with shots of the hero who, because of the subjective-camera technique, was never seen in the picture. Startling camera effects with mirrors can be achieved: reflections of background action while the foreground action is being conducted in front of the mirror; revelation shots, when the camera pans to a mirror to reveal some startling addition to the shot; revelation shots when, after opening with a close-up on a mirror reflection, the camera pulls back to reveal the person whose image has been reflected, in conjunction with some other person or thing. Mirror reflections also come in handy as cutaway shots from the main action, to cover a very short lapse of time.

One of the first things a director looks for when he examines his set initially is a mirror. For, with it, he realizes he has a filmic tool that can give him added angles and shots. The screen writer, then, should arrange for a mirror to be put on the set. More, he should plumb all the possibilities of mirror-reflection shots, and then write a few into his script. He can feel reasonably sure that, if the mirror shot is apt, if it does not disturb the forward flow, the director will use it.

Props are tools for action movement, story development, character development, acting aids, suspense, comedy, and for countless other purposes. The screen-play writer's bag of motion-picture tools should include a vast assortment of such props. With them, he can include a multitude of "business" bits—without them, he can be pictorially bankrupt.

The subjective camera

Under ordinary conditions, the camera lens furnishes a number of viewpoints to the audience, first of one character and then of another.

Lost Weekend concentrated, in the main, on the viewpoint of the protagonist, as played by Ray Milland. In *Lady in the Lake,* Robert Montgomery concentrated exclusively on the viewpoint of Philip Marlowe, the tough Raymond Chandler detective character he played in the picture. His idea was to use the camera as the eye of his character, so as to keep the audience's attention consistently on the character he was playing.

In Montgomery's picture, a number of trick devices were resorted to in order to further this illusion. He was seen only twice in the film. At other times his presence was suggested by means of shadows, by reflections in mirrors, by shots of hands and feet, by cigarette smoke in front of his face, by having the camera dip when he sat into a chair, and by having a glass of whisky pushed head on into the camera.

The result was a picture that was not too brilliant as far as quality was concerned, for reasons which will be gone into shortly. It created a mild stir, only because of the technique which made the picture a vehicle for a tour-de-force.

This same technique was used in the opening sequence of Mamoulian's *Dr. Jekyll and Mr. Hyde,* where the camera was supposed to be the eyes of Dr. Jekyll. In Pichel's *The Great Commandment,* the camera became the eyes of Dr. Muncheson, as he watched Ingrid Bergman crossing the room to the door.

The pioneer of the subjective camera was Abel Gance, in his *Napoleon,* made about 1926. In it, he strapped a camera to a singer's chest to record the reactions of the theater audience to the singer's rendition of the *La Marseillaise.* In the same picture, he attached a camera to the tail of a runaway horse. He even had it take part in a snowball fight, where it was struck by snowballs, ducked, ran away, and returned.

To present a film that is purely subjective, it is necessary that no compromise be made with objectivity. At no time should the point of view vary. Everything the camera reveals must, of necessity, be only what is seen through the eyes of the protagonist.

This means that the camera must simulate every action performed by the protagonist. When he descends the stairs, it must not slide down smoothly, but must go down swaying from side to side, in rhythmic jerks. Pans must be performed so as to give the effect of glossing over nonessentials, as the human eye does, and concentrating only on important details. And there must be a steady stream of pans, for the eyes are restless and are continually roving from side to side, searching out points of interest. What is more, there must be an intermittent blacking out of the screen, to indicate occasional blinking of the eyes. Then again, a great many more eye-level shots than are necessary in the ordinary picture must be photographed in the subjective film, because that is the normal level of most people. This necessitates building seven-foot doors to accommodate the film magazine and permit it to follow the protagonist through doors.

It is also essential for the other characters to talk directly into the camera while conversing with the protagonist. When this is done time after time, the device begins to become monotonous.

If the object of the subjective camera film is to put the audience into a position of identification with the protagonist, then his conversation and narration must tend to destroy the illusion. For the audience's reactions to what it is made to see through the camera lens may not jibe at all with what the protagonist is saying or thinking.

Thus, it can be seen that the subjective camera technique is at best just another trick device which, when overdone, as it was in *Lady in the Lake,* betrays its technique, and thus nullifies the results desired.

The subjective treatment has been and can continue to be used only if it is handled sparingly and judiciously. If it is employed only as an *aid* to audience participation—in not one character but in most of the major characters—then it can serve its purpose. And it must be used only in those story-line situations that call for this specialized treatment. Finally, the scenes in which the subjective treatment is used must be written and produced so that they flow out of the preceding scene and into the following scene, so that the technique will not obtrude and interrupt the continuity.

Needless to say, because of the costs involved in the many time-consuming takes necessary to obtain an OK take in the subjective-camera treatment, and the work involved in lighting up such long-running takes and of rehearsing camera crews and others in the intricate camera movements, the subjective technique is out of line in the average television film script.

Conventions

Audience acceptance of certain dramatic conventions is necessary to establish rapport between the performers and the audience. The audience, for example, accepts the convention of the missing "fourth wall" on the stage. At the same time, it will accept the shadowy figures flickering on the screen as humans, because such an acceptance must be present if there is to be enjoyment and understanding.

Thus, the audience has come to accept the presence of an orchestra accompanying a singer on a roof top, for instance, where no orchestra is visible or could even be present.

The point is this: In utterly realistic pictures, where everything must contribute to the sum total of the realistic effect to be achieved, such conventions should be resorted to only sparingly. Milestone's picture *The Grapes of Wrath* is an excellent example of this type of realistic picture. It would have suffered if the usual motion-picture conventions had been used. For, in it, only that which served to fill in the details of the mosaic of the lives of the California Okies was recorded, and the result was a picture that faithfully re-created the life of the itinerant worker. The audience was almost able, at times, to smell their variegated odors. Rossellini's *Open City* is another example of cinematic realism that excluded the use of unrealistic conventions.

But there are other types of pictures in which many of the cinematic conventions are completely accepted by the audience; musicals, especially the lavish musical productions of Warner Brothers, contain many of these conventions, which the audience accepts as blithely as they do the shadowed images on the screen.

A story is told of an argument Hitchcock had with his composer for the picture *Lifeboat*. The composer was insisting that he be permitted to compose some music to be laid under the shipwreck scene.

"Who ever heard of an orchestra playing at a shipwreck?" Hitchcock is reported to have said.

The composer was quick with his retort, "Who ever heard of a cameraman being at one?"

Composition

It may have become obvious that various attempts have been made in this book to deal with subjects that heretofore have been considered outside the pale of the screen-play writer's domain. Much attention, for instance, has been given to certain aspects of cutting, which are in the film editor's province, and of shot sequences, and so on, which have been the director's job. An attempt will now be made to give the screen writer some idea of the composition of the images on the screen: that is, the place and position of the physical, decorative elements of the shot, so as to make for an artistic and esthetically satisfying presentation. These have been the consideration of the director, the set designer, and the set decorator.

This is being done with a definite purpose in mind. The role of the screen-play writer has been relegated to a position of minor importance, because he has permitted himself to be jobbed out of certain responsibilities which were inherently his. As a matter of fact, a survey at the Hollywood studios showed that the writer's minimum salary is less than the minimum established for the second assistant hairdressers! This, in spite of the fact that it is only with the work of the screen-play writer that the business of making a picture can begin!

It is for this reason, then, that this book has included a discussion of composition in motion pictures. For the screen writer creates the actions and dialogue of a group of people, not in a vacuum, but set against certain scenic and architectural backgrounds. And if the people and their actions and their speech are to be integrated into their background, the best place in which to do so, naturally, is at the source of their inception as characters—with the screen-play writer himself.

It would be impossible, in the short space given to this subject, to cover it in complete detail. Nevertheless, certain of the basic principles can be given, so that the writer will be equipped with enough information to be able to suggest composition in his screen plays, intelligently and effectively.

Composition definition. In motion pictures, composition is that quality of the set-content arrangement, animate and inanimate, which focuses audience attention on important details in an orderly, esthetically satisfying manner.

Three-way composition. This composition is achieved in three ways: with lights, with set-content position, and with character movement. The screen-play writer should be concerned, in the main, with the last two, although a basic knowledge of set lighting could be of considerable aid.

In writing set descriptions and in suggesting set props, character movements, and camera movement, the screen writer must always keep in mind the important fact that the audience's eye will travel naturally from one point of attention to another. In order to take advantage of this natural tendency—to make sure, in other words, that the eye will be invited to follow, rather than discouraged—the following principles must be kept in mind constantly:

Emotional content analysis. Determine beforehand what is the key emotion to be portrayed. Is it to be comic, dramatic, brilliant, formal, informal, factual, bizarre, frothy, gruesome, or gay?

Establish mood patterns. With the proper over-all pattern of mood established, plan your sets so that they fit into that particular mood. That accomplished, go into the mood pattern scene by scene, and try to establish each specific mood pattern so that it fits in, in some way—even by contrast—with the general over-all mood pattern.

Von Sternberg was especially successful in establishing such mood patterns, and in sustaining them throughout his pictures. His innovation of painting sets white to control his lighting more perfectly served to unify the picture's pictorial qualities so that he was able to achieve pictorial continuity in addition to the other types of continuity.

In the same director's *Salvation Hunters,* the slum background was faithfully and realistically limned throughout the picture. At the same time, he used the exterior ugliness to mirror the interior ugliness in the lives of his characters.

Gregg Toland, perhaps the finest cameraman in the business, wrote of his lighting of *Wuthering Heights:* " (it) was a soft picture, diffused with soft, candle-lighting effects. I tried to make the love scenes beautiful in a romantic way. It was a love story, a story of escape and fantasy. So I tried to keep it that way photographically, and let the audience dream through a whirl of beautiful close-ups."

Simplicity. Once the mood pattern for each scene has been established, the writer should begin to consider what his sets should contain in the way of architectural design, set decoration, and props.

Old-fashioned attraction. He should remember, for instance, that the old-fashioned has a strange attraction for both young and old. Wherever possible, he should indicate old-fashioned residences for interiors, with old-fashioned architectural features, all modified, of course, for modern appreciation. Only for an absolutely realistic representation of a Victorian parlor, for instance, would it be advisable to suggest a clutter of whang-doodles, antimacassars, and whatnots. Refurbished attics, modernized brownstones, period country architecture—these, and many others, are constantly being used as sets because of their color and uniqueness.

Keep it simple. But in describing such a set for use, the screenplay writer must keep it simple. Only those things that contribute to the over-all mood pattern should be suggested. The set-decoration props should be confined to the absolute essentials. They should all be predetermined to suit the action of the scene, so that they will not serve to distract the eye of the audience which, as has been explained, tends to move freely from one point of attention to the next.

This simplicity should be especially considered by the writer of television films. Again, because of the comparatively small screen on which his drama will be viewed, he should suggest no finely wrought, delicately detailed backgrounds. Instead, he should indicate backgrounds, furniture, and props composed of large patterns, with sharp changes in contrast. Areas that are large and have an over-all color should not be used, especially in the foreground, so as to obtain variegated density and avoid "horizontal smear."

The television writer should also avoid sets in which large white expanses of walls are contiguous to large black walls or props or furnishings. On the television screen the result would be a bleeding over from one to the other.

Variety.   But, at the same time, for theater-presentation pictures, the fact should not be forgotten that variety can be a powerful means of retaining the roving attention of the audience. This variety, in the matter of set content, will be useful when shooting from various angles on the set, so that the background can furnish a sufficient number of pictorially different shots on the same set.

While furnishing specific space-filling set props, the writer should also suggest that there be sufficient *space between* props. Not only will this permit character and camera movement, but it will also serve as a frame of reference for the props themselves, and will allow for the very important quality of balance.

Balance

For composition concerns itself largely with this most important quality. It is the well-balanced picture that attracts the eye and satisfies the innate desire of the onlooker for the symmetrical. The "symmetrical," however, does not necessarily mean that one side of the picture should contain the same number of elements—in size, in weight, in rhythm, and so on—as the opposite side. This formal type of balance is entirely too pat for the eye to accept. It is static in quality and so tends to retard the flow of pictorial movement. Balance, too, should furnish movement to the over-all flow of continuity.

Off-center balance. Balance should be achieved by setting the center off the actual center of the picture, and then weighting the smaller segment with more content than the larger segment. This suggestion should be remembered in describing close two-shots or three-shots. Close-ups of one-shot subjects should be arranged so that the person is a little to the right of, and a little above, center.

The same effect should be striven for vertically as well as horizontally. For example, instead of having all the characters seated, some of them should be permitted to stand while others remain seated to achieve variety in height with pictorial rhythm.

Lower left to upper right. It is a well-known fact to cameramen that the most interesting portion of the frame is a diagonal, from the lower left-hand corner to the upper right-hand corner. Attention is centered on this diagonal flow. Take advantage of this, then, by suggesting that important action take place in that portion. Have that action move from the lower left frame to the upper right frame.

Strive for depth. At the same time, strive to get depth into each picture, by the use of two strongly defined planes. This can be done, of course, with a wide-angle lens and special lighting. But it can be aided considerably if the screen writer suggests that the set contain in it elements for effecting this desirable quality. For instance, in long scenic shots, suggest that the foreground contain a tree, a rock, or some other close object in one plane, to set off the distant scenic view in another plane. In long interior shots, a significant prop can be used in the immediate foreground while action, in focus, takes place in the background; or a close-up—or even extreme close-up— is effective, while action takes place in the middle and extreme distance.

Frame foregrounds. Try to arrange for arches, for doorways, for anything that may serve as a frame in the foreground so as to highlight the object of chief interest in the background. The foreground action can also be in silhouette, an innovation of Von Sternberg, who first used it in *The Case of Lena Smith.*

Most of William Wyler's later pictures—photographed by Gregg Toland—feature this quality of compositional depth. In *The Letter,*

The Little Foxes, and *The Best Years of Our Lives,* he resorted to photography in depth and succeeded admirably. As Wyler wrote, "Gregg Toland's remarkable facility for handling background and foreground action has enabled me . . . to develop a better technique of staging my scenes. For example, I can have action and reaction in the same shot without having to cut back and forth from individual cuts of the characters. This makes for smooth continuity, an almost effortless flow of scene, for much more interesting composition in each shot, and lets the spectator look from one to the other character at his own will, do his own cutting."

Movement composition

It is common knowledge that movement of any sort has more attraction value than the static. This is especially true in the motion picture, which depends so much on character movement to achieve the all-important flow of continuity.

Limit background movement. Extraneous movement, however, can negate this flow, especially when it is thrown into the background while the main-action movement takes place in the foreground. This fact is well appreciated by scene-stealing actors who manage to distract attention from the main action in the foreground by fiddling with a handkerchief, pulling an ear, reacting unnecessarily, and so on.

If a beach scene is to be indicated, for instance, make certain that important action is not photographed with the rolling surf in the background. In Carol Reed's *The Third Man,* the effectiveness of the ferris wheel scene was lost completely, because it was photographed with a close-up of Welles and Cotten in one of the wheel's cars as the other cars rotated in the background. This continuous movement was seen through the car's windows (in process-screen projection). The result was that some important plot points were lost and the audience was left with the impression that there were many plot holes in the story.

So, be careful of background movement such as candle-flame

flickers, clock pendulums, fireplace flames, character movements, and so on, while setting up important main-action shots in the foreground.

At the same time, when there is no foreground action taking place —as in a scenic long shot—try to inject some sort of distant background action into the shot, so as to carry audience attention, which can become lost in scenic beauty. Try to suggest some moving animal or vehicle in the background—a horse, a wagon, a ship, or a sea gull, a train, a moving cloud even, to insure audience interest.

Dynamic symmetry

In art, dynamic symmetry is a device long used to furnish motion to what is, patently, a static picture. It utilizes a system of giving lines perspective, so that they converge to a point on the horizon, usually the point of main attraction, for the purpose of drawing the eye to it.

Dynamic symmetry can be applied to the motion-picture image as well, to endow an otherwise static shot with action and movement dynamically suggested.

Dynamic symmetry with low angles.   Thus, in a low-angle shot of a tall building, the picture should be shot so that the lines of the building, instead of flowing up parallel to the sky, would converge, so that they could meet at some spot off frame.

Dynamic symmetry with set furnishings.   In interiors, this same principle could be used to focus the center of attraction on whatever the writer has in mind. Thus, if an important entrance is to be made through a door, a full shot of the room should be indicated first. It should be shot at such an angle that the door would serve as the point where all the perspective lines meet. With this established, the writer can then, in his set description, indicate that certain furnishings be included on the set. These could lend themselves ideally to focusing the door by means of dynamic symmetry. A couch, for example, could be put in the foreground, camera left, and running lengthwise to the camera. To camera right, against the wall, could be a fireplace, with its lines converging to the door as a focal point. The wall to camera left could contain a bookcase or a window with its lines converging to the door. And overhead, a chandelier could be so placed that its lines would converge to the door as well. So, although this static shot could be an an opening scene, the more dynamic composition would give it movement and, in addition, furnish a pictorial continuity for the audience, thus preparing them for the dramatic entrance.

Static close-up with dynamic symmetry. The same principles can be applied to the static close-up. Even a close-up of an ordinary matchbox, for example, can be made more dynamic with suggested movement. With a pen at one side, an envelope opener on the other side and, above it, a slash of paper placed in an opposing angle, to furnish counterbalance, this ordinary, static matchbox can be given movement that would not deter the flow of pictorial movement necessary to the film.

Orson Welles's pictures contain dozens of examples of this use of dynamic symmetry for pictures. They should be studied well, for they can furnish more material regarding this vital subject than an entire book.

Television film writers, on the other hand, should remember to suggest that all important action be photographed center screen. The outer edges of a television screen project poor image definition, and the pictures have a tendency to become distorted in those areas. Also, the lower and right edges of a television screen are more susceptible to edge-flare. The television film writer, therefore, should not suggest that any dark subject, sets, props, costumes, etc., be used in those particular areas.

The foregoing should be considered only as tips for effecting better composition by means of indicating suggestions in screen plays. It is entirely within the scope of the cameraman to arrange for composition at the behest of the director. But there is no reason why the screen-play writer should not be able to furnish certain basic essentials, so as to aid in achieving the best composition available.

Epiphanies

An epiphany, according to the dictionary, is a Greek word that means a manifestation. It originated as a name for a religious feast, celebrated on January 6, to commemorate the arrival of the Magi, which was supposed to be the occasion of the first manifestation of Christ to the Gentiles of his time.

Now just what has this religious rite to do with literary life in general and screen-play writing in particular? James Joyce first used the term in *Stephen Hero*, to illustrate, as he put it, "a sudden spiritual manifestation, whether in the vulgarity of speech or of gesture, of a memorable phase of the mind itself."

Joyce's use of the epiphany can be illustrated with his thoughts on the Ballast Office dock.

"Yes," said Stephen, "I will pass it time after time, allude to it, refer to it, catch a glimpse of it. It is only an item in the catalogue of Dublin's street furniture. Then all at once I see it and I know at once what it is: epiphany. Imagine my glimpses at that dock as the gropings of a spiritual eye which seeks to adjust its vision to an exact focus. The moment the focus is reached the object is epiphanized. It is just in this epiphany that I find the . . . supreme quality of beauty."

How, then, can the epiphany be adapted to the motion picture?

It can be done in three ways: first, by the characters' psychological traits which, in turn, can be epiphanized by means of their dialogue, and then by means of their physical actions and reactions—that is, their gestures, expressions, manner of walking, and so on.

Such epiphanies have been created in many films, and these isolated bits stand out in memory with that "supreme quality of beauty." Bette Davis' vitriolic reading of "You disgust me!" in Somerset Maugham's *Of Human Bondage* is a beautiful example of epiphanizing, because it includes a perfect synthesis of dialogue and expression.

On the other hand, Cagney's sudden smacking of the grapefruit half in the girl's face, in one of his early pictures, epiphanized something that many men, at some time or other, have been wanting to do with some woman or other.

The screen's first cut-in close-up, the pan of beans in Griffith's *Birth of a Nation,* had this same effect on audiences—it was electrifying.

Laughton's Bronx cheer in *If I Had a Million;* the tinkle of the Judas silver falling to the floor in the wake scene of *The Informer;* the aimless chatter of Dolly in *Brief Encounter,* wasting the precious last moments of the two lovers; the entire staircase scene in *Potemkin;* the horse dangling in mid-air from the upraised drawbridge in *Ten Days That Shook the World;* Ray Milland's typewriter-hocking sequence in *Lost Weekend;* the expression on Chaplin's face when the girl did not arrive to partake of the dinner he had prepared for her, in *The Gold Rush;* the Louise Rainer telephone bit in *The Great Ziegfeld;* the land rush in *Cimarron;* the cockroach race in *Lives of a Bengal Lancer;* the feathered Scot's cap falling to the ground in René Clair's *The Ghost Goes West;* the idyllic marriage of Poil de Carotte, in Duvivier's film of the same name, in which the two children walk through a lovely countryside scene together, followed by a long line of farm animals; the close-up of the spy's little finger in *The 39 Steps;* the hilarious scene in *Rake's Progress* when Rex Harrison breaks up the chairman's speech by interrupting him with replies to rhetorical questions; the poignant moment in *Bicycle Thief* when the little son veered off petulantly from his father, who was also in a pique, and walked parallel with him on the sidewalk; that moment of nonrecognition, when the lady suddenly discovers that all the people have changed, in *The Lady Vanishes*—these are all unforgettable examples of Joyce's "a sudden spiritual manifestation" that makes for the filmic epiphany.

These are the rare touches of genius which often glow in an otherwise mass of dross. They are not accidents. They are the result of experience, knowledge, and a conditioned intuition that make for the difference between a hack screen-play writer and one who, like the Elizabethan dramatists, is to be considered a poet.

For these bits of filmic epiphany can be construed as pure poetry. They are lyrical interpolations that soar with unalloyed beauty. They are, to use a clichéd but apt phrase, "poetry in motion."

Symbolism

A symbol should serve a definite purpose. It is the screen writer's personal poetics and creative *representation* of what is otherwise a baldly stated fact. In a motion picture, the symbol can show something more beautifully, more startlingly, more feelingly, more pictorially than if it were shown in the traditional, prosaic *presentational* manner.

The motion picture is an ideal vehicle for the literary and pictorial symbol—properly used. Improperly used, it can only deter the forward flow of movement. In a literary work, the symbol may be one which is not immediately obvious but which can be thought out until its meaning becomes known. But in a motion picture, the symbol must be strictly on the conscious level. It must be obvious, clear-cut, easily identifiable, and capable of being instantly grasped by the audience.

This is so because, unlike a book, where the reader can go back and reread the passage containing the symbol, the motion-picture audience is unable to look back to the improperly understood symbol for further simplification. It flashes by on the screen, and then it is off again and will be lost completely if it is not immediately comprehended.

The motion-picture symbol, then, must have universality of appeal. It cannot be so esoteric that its meaning and relationships are known only to its creator, or else the audience will be left with a vague feeling of dissatisfaction and obscurity.

Symbolism has a definite place in the motion picture. It has always been so, as far back as the time when stock shots of London and Paris were first flashed on the screen to set the scene for the following sequence, which was supposed to take place in those locales.

In the old silent picture—and especially in those from Europe—the pictorial symbol was used to obtain cross-reference effects. In Lang's *Destiny*, Death was represented by three lighted candles, each symbolizing the span of life of one of the characters. As each of the candles flickered out, one character died.

A number of examples of the use of the motion-picture symbol come to mind. Like those lambent directorial touches that suddenly light up an otherwise drab scene, the felicitous symbol can make a totally unprepossessing shot glow with meaning.

In Pick's *Shattered,* the shot of the railroad trackwalker swinging his lantern was intercut a number of times to symbolize the monotony of his life.

In Griffith's *Dream Street,* the masked violinist was supposed to symbolize Evil, while the rapt crowd, listening, represented suffering humanity.

In Gance's *Napoleon,* the tumultuous session of the convention was symbolized by a storm shot, and Bonaparte's angry face was dissolved into a rugged eagle, while the cast-off women became dead leaves in the wind.

In Eisenstein's *Potemkin* the opening shot of the picture showed an enormous frothy wave breaking against the shore, a symbol of revolution. The shot of the haunch of meat infested with maggots was supposed to symbolize the condition of Russia before the revolution.

In *Cimarron,* when George Stone, the Jewish peddler, was beaten up and thrown to the ground, his sprawled arms fell on a couple of crossed sticks to symbolize the death of another Jew on another wooden cross.

Symbolism found its most sophisticated use in Czinner's *Ecstasy,* which was loaded with symbols to the point of satiety.

In Lang's *Metropole,* the beam from the mad inventor's flashlight, encircling Maris, whom he was chasing, was used to symbolize the nonescapable wall that trapped her.

In the same director's *Scarlet Street,* the intermittent flicking on and off of the off-scene electric sign symbolized the flashes of sanity and insanity in the mind of the murderous cashier.

The same effect, in Technicolor, was obtained in the same manner by Hitchcock in the closing scenes of *The Rope,* when the two psychotic young murderers were confronted with their guilt by their former professor. Reflections of an electric sign just outside the penthouse windows illumined their faces alternately with the color red—associated with insanity and symbolizing their warped brains; the color white—symbolizing their youth; and the color green—symbolizing their sane, lucid moments. The phantasmagoria of colors all symbolized the obvious schizophrenia of Branden, the evil genius of the picture.

In the picture *M*, the shot of Lorre's shadow hovering over the frightened little girl graphically symbolized the tragedy that was soon to take place. In the same picture, the shot of the little girl's ball rolling out of the bushes symbolized her death at Lorre's hands better than any more literal shot, even of the murder, itself.

The same type of symbol was used in *Hangmen Also Die,* when the Gestapo man's derby was seen to roll around comically and come to a dead stop under the table on which his murdered body lay outsprawled.

Ford's *The Informer,* according to Dudley Nichols, its screen-play writer, was replete with symbols, some "obvious, much of it concealed except from the close observer."

The foggy night in which the entire action played was supposed to symbolize groping humanity and the mental fog in which Gypo moved that night. The reward poster was a symbol of betrayal; the Black and Tan officer's stick that pushed Gypo's reward money across the desk was a symbol of contempt; the blind man's tap-tap-tapping symbolized Gypo's conscience; and the carved image of Christ at the picture's end symbolized, of course, Gypo's salvation in his Lord.

In the more recently produced British film *Gone to Earth,* a shot of a shoe crushing a flower symbolized the seduction of the girl played by Jennifer Jones.

There is a school of thought that objects to the obvious symbol as gauche and inartistic. The same school operates in other media of expression and communication. It is the school of obfuscationists. The fact remains that motion pictures are *primarily* an instrument of communication. First, they must communicate ideas and sensations. They cannot do this by making symbols so unidentifiable that, only by re-viewing the picture a number of times, can the symbols become clothed with meaning. Nor can dozens of explanatory commentaries be published, as was necessary with Joyce's work in order to bring his hundreds of symbols into recognizable focus.

Certainly the more obvious symbols—the clichés, in other words—should be avoided. But, just as it is the duty of the screen-play writer to create fresh characters and situations and dialogue, so it is part of his job to create fresh symbols—and re-create fresh uses of clichéd symbols—in order to illumine the prosaic with the poetic.

But these symbols must be understood at first glance, at least partially. For the symbol need not be *completely* obvious at once. It can create a sensation of understanding in the subconscious, so that the cumulative result will create the effect desired in the audience.

The pictorial symbol can be of great use to the screen writer if it is used intelligibly. If it cannot be understood immediately, and absorbed, then it serves only to obscure, to clutter up and, thus, retard filmic movement and continuity.

Topicalisms

Motion-picture production is such that a great deal of time elapses between the period in which a screen play is written and the time when it is released for public viewing. In some rare instances—as when a picture is rushed through production and released as soon as possible in order to jump the gun on a competing studio that is making a similar picture, or when early release is essential to permit the picture to become a current year Academy award participant—a picture's release date may not be too far separated from the time when its screen play was written.

Ordinarily, however, for a number of reasons—such as a backlog of sound-stage or Technicolor commitments, constant rewrites and polish jobs on the script, casting delays, and the like—from eight months to two years may elapse before the writer can obtain theater audience reactions to his work.

This delay can lead to some serious pitfalls for topicalisms. At the time the screen writer is fashioning his script, Sugar Ray Robinson may still be a boxing champ and one of the writer's lines may run, "Yeah! he may have a Casper Milquetoast build, but he sure packs a Joe Walcott wallop."

But during the interim that elapses before the picture (or even this book) is released, old Joe may have been KO'd by a more effective puncher. Hence, when the picture is released, the allusion to Walcott will have been outmoded, and will definitely date the picture as being out of step with the times.

MacKinlay Kantor's story for the picture *Best Years of Our Lives* was written in 1945. But by the time the picture was produced, in 1946, and finally released, in 1947, a considerable number of changes from the original story had to be made to avoid obvious dating and topical references which would have made a period piece out of what was intended to have almost newsreel immediacy.

Avoid year dates. Unless it is absolutely required by script demands, the screen-play writer should avoid any reference to specific year dates. That is why, when calendars are photographed on desks, walls, or in time lapses, the year is not shown unless it is demanded by the story.

Avoid dated gags. The writer should never resort to topical gags, or to gag phrases, unless they have become stabilized by universal usage and, of course, unless their use is intended to establish the period as the one in which the gag was being used, or to establish character. An older, conservative man, whose character is such that he is inflexibly part of the past, could be made to say, "Twenty-three skidoo," or "Oh, you kid!" without courting dating trouble. But the difficulty arises with the indisputable fact that the average gag phrase of more recent years—the "is zat so," the "Confucius say" and the "but definitely"—become outdated in a comparatively short time and, like short skirts seen in a long-skirt era, create only a sense of ludicrousness rather than of topical style.

To sum up: Unless story demands call for it, the screen-play writer should never permit any topical reference to remain in his script—an actual date; a historical reference (alluding, for example, to the current president, who may die the next day) ; a currently popular phrase; a currently popular song title; a current bit of newspaper gossip; or a current newspaper headline—anything that may become a disturbing factor in the audience's picture attention when the motion picture is finally released.

Sound

Until the movies began to talk, they were only two-dimensional. An attempt was made to give silent pictures a third-dimensional quality by adding a musical background—usually a tinny, out-of-tune piano —that furnished, in addition to mood music, music that simulated suggestive sound background.

It was when the talkies arrived that sound came into its own as an integral part of motion-picture making. For, with it, it brought perfectly synchronized mood music, instrumental music to suit the action being played on the screen, spoken dialogue, and sound effects.

You have only to try this experiment to realize how important sound effects are to motion pictures: close your eyes at the next movie you attend and notice that, to a certain degree, depending on the type of action being played, you will be able to follow that action. Again, you may have noticed, when the sound apparatus in a projector fails, how flat, how unreal, how shadowlike the shadows on the screen suddenly become. It is as though the life blood had suddenly been drained out of the characters.

When electronic sound was first perfected in Germany, Walter Ruttman, a painter who had been experimenting with abstract films, recorded a three-hundred-foot sound montage called *Week End*. In it, solely through the use of sound effects, he told a story (which was radio-broadcast) of two lovers who take a week end in the country. With only a few lines of dialogue, with depot sounds, train sounds, bird calls, leaf rustling sounds, crowd noises—even with fragments of silence—Ruttman was able to present what amounted to a sound symphony.

For sound can be quite important to motion pictures. Properly handled, it can give verisimilitude to any scene, exterior or interior, action or otherwise.

Unfortunately, though, the quality of sound is out of the hands of the screen-play writer. A complex setup of boom men, recordists, sound mixers, sound editors, sound dubbers, and the like, become the eventual arbiters of the quality and, quite often, the nature of the sound that comes out of the sound track. But the writer, to a great extent, can suggest that certain sounds be used, *when* they should be used, and *how* they should be used, and hope that when the picture is completed some of his suggestions will have been followed.

Know your sound effects. The screen-play writer should realize, first, that the studio and specialized service sound departments possess sound effects of almost every noise to which the ears of man have been subjected—from a volcanic eruption to the sound of bacon frying in a pan or of mice squeaking on the floor.

Selectivity. But because these sounds are available—either from stock sound tracks, or from live-sound, "wild" sound tracks shot on the set—the writer must realize that he should practice the same selectivity with sound effects as he does with action and with dialogue.

Sound effects should be built and orchestrated and afforded the same attention as is given to all the other elements of picture making. Sound effects should be used selectively. The human ear itself when listening to normal, workaday sounds, practices an almost instinctive process of sound mixing and sound selection. It rejects and channels into the subconscious sounds that are extraneous to understanding, and accepts only those that are related to what the conscious is aware of.

This selectivity also operates in disassociating sound from sight. For it is quite possible to give visual attention to one thing and, at the same time, be listening to the sound of something outside the scope of vision. These are physiological factors that must be often considered by the screen-play writer.

An important advantage of sound effects is that, as far as film length is concerned, they are not additive. Because they can be laid behind a scene's action, they require no extra footage. That is why they can round out, with a three-dimensional effect, what could be flat and only two-dimensional.

Establish sound. The sound effect of heavy footsteps in a murder mystery, or in any other type of suspense scene, can lend an air of approaching danger to a close-up of feet walking across a creaking floor. This sound effect, however, must first be established, not only aurally but visually, in a close-up. After that, only the sound may be used. This is so because the sound of footsteps in itself is not distinctive enough—compared, say, to the sound of a dog's bark—to be comprehended by itself alone. In addition, the sight of unidentified feet adds to the suspense.

Indirection with sound. Sound effects can do more than merely add to what is being seen. They can suggest, by indirection, what is not being seen, provided, of course, that the sound effect—unlike that of footsteps—is easily identifiable.

When Chaplin made his *Woman of Paris,* he was forced to suggest the leave-taking of a French train, because French coaches were unavailable in Hollywood. So, by means of lights and shadows flashing across the faces of the characters—by indirection—he suggested the presence of the train. Had he been able to lay in a sound track (this was in pretalkie days) he would have been doubly successful for, in addition to sight, he could have used the huff and puff of escaping steam, the roar and jangle of the wheels, the thin, piping whistle of the station starter, together with the other sounds, authentically French, that are the aural accompaniments to a starting train.

A perfect example of sound being used indirectly was seen in Hitchcock's *The Rope.* In almost the entire closing reel, after Stewart had fired the shots through the open penthouse window, the sound track began to carry (considerably diminished in volume) first, the voice of one person who had heard the shot, then the voice of another person. and then still another person until finally the voice of a policeman was introduced to cap the babble of excited voices. The whole sound sequence was then capped by the sound of a squad car's siren—introduced first in the extreme distance, and then faded in gradually—whining in the street below the penthouse and thus symbolizing, without its ever being shown visually, the eventual electric chair demise of the two murderers.

Sound sequences. In King Vidor's *Hallelujah,* the last ten minutes of the film—the chase sequence through the swamps—used only a sound-effects sound track to carry the action: the swish of water, the sucking squoosh of feet in the mud, the rustle of shrubbery, and the shrill cries of birds. The last-mentioned sound effect, by the way, was in the form of three bird cries punctuating a period of intense silence. The over-all effect of this sound-effect montage was to make the chase fraught with terror.

Fill in with sound. Sound effects can also suggest the whole of some thing while only part of it is being photographed. Train interiors, for example, especially tight shots which do not furnish sufficient background architecture and furnishings for quick identification, can be ideally suggested merely by indicating that running train sounds (in considerably decreased volume) be laid in behind the shot.

Writers of cheaply produced theater and television films should lean heavily on these subterfuges for the economies they can bring.

Recalled sound. Memory recalls of sounds previously heard can be used as aural flash backs in a sound superimposure, to bring back some sound effect from the past in order to motivate an action of the present.

Usually such sound superimposures are distorted electronically from the natural sound, to avoid leaving the impression that they are actually being heard.

In *Scarlet Street,* this effect was used as a climax motivator when Edward Robinson hanged himself after hearing the muffled memory recalls of the girl who was condemned to death for the murder he had committed.

Sound transitions. Sound effects—as was explained in the time lapse section—make ideal time lapses and scene transitions. As symbols, too, the sound effect is an esthetically satisfying device.

Sound leitmotifs. Another very important use for sound effects is their ready adaptation as leitmotifs and thus as over-all transition devices. In Hans Richter's *Everything Turns, Everything Moves,* the sound effects of a carnival setting were used, and referred back to constantly, as a connective device for the entire picture.

Three-dimensional sound. Within the shot itself the screen-play writer should make use of sound to its fullest extent. A street scene, for example, is not truly a street scene if the audience hears only the sound of the dialogue. This is particularly so when street scenes are shot indoors, on a sound stage. Studio acoustics tend to enliven the quality of the voices, whereas, outdoors, they would be recorded with a more natural quality. This unreality becomes exaggerated when background street sounds are not dubbed in. To compensate for this deficiency, street sounds, such as passing autos, distant street-cars, and even unidentified human voices should be introduced. They should be sufficiently diminished in volume so as not to inter-fere with the main dialogue. These voices need have no immediate relevance to the action being shot. But they can offset phony sound-stage acoustics and, at the same time, give background verisimilitude to the foreground main action.

In the French picture *Women of the Forest,* most of the action takes place in a few interior sets. But a sense of the world outside is furnished by a brilliantly detailed sound track of a variety of street noises, as a sort of antiphonal background to the drama being enacted indoors.

Avoid sound on cue.   A serious fault encountered in the use of background sound effects is to be found in the manner in which they are introduced. In the picture *The Good Earth,* for example, sound effects of all sorts were introduced—the whir of locusts, rain, thunder, wind, and so on. But there was something mechanical about them. They all seemed to come in right on cue, as though a director or prompt man were in the wings telling the sound-effects man when and where he should turn on the particular sound and turn it off again. Some of this could be attributed to the sound dubber, who neglected to fade in and fade out his sounds. But much was also due to the screen-play writer, who should have indicated that the sounds be introduced gradually, that is by building sound effects as well as visual effects.

Cap with sound.   When a sound effect is to be used as a scene-capper, as is often the case, it should always be introduced before-hand. In Laughton's *The Beachcomber,* for instance, a cuckoo clock was used to cap the scene in which Elsa Lanchester had made a silly remark. The clock's "cuckoo" was an apt ironic comment on it. But the effect could have been heightened had the audience been intro-duced to it previously by way of having it "cuckoo" once or twice in the background and without pointing it up with a close-up.

As a matter of fact, this was done *after* the cuckoo was used, to cap the scene in which Lanchester's brother was alone and the cuckoo clock sounded once. This suggests that the writer may have originally written in the shot with the brother at the correct time—that is, preceding the clock's commentary "cuckoo"—but that the film editor cut the shot into the wrong place.

In Ruttman's *Melody of the World*, the war sequence, which was replete with the roar of cannon and other battle sounds, was suddenly cut to a close-up of a woman screaming in anguish. The effect was made even more stunning when a cut was made to a field of white crosses, brooding in dead silence. The same effect was achieved in *The Life of Beethoven*, where, after loud claps of thunder were established outside Beethoven's house, a cut to a close-up on Beethoven, inside the house, was accompanied by utter silence, pointing up his tragic deafness.

Volume important. Another fault in sound that can be laid to inept sound-dubbing is the insistence on keeping the sound levels of all the people in a scene at the same volume, despite their varying distances from the camera. This occurs because when live dialogue is being recorded on the stage the sound recordists are afraid of losing a voice. Hence, they ride gain so that all the voices emerge on the sound track with exactly the same volume, tempo, and pitch.

Sound volume, like sound itself, can give a third-dimensional reality which should be retained as often as possible. In Hitchcock's *The Rope*, where for the most part live dialogue was recorded on the stage, this effect was striven for and achieved. But in those shots that were shot silent, with the dialogue post-synced in, no attempt was made to vary the sound levels. The result was that when one of the characters walked away from the camera—almost to the other side of the room—his voice retained its volume, and did not give the impression that he was some distance from the camera and from the other character conducting the dialogue.

Although this is the sound dubber's fault, the screen-play writer can suggest, in his sound directions, that the individual levels vary according to their distance from each other and from the camera. Such suggestions may serve to keep this important fact in mind, and can give the sound recordist a chance, if he works with a script, to prepare for the desired effect.

Sound volume increases.   There may be times when it is necessary to increase sound volume above the realistic level. The ticking of a watch or clock may have to be brought up in volume if it is essential to the action. Footsteps, creaking floors, doors and the like, may have to be increased in volume. But for most purposes, an attempt should be made to re-create sounds and sound effects realistically.

Sound filters.   The screen writer should also be conversant with the work of the electronic voice-filtering devices: echo chamber effects, the Sonovox, and other such sound devices.

Phone filter.   The sound filter should be used to simulate the effect of a voice on the receiving end of a telephone. It can also be used to distort the sound of a voice on other occasions, as in simulating the voice of a radio announcer or the voice of a person on the receiving end of an office intercom system, or as a memory recall, when the character is remembering some remark or sound, or music heard in the past.

Echo chamber.   The echo chamber is an electronic device that imparts an echo effect to a voice, even though it may not be spoken in a place that produces an echo. It should be suggested when a speech is being made in a hall, when a conversation is being conducted over the phone in a phone booth, when dialogue, in other words, is spoken in any place that may result in an echoed quality, such as in subterranean caves and tunnels, empty rooms, basements, and the like. Once again, this should be strictly within the domain of the sound dubber, but the writer should suggest the use of these effects and hope that the suggestions will be taken.

Sonovox.   The Sonovox is an electronic device that gives a human-voice quality to what is ordinarily a nonhuman sound. Thus, a violin can be made to talk, or a train siren (as in the well-known Bromo Seltzer commercial), or even a cow. The use of this effect, though, is limited. It can be resorted to as a comedy effect in farces, as a strange, eerie effect in fantasies or dream sequences.

Budget with sound.   The use of sound effects in cheaply made budget pictures for movie houses and television films is almost imperative. A café or restaurant scene can be shot by building only a small corner set and then laying in a sound track containing the background hum of voices, the tinkle of glassware and plates, and the sound of a small orchestra, to give the impression that the corner is actually part of a larger set.

Similar subterfuges suggest themselves: corners of large railroad stations, hotel lobbies, street corners, airports, and the like. An enterprising producer can get the effect of a whole theater simply by resorting to such tight shots as: a segment of the stage on which the action takes place, a shot of a small part of the orchestra, a shot of a small part of the audience for reaction shots, and a shot, from the wings, of the action taking place on the stage, with the camera focused so as to catch only a few faces in the audience. And overriding all these tight shots are laid in the sounds of audience reactions—handclapping, coughs, and so on—plus the music of the orchestra, dubbed in from another sound track.

Orson Welles was able to do away with these audience reaction shots entirely, simply by shooting into a bed of lights that were supposed to represent the footlights, which were to give the effect of blinding the performers—and the movie audience—to the theater audience apparently seated out front.

Music

Because music has become such an integral part of motion-picture making, and because the screen-play writer is the prime mover of all motion pictures, it is incumbent on him to familiarize himself with music as one of the elements of motion-picture making.

Good music can improve a bad screen play. Bad music can also break a good screen play. If the writer is anxious to regain those prerogatives which he has permitted to slip through his fingers, then he should begin to assert himself and his wishes, by suggesting elements—outside the fashioning of the screen play proper—which can have so much effect on the finished picture.

Music is one of these elements. For, with his suggestions for music, the writer has a tool that can supplement the words he has written, and implement the other workers in the picture with elements that will be completely integrated into the picture as a whole.

It is not necessary for the screen-play writer to be completely conversant with music. He need not be able to distinguish one note from the next, or even be able to sing on key. He may even be tone deaf. But he should know how music can be adapted to his screen play so as to take full advantage of its possibilities.

Plot music.   There are two broad types of music used in motion pictures. The first and least important, as far as the screen-play writer is concerned, is the plot music injected into a script as part of the action itself: the song the heroine sings; the music the night-club orchestra plays; the music used for dance scenes; and the music for such off-scene events as carnivals, circuses, parades, and theater presentations. The theater-scene music in *A Double Life* was in this category. This music is usually written before the picture is shot so that recordings can be made of it. These recordings are then played back while the scenes are being photographed, so as to make for perfect action and lip synchronizing. Later on, in the dubbing theater, the music tracks are laid in behind the photographed scenes and matched perfectly.

Background music.   It is with the second broad type of screen music—the background music—that the screen writer should be more concerned. Because of the rigid conventions which have attached themselves to the composition of music for motion-pictures, much of the music used is of the hackneyed "Hearts and Flowers" variety that has become as standardized, in many aspects, as the old-time cue music played for silent pictures on tuneless pianos.

If the writer is a sincere, creative worker, if he strives to avoid the cliché in his verbalizing and achieve new-minted freshness, he should be vitally concerned with the quality of the musical material that is to complement his writing. Since the average motion-picture musical score—with sequences running from a few seconds to several minutes—covers a total running time of between forty and ninety minutes, the writer should offer his suggestions and try to make certain that the background music will be in accord with the foreground action and dialogue.

From a note in his files, we can see how a British director, David Lean, was able to tell his composer the kind of background music he wanted for his *Oliver Twist*. "I should like music," he wrote, "to accompany the whole scene of Fagin donning his hat, taking the walking stick and walking around like an old gentleman, and finally having his foot trodden on and his pockets picked, causing him to search frantically for his lost wallet and watch, which makes Oliver laugh so much. I think the music should start immediately after 'To work' and end on the dissolve to Oliver lying asleep. This is to me almost the most important piece of music so far, and I should like it to transform the scene into a comic ballet." If the creative director can give such suggestions and instructions, there is no reason why the creative screen-play writer cannot do likewise.

Avoid familiar music.   One important injunction should be applied to almost all background music. Unless it is used as a gag, the music should be original and not familiar. That is, it should not derive from any known music. Music that can be recognized, and thus identified, is disconcerting. It can detract the audience's attention from the action and call attention to itself.

Functions of background music.   Background music has a number of definite functions: it can supply additional information; it can intensify emotional content; it can heighten dramatic impact; it can clarify ideas; it can help to build a scene and then cap it; it can contribute to continuity by integrating separate actions and scenes; it can identify characters and atmospheric time and place; it can amplify psychological states of mind; and it can bridge and point up otherwise comparatively uninteresting pictorial scenes.

For the screen-play writer to consider all of these functions with the necessary attention when writing his script, it would be essential that he work in direct co-operation with the music composer. Since this is a virtual impossibility in the present studio setup—where the writer seldom confers even with the director or film editor before he starts to write the screen play—he should try to estimate the musical needs of his script and at least attempt to assure his work of the proper musical accompaniment by suggesting certain requirements.

The ideal setup would be one in which there was complete co-operation between the writer, the director, the composer, the music department, and the sound-effects people, so that there could be complete integration of all the elements. This was done in H. G. Wells' picture, *The Shape of Things to Come,* which elicited from Wells the remark that "This Bliss music is not intended to be tacked on: it is part of the design."

Informative music. To make use of the first function of background music—*to supply additional information*—the screen-play writer may suggest that the music imitate the sound of certain of the actions. In the wake scene of *The Informer,* for instance, the music was so written that it imitated musically the tinkle of the silver coins as they fell to the floor from McLaglen's pocket. At another time, the music convincingly imitated the burble-burble-burble sound of the Guinness' stout as it was being swallowed by McLaglen.

In Gance's *Life of Beethoven,* the composer's tragic deafness was beautifully conveyed to the audience in the scene in which Beethoven walked down the street and passed an itinerant street violinist. The violinist had just been established, together with the music he was playing. Then, as Beethoven approached the violinist, the music was slowly faded out, until by the time Beethoven was close up, the music was completely faded out. And, as Beethoven walked away, the violin music was brought up again to re-establish it.

Foreshadowing music. Background music can also foreshadow events to come. The screen-play writer may, at a certain point in his script, indicate to the composer that the foreshadowing should appear musically. In *Chapayev,* this was done when the army set out to do battle with an obviously superior force. The music at that point was in a minor key, so that a foreshadowing of the defeat of the army was incised subtly into the minds of the audience—this without telegraphing, because music, by its very nature, and unlike diction, has the faculty of suggesting without disclosing.

Intensifying music. Intensifying emotional content is, perhaps, the most important of music's functions. The frank, forthright music used in the opening sequence of *Valley of Decision* reflected the dominating influence of the steel mills over the lives of the workers and, at the same time, gave a dominating coloration to the characters of the steel bosses. A suggestion as to the mood that the music is to establish and sustain can be written in by the screen writer, indicating the time he feels it should be introduced and other times when he believes it should be reintroduced, as a sort of leitmotif.

In *Algiers,* in the scene in which the informer is confronted by the killers, he backs away and bumps into a mechanical piano which is set off. Then, with this tinny, robot-like ragtime music grinding out as an ironic counterpoint, the informer is murdered.

Identification music. These same leitmotifs can be suggested by the writer when asking for music to *identify characters.* The introduction of a character can be accompanied by a certain characteristic musical phrase—as is done in opera—so that whenever that character appears, or is about to appear, the accompanying music can add an identifying commentary.

In Powell's *The Edge of the World,* a horn call is used as a leitmotif for Peter Manson, one of the main characters. Later it is integrated into a departure theme, when he is about to leave his beloved island. And when he falls to his death, full minor-key brass chords enunciate an island theme suggesting the desolation of those remaining on the island. The entire last reel of film, over which this music is laid, contains but ten words of dialogue, and runs for more than eight minutes.

In Fritz Lang's *M,* Lorre, the psychopathic murderer, is characterized by his whistling a few bars from Grieg's "Troll Song" whenever he is bent on murder. In fact, his identification is made by a blind man who remembers his song.

Two or more themes can then be introduced, in counterpoint, whenever the action is such that two or more characters are involved.

A comedy character, for example, could be introduced with a light, tripping pizzicato theme; a dignified person could be characterized, musically, by a theme in a slow tempo and at a low pitch; the same theme, but in a minor key, could be used to typify a sentimental person, with sad and dreamy proclivities.

Psychological music. Psychological states of mind are particularly conducive to musical interpretation because of their evanescent quality, with which music, with its many subjective nuances, is able to supplement the objective, pictorial image.

In *The Red Pony*, when the boy began to daydream about white circus horses, the picture showed the white chickens in the farmyard being transformed into white circus horses. And the bucolic music that accompanied the barnyard scene was subtly segued into circus music, to underscore the imaginative change.

Dramatic music. There is nothing so effective, *for heightening dramatic impact* or *for capping a dramatic scene*, as a chord of appropriate music. In radio, this function is called for by the word "sting."

Thus, in *The Picture of Dorian Gray*, a sharp, dissonant chord was used to punctuate the dramatic intensity that came with the shock Dorian experienced when he learned of his sweetheart's suicide.

Such "sting" chords can be called for at the proper time by the screen-play writer, and partially described, so that the composer may have the writer's conception of what is necessary, in lieu of a personal conference with him.

Chase music. Even a comic situation can be underlined with appropriate music. A comedy chase, for instance, lends itself admirably to musical interpretation. The lumbering, elephantine notes of a bassoon or a bull fiddle can be used to portray the antics of a fat man chasing his hat, or a blonde, or whatever it is a fat man can chase that is intended to be funny. The same instruments playing in a minor key can suggest the pathos of such a character involved in unrequited love. In *The Boy with Green Hair*, special chase music played under the chase scene, when the boy, Peter, was being pursued by the gang of boys. This aided in heightening the dramatic impact and pacing the tempo.

Atmospheric music. The function of *identifying atmospheric time and place* is a natural for background music. Historical eras can be represented musically so that, even without the addition of picture, the time and place can be deduced. The old-fashioned minuet pattern can easily identify the seventeenth and eighteenth centuries; drum patterns (either of the African or of the American Indian type) can set the scene for their respective locales; calliope music can do more for setting a circus scene than almost any other element; the sharp, brittle tempo of current popular songs is perfect for introducing a dance hall sequence or a night club; dock scenes call for sailor chanty patterns; and country scenes for patterns on the order of those used in Beethoven's *Pastoral Symphony*. There is no end to the manner in which atmospheric time and place can be supplemented by music.

In the British film *Western Approaches,* Clifton Parker's "Seascape" was beautifully incorporated into the background as atmosphere music to suggest the tremendous upheaval of the ocean, the menace of the sea to shipwrecked men, and the ocean's desolation.

The mechanical piano playing of the theme music in *Casablanca* conveyed the shoddy dissoluteness of the North African fleshpot.

Building with music. The function of *building* dramatic content with *music* can be seen to work perfectly in montages. Because these montages are unrealistic representations that condense time, the accompanying music serves as a sort of realistic cement, because it supplies what appears, momentarily, to be a series of disjointed silent shots, with the unifying coherence of a musical idea or phrase.

Transition music. Because music can furnish a continuity of sound, it can be used as a transition device to link otherwise disconnected scenes that have been neglected in the writing of the script or in its shooting. This function, then, can be relied upon by the screen-play writer in order to vary his transitions, or as a sound-track relief of a series of pictorial transitions. Although this sort of continuity is not intrinsically motion, it has sufficient surface movement to supply the necessary continuity.

In *Brief Encounter,* music combined with train sound effects and dialogue was especially helpful in creating extremely successful transitions.

Background music can also be used in combination with a sound effect, as a matched musical dissolve, to connect two sharply different scenes. Thus, the sound of a woman's scream, at a certain note, to top off one scene, could be segued into a corresponding musical note of the same pitch, in the following scene.

Crutch music.   Dialogue sequences that in themselves are not sufficiently dramatic—as in certain obligatory expository scenes—can
be enlivened considerably with suitable background music, which
can serve to carry forward lagging action.

There are many such sequences in a film that require a stiff dose
of music in order to achieve movement. Vacant spots between dialogue sequences can often be filled in with a background of neutral
music that can carry audience interest by the sheer power of its
compelling rhythm.

Commenting music.   Background music can be called on to comment ironically on pictorial content. In Painleve's *Hypocampes,* a
shot of a sea horse in the ocean was accompanied by a melange of
clichéd race-track, newsreel music, and served to point up humorously the composer's quaint notions about horse racing in general
and newsreel horse-race musical clips in particular. The sad, haunt-
ing zither music of *The Third Man* served as a sort of Viennese off-
stage commentator on the action it buttressed.

The screen-play writer can make his own musical comments, not
in actual content, but in the form of suggestions to the composer.
He has only to be aware of the potentialities of music, and the place
it can play in the fashioning of his screen play.

Dialogue-displacing music.   In such places in a script where only
silent action is being portrayed, background music can fill in a
third-dimensional sound track.

In Chaplin's *Monsieur Verdoux,* after Chaplin had gone to bed
with one of his wives, the camera discreetly remained outside the
closed door of their bedroom. But the music suggested what was
going on, presenting first a melody that suggested marital bliss; then
changing to a series of phrases that betokened the murderous passions taking place; and, finally, banging into a resonant *fortissimo,*
representing the murder itself. Concluding, came a rhapsodic idyll
of moving music, suggesting passions spent. And Chaplin emerged
from the room, insouciant and debonair, as fresh as one of the roses
from his garden.

There are times, however, when completely silent sequences can
add to the effectiveness of the action. The effect of the pause in Han-

del's resounding Hallelujah chorus is tremendous. In the same way, Prokofiev highlighted many of the climaxes in his excellent score for *Alexander Nevsky* with impressive silences. But many producers abhor silence. Like unimaginative advertisers, they cannot understand why they should pay for so much dead "white space" in their product. So they insist that, no matter what reasons you may have for desiring a silent sequence, overriding music be used. To avoid their injecting an inharmonious element, then, suggest that some sort of appropriate but neutral music be played over your silent sequences.

Format

For those screen-play writers who are now working at established studios the following section may be unnecessary. Their completed scripts are typed from their originals by experienced secretaries who are conversant with the standard type-script format demanded by their studio.

But for those who do their own retyping, or who have their scripts typed by a stenographer, the following information regarding the standard format required by the studios should be of importance.

Scripts must be clean, of course. They can be duplicate sheets, but with the typing sufficiently dark to insure legibility. The paper must be onion skin, 8 x 10 or thereabouts, and the entire script must be bound in colored binding paper, stapled, and suitably identified as to title, author, and author's address.

The format of the screen play itself, however, varies from studio to studio. But certain generalizations can be made so that a type script may be acceptable to most studios and independent producers.

Following is a copy of the first pages of a screen play. It shows the number of typewriter spaces that should separate the lines, and the number of spaces, from the *left* tabulating stop, that should separate the line-beginning margin words.

(top of the page)

(2)

THE LAST CHANCE

(3)
SCREEN PLAY
(2)

by

(2)
LEWIS HERMAN
(4)

(15)   FADE IN

(2)

INT. LIVING ROOM—BAKER HOUSE—DAY

(2)

(8)   1. MED. SHOT—JOE BAKER. He is stretched out on   (1)
the sofa as though unconscious. LIBBY DALE rushes   (1)
into the shot and starts to shake him.

(3)
(40)   LIBBY
(30)   (anguished)   (1)
(25)   Joe! Joe! why did you do it, Joe?

(2)
(40)   JOE
(30)   (opening his eyes)   (1)
(25)   What are you talking about?

(2)

Libby is taken aback by his awakening.
She pouts prettily as she gets up from the sofa.   (1)

(3)
LIBBY
(disgruntledly)   (1)
Hm! then this letter was a fake.   (1)

She throws the letter in Joe's lap. He picks it   (1)
up and starts to read it.

(2)

INSERT   LETTER which reads:

Dear Libby: Joe may do it yet.   (1)
Toby   (1)

(2)

BACK TO SCENE: Joe throws the letter to the floor.

> JOE   (1)
> (grinning)
> So you thought I was ready to kill
> myself, huh?
> (3)

EXT. FRONT LAWN—BAKER HOUSE—DAY
(2)
2. FULL SHOT on the yard as BOBBY BAKER runs across
the lawn to the house.
(3)

3. MED. SHOT on Bobby running up the steps as he trips (1)
and falls on the upper stair sprawling out on the   (1)
porch. He gets up and limps hurriedly to the front   (1)
door.

(2)

(55)   WIPE
(3)

INT. LIVING ROOM—BAKER HOUSE—DAY
4. MED. SHOT on Bobby as he limps into the room and (1)
sees his brother and Libby eyeing each other warily. (1)
(2)

> BOBBY
> (disgustedly)   (1)
> At it again, huh?   (1)
> (3)

DISSOLVE

The following examples illustrating the use of capital and lower
case letters, should be used for camera action. When the camera is
stationary, use upper case letters for:

MED. SHOT with a group in b. g.
CLOSE SHOT toward door.
LONG SHOT through window.
CLOSE-UP over shoulder.
SUPERIMPOSE over MAIN TITLE.
CLOSE MOVING SHOT—REVERSE ANGLE—shows:
CLOSE SHOT—ANGLING UPWARD—to reveal.

When the camera is moving, use upper case letters for:

CAMERA PANS BACK—TO—UP—DOWN—
WITH—FROM—THROUGH—TOWARD—
OVER—LEFT—RIGHT.
CAMERA ANGLES DOWN—HOLDING to show
CAMERA MOVES DOWN SLIGHTLY revealing

DISSOLVE AND WIPE may occur any place on the page. When they become DISSOLVE OUT and WIPE OUT at the end of a page, be sure to begin the next page with DISSOLVE IN or WIPE IN.

The same is true of FADE OUT and FADE IN, which may occur, three spaces apart, any place on the page. But, when FADE OUT occurs at the end of a page, be sure to begin the next page with FADE IN.

Whenever MUSIC or SOUND occurs, these identifying words should precede the sentence, as, for example:
MUSIC. Singing is heard.
SOUND. The train is heard approaching.

When adding scenes or pages, identify them with capitals, as in 1A or 5B and so on.

Do not use a new scene number as long as the camera is in action, for example, CAMERA DOLLIES IN, ANGLES UP, PANS BACK TO, TRUCKS TOWARD, and so on.

Lower case letters should be used for "disclosing," "showing," "including," "revealing," and "favoring"; as well as for character names.

The following material does not apply to punctuation marks in dialogue but to the rest of the screen play, excluding the dialogue.

Do not hyphenate words at the end of a line, except in the case of a normally hyphenated word.

Quotation marks should always be placed *outside* the comma and period. This is an invariable rule. Place quotation marks *inside* the colon and semicolon; *outside* or *inside* the marks of exclamation and interrogation, depending on whether those marks belong to the quoted matter; *outside* the dash when it stands for something left *unsaid,* and *inside* when it is used as an ordinary punctuation mark; *inside* parentheses when the parenthetical clause is quoted, otherwise outside.

Place a semicolon after the expressions: "namely," "viz," "for example," "e.g.," "that is," "i.e.," "for instance," "however," "hence," "moreover." This should be *done when they introduce* a sentence, a principal statement, or an enumeration of examples or explanations.

Use dashes in scene location, never commas, as in: INT. LIVING ROOM—BAKER HOUSE—NIGHT.

Bound in with the script, following the title page—which should have the title, in caps, typed across the middle of the page, and underlined—should come a page with the following:

CAST OF CHARACTERS

Joe Baker .... a young man, about 23.

Libby Gells .... a young woman, about 18, in love with Joe.

Tony Zale .... about 30, in love with Libby.

Mrs. Tilly Baker .... about 45, Joe's mother.

Mr. Piat .... about 55, town banker.

Mrs. Piat .... about 40, Mr. Piat's wife.

AND OTHERS

In the above cast of characters, the character descriptions should include, in addition to what is shown, a thumbnail characterization of each major character. Description of the leads should include a mention of the type the character represents: "Cary Grant type," "she has Ida Lupino's vivacity" or "could be played by sour-puss Ned Sparks."

Although a set list is not always essential, it could be included, provided, of course, there are few enough sets to warrant using it as a selling idea, if it is to be a B picture. If not, forget about it.

Following is a series of brief injunctions which should be followed.

1. Typewrite all scripts.

2. Use only black typewriter ribbons.
3. Use pica-size type, if possible.
4. Do not bind the script with gay, colored ribbons. Wire staples are enough.
5. Register a copy of the script with the Screen Writers' Guild. Motion picture scripts can be copyrighted, but Guild registration is sufficient.
6. Retain a copy of the script yourself.
7. Keep your fingers crossed. Continue to keep them crossed even if, *mirabile dictu,* the script is sold.

INDEX